ker

Plays: Two

**The Marrying of Ann Leete, The Madras House,
His Majesty, Farewell to the Theatre**

Harley Granville Barker (1877–1946) was the author of the most
thoughtful English plays of the first half of this century, ranging
from intimate to epic. Brilliantly written (Shaw called them
'masterpieces'), they were judged to be far ahead of their time on
first performance. They have been gradually rediscovered over
the past fifteen years, with highly praised productions of *The
Marrying of Ann Leete* and *Waste* by the RSC, *The Madras House*
at the Royal National Theatre and several productions of *The
Voysey Inheritance*. A retrospective exploration of his drama was a
main feature of the 1992 Edinburgh Festival.

This is a companion volume to *Granville Barker Plays: One*,
which contains *The Voysey Inheritance*, *Waste*, *The Secret Life*,
Rococo and *Vote by Ballot*.

Harley Granville Barker's plays include: *The Marrying of Ann
Leete*, written 1899, first presented by the Stage Society, 1902,
first public production by the Royal Shakespeare Company at the
Aldwych Theatre, London 1975; *The Voysey Inheritance*, written
1903–5, first produced at the Court Theatre, 1905, revised
version produced at Sadler's Wells Theatre, 1934; *Waste*, written
1906–7, first presented by the Stage Society, 1907, second
version written 1925–6, first produced at Westminster Theatre,
1936; *The Madras House*, written 1909–10, first produced 1910 at
the Duke of York's Theatre, revised 1925 for production at the
Ambassadors Theatre; *The Secret Life*, written 1919–22, first
professional production at the Orange Tree Theatre, Richmond,
1989; *His Majesty*, written 1923–28, first produced at the
Edinburgh International Festival at St Bride's Centre by the
Orange Tree Theatre Company in 1992.

HARLEY GRANVILLE BARKER

Plays: Two

The Marrying of Ann Leete
The Madras House (1925 revision)
His Majesty
Farewell to the Theatre

with an introduction by Margery Morgan

Methuen Drama

METHUEN WORLD CLASSICS

This edition first published in Great Britain 1994
by Methuen Drama
an imprint of Reed Consumer Books Ltd
Michelin House, 81 Fulham Road, London SW3 6RB
and Auckland, Melbourne, Singapore and Toronto
and distributed in the United States of America
by Heinemann a division of Reed Publishing (USA) Inc
361 Hanover Street, Portsmouth, New Hampshire NH 03801 3959

Reprinted 1994

ISBN 0-413-67980-2

A CIP catalogue record for this book is available from the British
Library

Typeset by Wilmaset Ltd, Birkenhead, Wirral
Printed and bound in Great Britain by Cox & Wyman Ltd, Reading, Berks

Contents

Chronology

1877   Born, 25 November, in an apartment in Sheffield Terrace, Kensington, first child and only son of a young surveyor and his half-Italian, half-Scottish wife, who earned her living with drawing-room and platform recitations.

1882   Birth of his only sister, Grace.

1891   After years of reciting in his mother's programme, Granville Barker appeared with a company of juveniles in a dramatisation of Anstey's *Vice Versa* at Harrogate Spa Rooms, in May. Then embarked on six months' training for the stage with Sarah Thorne, lessee of the Theatre Royal, Margate.

1892   First London engagement, as Third Young Man in *The Poet and the Puppets*, a skit on Oscar Wilde, at the Comedy Theatre.

1894   Understudied during Florence Farr's season at the Royalty Theatre, when Shaw's *Arms and the Man* and Yeats's *Land of Heart's Desire* were first performed. Appeared in charity performance of *King Robert of Sicily*, at the Lyric Theatre in July. The cast included his mother and sister, Berte Thomas, Ben Webster (in the title role) and the young Clara Butt. (May have been his first production.)

1895–6   Toured with Ben Greet's Company, playing minor roles in Shakespeare plays. Wrote *The Family of the Oldroyds*, first of a series of unpublished plays, in collaboration with fellow-actor, Berte Thomas.

1897   July, played Hastings, in *She Stoops to Conquer*, to Gordon Craig's Young Marlow, at Kingston-on-Thames.

1899   Production of *The Weather-Hen* by Granville Barker and Berte Thomas at Terry's Theatre, then at the Comedy. Played lead in *Richard II* for William Poel's Elizabethan Stage Society. Joined committee working for a National Theatre, along with Gilbert Murray and William Archer.

1900   Involved with the newly-founded Stage Society, acting in plays by Ibsen, Hauptmann and Shaw (especially as Marchbanks in *Candida*), and directing short plays by Maeterlinck, Yeats and Fiona MacLeod.

1901   Joined the Fabian Society.

1902   Directed his own play, *The Marrying of Ann Leete*, for the Stage Society, and played Frank in the Society's presentation of Shaw's banned *Mrs Warren's Profession*. Played Osric in *Hamlet* for Forbes Robertson at the Lyric Theatre.

1903   10 August, took the lead in William Poel's production of Marlowe's *Edward II*.

1904   *Scheme and Estimates for a National Theatre*, by William Archer and Granville Barker, privately printed and distributed. Barker's productions of Shakespeare's *Two Gentlemen of Verona* and Euripides's *Hippolytus* (translated by Gilbert Murray) led to the first of the Vedrenne-Barker seasons at the Court Theatre, Sloane Square. First production of *Prunella* by Laurence Housman and Granville Barker in December.

1905   February, first production of *The Voysey Inheritance*.

1906   24 April, marriage of Granville Barker to Lillah McCarthy, leading actress in the Court Theatre Company.

1907   Elected to Executive of the Fabian Society. The Vedrenne-Barker management closed at the Court Theatre in May, re-opening at the Savoy Theatre in autumn. *Waste*, scheduled for November, was banned by the Lord Chamberlain.

1908   Visited USA on invitation of would-be sponsors of an American national theatre, but the scheme fell through for lack of a suitable building. On tour in Dublin, Barker almost died of typhoid fever.

1909   Visited theatres in Germany. Returned to direct Galsworthy's *Strife* to be followed by *Justice*. Albert Barker, his father, died of tuberculosis in Monaco.

1910   Principal director of plays for Charles Frohman's Repertory Theatre at the Duke of York's. *The Madras House* produced, alongside Shaw's *Misalliance*. Season closed prematurely at the death of King Edward VII. Visited Royalty Theatre, Glasgow, as actor and director, lecturing on 'A Citizens' Theatre'.

1911   Translated Schnitzler's *Anatol* dialogues, performing them at the Little Theatre, with Nigel Playfair and Lillah McCarthy. *Rococo* presented there in October.

1912   Revolutionary productions of Shakespeare's *A Winter's Tale* and *Twelfth Night* at the Savoy Theatre.

1913   In management at the St James's Theatre, until

money ran out, directing Molière, Ibsen, Shaw, Maeterlinck, etc., including *The Harlequinade* by D C Calthrop and Granville Barker. Took a long lease of the Kingsway Theatre, with Lillah, and produced Arnold Bennett's *The Great Adventure*, which ran there for twenty months.

1914   Visited Russia to observe Stanislavsky's Moscow Art Theatre at work. Celebrated production of *A Midsummer Night's Dream* at the Savoy Theatre. In November, presented Masefield's *Philip the King*, at Covent Garden, and Hardy's *The Dynasts* at the Kingsway. Wrote *Vote by Ballot*, probably early in the year.

1915   American tour, most remarkable for outdoor, arena performances of Greek tragedies.

1916   Wrote *Farewell to the Theatre*. Enlisted in the Army, later transferred to Intelligence. Wrote *The Red Cross in France*, based on a visit to the Front.

1917   Grace Barker, his sister, died of tuberculosis, in France.

1918   Translated Sacha Guitry's *Deburau*, first produced in America. Divorce from Lillah McCarthy and marriage to wealthy American authoress, Helen Huntington.

1919   Became first Chairman of the British Drama League.

1920   Directed G M Sierra's *The Romantic Young Lady* (first of the translations of Spanish plays made collaboratively with Helen) at the Royalty Theatre. Began to hyphenate his name.

1921   Directed Maeterlinck's *The Betrothal* at the Gaiety Theatre. The Granville-Barkers acquired a country house in Devon.

1922   Published *The Exemplary Theatre*.

1923   Published *The Secret Life*, 'The Heritage of the Actor', in the *Quarterly Review*, and long Prefaces to the first three volumes of *The Players' Shakespeare*; also, with Helen, *Collected Plays* of Sierra in English.

1925   Revised and directed *The Madras House* at the Ambassadors Theatre. Gave British Academy lecture, 'From *Henry V* to *Hamlet*'. Break with Shaw. Published English version of Jules Romains's *Doctor Knock*. His mother died at her home in Monte Carlo.

1926   Re-wrote *Waste* for a production which did not materialise.

1927   Publication of first collected volume of revised *Prefaces to Shakespeare*, English version of *Six Gentlemen in a Row* by Jules Romains and English versions of *Four Plays* by Serafín and Joaquín Álvarez Quintero, with Helen.

1928   *His Majesty* published.

1929   Elected President of the Royal Society of Literature.

1930   Published *A National Theatre* and second series of *Prefaces to Shakespeare*. Gave Clark Lectures at Cambridge, published as *On Dramatic Method*.

1932   Publication of *Four Comedies* by S and J Á Quintero, in English versions by Helen and Harley Granville-Barker.

1934   Co-directed *The Voysey Inheritance* with Harcourt Williams at the Old Vic. Co-edited *A Companion to Shakespeare Studies* with G B Harrison.

1936   Co-directed the first public production of *Waste* with Michael MacOwan at the Westminster Theatre.

1937   Became Director of the British Institute in Paris. Gave Romanes Lecture at Oxford (*On Poetry in Drama*).

1940   Directed *King Lear* at the Old Vic in association with Lewis Casson (John Gielgud as Lear, Jessica Tandy as Cordelia). He and Helen escaped from France and made their way to New York.

1941–2 Worked for British Information Services in New York.

1942–44 Gave lectures at Toronto, Harvard and Princeton, which formed the basis of further *Prefaces to Shakespeare*.

1945   Published 'A Theatre that Might Be' in *Theatre Arts Monthly*, July. Returned to England and thence to Paris.

1946   Died of arterio-sclerosis on 31 August.

1947   Fifth series of *Prefaces to Shakespeare* published posthumously.

compiled by Margery Morgan

Introduction

When Harley Granville Barker died in 1946, he was most widely know as a Shakespeare scholar. Bernard Shaw, already an octogenarian, wrote about him to *The Times* and then at greater length for *Drama*, the magazine of the British Drama League, recalling the heady days at the beginning of the century when he and young Barker had worked together in the theatre. He reminded his readers of a very talented actor, a brilliant director for some types of play (Shaw always had his reservations in this area), a theatre manager of great achievement and yet more ambitious purpose. It was as a playwright, Shaw held, that Barker was still most under-estimated. The older dramatist, who owed his own establishment as a great comic dramatist largely to Barker's work, was not an impartial witness: he regarded the latter's first marriage, to Lillah McCarthy, the leading actress of the Vedrenne-Barker company and creator of a long line of Shaw heroines, as folly; and he made no secret of regarding his second marriage, to a wealthy American writer, Helen Huntington, as a disaster. The view had broken up the long, friendly association. Shaw, who had always begrudged the energies the younger man had spent on producing Shakespeare, denounced writing on Shakespeare as even greater waste. So he lent weight to a growing legend that Granville Barker's second marriage had led to a decline in his artistic powers as well as to a desertion of the theatre in its need.

Barker, in fact, never ceased to work in various ways for the kind of theatre he wanted, which would provide conditions for performances of the highest technical and imaginative quality, training grounds for actors, and stages where new plays would be faithfully and imaginatively explored. The publicly subsidised theatre which alone, he had come to believe, could guarantee such conditions, did not come into

being until shortly before his death. He had been writing all
his life for his ideal theatre: plays with large casts, requiring
highly skilled actors and long periods of ensemble rehearsal
under intelligent and sensitive direction. Such conditions
were rare indeed in England between 1914 and 1945. Barker
had never thrust his own plays on the theatre. After his
death, they were all allowed to go out of print and so
generally out of mind. The last twenty years have seen a
gradual, but startling rediscovery of their vitality and rich-
ness of interest through stage performance.

Granville Barker was brought up to act and taught himself
to write. At the height of his fame, he recalled writing little
plays for his toy theatre as early as he could remember, while
his mother trained him to be 'that most objectionable of
juvenile creatures – an infant reciter'. She was well-known
for her own recitations in private salons and on public
platforms. The daughter of a cultured Anglican clergyman,
and proud to be the granddaughter of a Fellow of the Royal
Society who was also an Italian émigré, she was probably
influenced in her choice of profession by her other grandfather, Alexander Read. He had retired from the Madras
Civil Service to discover personal fulfilment in devotion to
his family accompanied by a passion for the theatre for which
he frequently thanked God. Elizabeth Bozzi-Granville had
taken as her husband a surveyor, eight years her junior, who
aspired to be an architect and would show off his powers as a
mesmerist to entertain guests. The family lived a somewhat
nomadic existence, changing addresses as Albert Barker
moved on from one job of house-conversion to another, and
as Mrs Barker did the rounds of inland spas, seaside kursaals
and metropolitan drawing-rooms. When he was thirteen, she
took her son to Margate, so that his elocution lessons and
platform experience could be supplemented by a season
training for the stage under Sarah Thorne, lessee of the
Theatre Royal. (Others who passed through the Sarah
Thorne 'school' included Ben Greet – an ex-schoolmaster
whose touring companies were to offer young actors useful
experience in playing the classics of English drama – and
Violet and Irene Vanbrugh.) Here he met Berte Thomas,

nine years older, but also a novice, who wrote a play which
Sarah Thorne put on at the theatre. Barker took note and
later approached Thomas with the suggestion that they
should try writing plays together. Manuscripts of three
survive from about 1895 to 1898 and make it clear that the
younger man was always the dominant partner in this
enterprise. Thomas admitted to becoming little more than a
sounding-board and an amanuensis. One play, *The Weather-
Hen*, was produced in London in 1899, over both their
names, and was praised for its freshness and individuality.

Meanwhile, Barker had served a further acting appren-
ticeship with companies touring the South-East and then
with Ben Greet. Small parts in London productions began to
come his way; they gave him a taste of the conditions
prevailing in the West End theatre and led him, with a group
of like-minded friends, to join the Stage Society, founded in
1899 to give club performances of Ibsen's *Ghosts* and other
distinguished modern plays which had no chance of production in the English public theatre of that period. In the
context of the Stage Society he got to know Bernard Shaw,
who had written a number of unperformed plays – some said
unactable – and William Archer, theatre critic and proselyt-
iser for Ibsen, and he renewed acquaintance with the Greek
scholar, Gilbert Murray.

Out of this conjunction came a revolution in the theatre.
The term 'National Theatre' is now identified with a
'brutalist' building on London's South Bank, though it is
occasionally remarked that the Royal Shakespeare Company
is a national theatre company too. The National Theatre
Committee, on which the young Barker sat alongside his
more distinguished seniors at the beginning of this century,
was in fierce and total agreement that what they wanted was a
living theatre, not a monument (for which there was a rival
committee). The members wanted to break the stranglehold
of purely commercial managements on imagination, inno-
vation and artistic quality, which actively discouraged
authors of talent from writing plays. They were also keenly
aware of the limitations upon actor-managers ever fearful of
bankruptcy, which drove them, also, to cut rehearsal time to

a minimum and to rely on long-running productions in order
to maximise profits. Another enemy was the 'star' system,
responsible – even in Irving's theatre – for neglect of the
standard of acting among 'supporting' players. Audiences,
too, were at fault: ignorant of the general excellence which
could be achieved under other conditions, they allowed
'what the public wants' to become an excuse for poverty of
material and slovenliness of execution.

The existence of the Comédie Française in Paris certainly
cast its shadow on the Committee's discussions and on the
decision that Archer and Granville Barker should prepare a
'blue book' (like the report and recommendations of a
parliamentary commission) dealing with the unit of a single
theatre, for distribution to politicians open to persuasion,
leaders of the theatrical profession and other persons of
influence who were seriously interested in the arts. A note in
the text of *A National Theatre, Scheme and Estimates*, on sale
to the public in 1907, pointed out that the model offered
could be used for any number of other theatres, in the
provinces or in other parts of the Empire. By that time,
Granville Barker had given a practical demonstration, at the
Court Theatre from 1904 to 1907, of what their alternative
theatre would be like. It put him at the head of the theatrical
avant-garde and identified him with a cause he was to pursue
in various ways throughout the rest of his life, even in his
final years as the 'king over the water'. This dedication may
well have limited the number of plays he wrote; certainly it
helped determine some of their characteristics. These plays
are sometimes criticised for the size of cast they require and
the 'uneconomical' introduction of characters who appear in
one scene only – as if this were an artistic failing, rather than
a financial consideration. (The same criticism is not levelled
at Chekhov or Brecht.) The dirtiest words the young
Granville Barker knew were 'commercial' and 'market'. He
wanted a large, permanent company, giving employment
and training to many actors – training through such a rich
variety of experience that any of them could take on the
demanding roles of *Waste*, for instance, which even today are
thought to require expensive talent. Yet it is significant that

the Court Theatre enterprise went by the title of 'the Vedrenne-Barker Seasons', J. E. Vedrenne being the business manager.

The idea of opposing the long-run system with a repertory of plays alternating in the programmes – a pattern now familiar from the practice of the main subsidised theatres – proved possible only in modified form. But room was made for new work to be seen which showed promise rather than achievement, and actors were given a variety of parts in different types of play, which saved them from the staleness of repetition. Although there was a regular corps of actors, paid equally, it was not possible to cast all the plays from a permanent company; guest actors' sympathy with the experiment was tested by their willingness to take a much lower fee than they could expect elsewhere. Granville Barker himself had to play a number of leading roles for economic reasons, when no one else suitable was available. So he appeared, for instance, as Tanner in *Man and Superman*, Professor Cusins in *Major Barbara* (the character based on Gilbert Murray) and Dubedat in *The Doctor's Dilemma* and became closely identified in the public mind with Bernard Shaw, the writer he had proved to be a brilliant, actable dramatist, and who had indeed become a close associate and friend.

Much of Barker's time at the Court was taken up in seeking out new plays, persuading established authors who had made their reputations as novelists to come up with pieces for the theatre, or working with novices to get their efforts into stageworthy shape and, as a dramatist himself, supplying original plays to go into the repertory: first, completing *The Voysey Inheritance*, then going on to write *Waste*, only to have performance banned by the Lord Chamberlain at the last moment. He then headed a campaign against the system of theatrical censorship which got as far as a parliamentary committee. (In essentials, this history was to be repeated by George Devine's English Stage Company at the same theatre in the 1950s and 1960s. The struggle against official censorship was won, however, in 1968.) He would have preferred not to act, but to be a full-time director in the modern sense, bringing unity of conception and style to serve the play, and helping the actors to realise it as fully as possible. He was the first of a new breed in the English public theatre. Gordon Craig had pointed the way with a number of semi-private performances, from 1900 to 1902. Deciding that this country did not want the kind of work he wished to do, Craig took himself abroad for the rest of his life and, in fact, achieved few more theatrical productions. Primarily a designer-director, Craig made it clear in an essay *On the Art of the Theatre*, first published in 1905, that he had little time for actors, whose oversize egos were likely to destroy the harmony of effect he wanted in the theatre. During the past decade there has been a strong reaction from players against 'director's theatre', a modern variant on the protests which greeted Craig's contemptuous dismissal of the flesh-and-blood medium of drama. The testimony of many actors who worked with Barker at different periods confirms the evidence from critics who urged the public to visit the Court Theatre if they wished to see much the finest acting in London, consistently and even in the smallest roles; he was certainly not open to the same charge as Craig. His attitude is most fully stated in the essay, 'The Heritage of the Actor' (1923), which he originally intended as a Shavian-length preface to *The Secret Life*. One passage may be quoted here:

> If this is the dramatist's day, he will be wise to consider the actor, not as a mere appendage to his work, but as its very life-giver. Let him realise that the more he can learn to ask of the actor the more will he gain for his play. But asking is giving. He must give opportunity.

Craig's ideas on the new art of the theatre, though doubtless affected by the aesthetic aspect of Irving's theatre, were closely related to the theories of contemporary symbolist poets and painters: by bringing all the arts into unity, the artist hoped to address the soul, beyond the senses and the intellect. The essays of Wagner, the 'father' of the symbolist movement, published in English in 1892, seem to have been Craig's direct source in their presentation of the music-drama, in which all the arts combine, as re-creating the genius and power of ancient Greek theatre in the modern world. The soul Wagner was concerned to address and nourish was that of nascent German unity, after the failure of the 1848 revolution. This concept of a national theatre inspired Yeats, particularly, in the foundation of the Abbey Theatre, Dublin. Though the English National Theatre Committee, in the early years of this century, might have claimed to be Wagnerites all, they took the ancient theatre of Athens as a model in a considerably less mystical and less nationalistic spirit. Under the guidance of Gilbert Murray (Professor of Greek at Glasgow, then at Oxford), they regarded the theatre of the city state as offering opportunity for airing and debating public issues, educating and enlivening the citizens of a democracy, civilising them through excellence in the arts. Granville Barker and his friends were always aware that they were concerned with the general nature and structure of British society and its economy, in their attempt to change the theatre. Fabian socialist ideas combined with the influence of Gilbert Murray in the aspiration voiced by Philip Madras in the new Barker play, *The Madras House*, which was to be presented at the Duke of York's Theatre in 1910:

> I want an art and a culture that . . . must spring in good time from the happiness of a whole people. (Original version.)

In 1907, celebrating the end of their tenancy of the Court Theatre, and again when the Vedrenne-Barker management's funds ran out after the continuation of its work at the Savoy Theatre, the theatrical reformers looked hopefully towards the Government, which in turn did nothing to encourage notions that the people might finance their own theatres through the tax system. Only after two world wars did that come about.

Barker considered leaving the country, as Craig had done. He seized such chances as came up: notably at the Duke of York's, when a commercial impresario, Charles Frohman, briefly intoxicated by optimism after observing Vedrenne and Barker's success with the public, mounted and then abruptly curtailed a season of new plays in repertory, engaging Barker to direct some of them. A wealthy aristocrat sponsored three Shakespeare productions, directed by Barker, at the Savoy Theatre in 1912 and 1914. Fast-moving and rapidly spoken on an open stage in decorative or abstract settings and imaginatively costumed, these caused an immediate sensation and revolutionised the staging and speaking of Shakespeare for the future. There had been little money to spend on designers at the Court, though Charles Ricketts had been brought in for *Don Juan in Hell*. In 1910, Granville Barker started to build up his own team of artist-designers to work closely with him: Ricketts again, William and Albert Rothenstein, Norman Wilkinson of Four Oaks (who went on, later, to Nigel Playfair's Lyric Theatre at Hammersmith and then to Stratford) and, as an apprentice, young Paul Nash. Then, during an American tour in 1915, Barker gave a start to the theatrical career of Robert Edmond Jones, who was to become the most famous of these designers. No playwright has worked with fuller awareness of all the aspects of a play in performance.

He got together enough money for an uncompromising thirteen weeks at the St James's Theatre, in 1913; and for a while he and his actress wife, Lillah McCarthy, in joint management, had plays running concurrently in three London theatres. They were emboldened to take the Kingsway Theatre on a twenty-five year lease, in 1914, and presented Hardy's epic drama, *The Dynasts*, and Arnold Bennett's *The Great Adventure* there, before war swept everything away. For the rest of Granville Barker's life he was to be seen in London only as an occasional visiting director. He would not try to repeat what he had already done, but left his followers to continue as he had shown them – in Manchester, Liverpool, Birmingham, Glasgow, at Stratford, in London at the Lyric, Hammersmith, in the Phoenix Society and, later, the Arts Theatre Club, or in Australia. He was less in the public eye, but continued resolutely to plan, campaign, advise and write. His authority grew among decision makers; the Universities of Oxford,

Edinburgh and Reading gave him honorary doctorates; with his second wife, he lived in Paris as Director of the British Institute, while the British public forgot that he had ever been an actor and in theatrical management. His contribution to productions of Shakespeare has been enormous over at least two generations, as actors and directors turned first to his *Prefaces to Shakespeare*. He did not foresee the extent to which power in society would pass from theatre to television, or else did not acknowledge what he saw. But both his experience and his arguments are still pertinent to late twentieth-century debate over the arts in society and the problems of funding them.

The three full-length plays in this volume represent three distinct phases in Granville Barker's development as a dramatist.

The earliest, *The Marrying of Ann Leete*, uses costume drama to veil its relevance to the late nineteenth century in a delicate pastiche of the eighteenth, just touching in allusions to political and cultural revolution: 'My poor France,' sighs Carnaby Leete; while Ann and Dr Remnant are reading poems by Robert Burns. The veil seems to lift momentarily when her brother addresses Ann as a 'new woman', though the play's definition of the term is as unorthodox for the 1890s as it would be today. Most of the critics who saw the author's original production for the Stage Society recognised that the work was fresh, clever and innovative, but declared themselves totally baffled by it. A striking exception was Arthur Symons, interpreter of Symbolism to the English public, who registered 'the excitement of following a trail . . . of ideas', recognised that the unfamiliar technique was based as much on a sound, practical knowledge of the stage as on freedom from conventionality, and observed the conduct of Barker's civilised people who consciously live by lies as a deliberate manoeuvring around the gaps which open in the earth 'right in their path . . . at every moment'. Motives behind motives emerge gradually out of the physical darkness in which the play begins. Another aspect of that first production which Symons conveys was the power of the dialogue to alert and startle: 'like pistol shots, and he keeps up the firing from every corner of the stage'.

The opening dialogue is constructed in almost stanzaic form, incorporating deliberately staccato lines which express the careful artifice and self-conscious restraint of polite society. The prescribed setting conditions formal grouping and movement, so that the explicit metaphors of play, sport, game are joined by a subtextual metaphor of dance. This bursts out grotesquely in the Hogarthian dance of death which counterpoints the wedding in Act Four and induces a greater sense of intimacy, a deeper quietness, in the final scene. If they were not so subdued, the touches of seasonal myth, such symbols as rose and hyacinth, drought and rain, candlelight, cloister and the post-Edenic world would be merely trite. Something more potent than delicacy is at work in the creation of Carnaby Leete, the arch-intriguer and cynic who has lived for power. Appropriating the word 'pellucid' and the definition 'letting light through', he betrays a double consciousness, an undercurrent of reflection beyond his will. It is a trick of irony that invests the villain's role with the author's consciousness. Linking the tyrant intimately to his rebellious daughter, through touches of affection, even hints of deep understanding and consent, contributes to the play's peculiar poise between thought and feeling, its metaphysical quality.

The actress, Winifred Fraser, who first played Ann, had been associated with some of the earliest English productions of Ibsen: her Hedvig in *The Wild Duck* had been singled out for praise, and she had taken the role of Selma in the Stage Society's presentation of *The League of Youth*, a character sometimes seen as an anticipation of Nora in *A Doll's House* and even Hedda Gabler. The locked door of the cottage, in the final scene of *The Marrying of Ann Leete*, surely alludes to the door Nora slams behind her. Ann certainly accomplishes a revolt and an escape – from the great house and the hypocritical masquerade of aristocratic society. Her choice of authenticity in peasant life and the traditional female burden of physical labour and child-bearing is open to interpretation. Perhaps this is a conservative response to the feminist challenge. Yet Ann is conscious of her power to change the course of history, in the moment of her decision, and the cottage is dim with indefinable future possibilities.

Written in the same year as the Stage Society was founded, *The Marrying of Ann Leete* was exactly the type of play it had been set up to promote: a challenging work with no chance of an ordinary commercial production. It was a young man's play but it prompted Bernard Shaw to foretell a brilliant career for the author. There was no expectation that this particular work would enter the current theatrical repertoire: it was too difficult for audiences unaccustomed to innovative drama and it received no public performance until 1975. When the Royal Shakespeare Company presented it then at its London venue (at that time the Aldwych Theatre), under the direction of David Jones and with Mia Farrow embodying the cool innocence of Ann, a large part of the theatre-going public was receptive to new, experimental drama; and familiarity with a more recent wave of symbolist plays, associated with Samuel Beckett, made Granville Barker's spare, elliptical dialogue not just less daunting but positively up to date. Chekhov had long been a favourite in British theatre, and it seemed that *The Marrying of Ann Leete* was the work of an English Chekhov, comparable to *The Cherry Orchard* in its presentation of a dying culture half-dreaming of a new age. This was such a company as Barker had himself built up, adept at ensemble playing, able to match the script in the intelligence and elegant precision of their art; and equally able to catch the unusual, delicately moving, winter mood of the final intimate scene. The designers had been faithful to the playwright's descriptions, creating a visual style with an edge of artifice reminiscent of sets created by Norman Wilkinson for some of Granville Barker's own productions. As yet, there has been no further production in England to explore the play's potentialities.

A masquerade, using its eighteenth-century guise as a metaphor, *The Marrying of Ann Leete* stands strikingly apart from the other plays in this two-volume collection. (At the turn of the century, it could be associated with Beardsley's

illustrations for *The Rape of the Lock*, or Max Beerbohm's
The Happy Hypocrite. Today's analogue, yielding nothing to
Barker in seriousness, might be Peter Greenaway's film, *The
Draughtsman's Contract*.) Yet it is not so isolated in the
totality of Barker's writing for the theatre, which includes a
substantial output of translations, adaptations and directly
collaborative work, all bearing marks of his artistic personality. In particular, *Ann Leete* has affinities with three plays
linked with the commedia dell' arte tradition: *Prunella*,
written in collaboration with Laurence Housman; *The Harlequinade*, with Dion Clayton Calthrop; and Sacha Guitry's
Deburau, of which Barker made a free translation at the end
of the First World War. He first presented *Prunella* at the
Court Theatre in 1905, and his own performances as Pierrot,
with a bitter, almost sinister quality which disturbed the
audience, were reckoned among his finest acting achievements. Described by Max Beerbohm as 'the most sponta-
neously poetic' of contemporary plays, *Prunella*, like *The
Marrying of Ann Leete*, is set in a trim English garden and is
concerned with a young girl who escapes from its safety and
learns sadness and maturity through experience. Both plays
keep a careful distance from realism and offer emotion
distilled as mood.

Although *The Madras House* is a highly individual work
which no other playwright could have written, it emerged
from a collaboration of a different kind, with Shaw. Their
close association in the theatre and as friends outside it
involved reading and discussion of each other's plays in
progress, sharing and responding to each other's ideas. In
the last phase of the Barker and Vedrenne management,
after the lease of the Court had run out, Shaw's 'disquisitory'
play, *Getting Married*, was presented at the Haymarket
Theatre, against the topical background of a Divorce Law
Reform Association founded in 1906 and preparations for a
Royal Commission on Divorce and Matrimonial Causes
which would be in session from 1909 to 1912. There was an
element of 'anything you can do . . .' in Barker's capping of
this fantastic comedy, relating the marriage laws to human
nature and ideals, with his own witty panorama of English

society seen in terms of money and women, as laid down in the opening dialogue of *The Madras House*. (Shaw had set Dubedat's attitude to money and women in the scales against his artistic genius, in *The Doctor's Dilemma*.) Act Three shows Barker most obviously taking up the challenge to play Shaw at his own game: the meeting in the Board Room takes on an air of classical burlesque, as the god-like males give free rein to their views; what is un-Shavian is the gentle deflation of the characters as the meeting breaks up and the realities of ordinary life return.

The argument of Thorstein Veblen's *Theory of the Leisure Class* provided the basis for *The Madras House*. Veblen had represented the drive of patriarchal capitalism as reaching its zenith in a culture of luxury marked by conspicuous waste, conspicuous leisure and conspicuous consumption, permeating the arts and scholarship with the elevation of 'taste' and 'the classic', and finding its supreme human symbol in the *lady*, evolved over many generations out of the common labouring woman. One of the book's chapters is entitled 'Dress as an Expression of the Pecuniary Culture'; another, which may have influenced Barker's dramatisation of Sunday morning at Denmark Hill, is concerned with 'Religious Observances'.

The original production, in 1910, set *The Madras House* alongside Shaw's new play, *Misalliance*, in a programme of plays in repertory, carrying an intellectual and cultural assault into the theatre's commercial heartland. (This was the experimental scheme set up at the Duke of York's Theatre by Charles Frohman, supported by J. M. Barrie.) The two dramatists introduced cross-references to link their two plays: Constantine Madras knows Tarleton, the wealthy retailer of drapery in *Misalliance*; and Eustace Perrin State, the American who buys the Madras fashion emporium, shares Tarleton's conversational technique of literary quotation and allusion; less obviously, the two plays share a running imagery of domestic civilisation as a farmyard. The single set required for *Misalliance* is a conservatory, with a portable Turkish bath as its focal point; the Huxtables, in Act One of *The Madras House*, have a conservatory (which

produces a dead frog) and proudly show visitors its apotheo-
sis, the Crystal Palace of trade and industry, as the glory of
their view; the symbolism of the Turkish bath takes variant
form in Barker's play: his figure of political and sexual
imperialism, the aptly named Constantine Madras, has
become a Mohammedan, and the Madras House has a
Moorish Room. Few of the early reviews picked up on the
interplay, and audiences had little chance to do so: *Misalliance* had had only eleven performances and *The Madras
House* only ten when Frohman prematurely closed down the
enterprise, frightened by the slowness of business. So the
gloom of failure obscured *The Madras House* for fifteen years
and *Misalliance* for half a century. Now, when the two are
performed separately, what each retains from the early
association is the sense of fun, an effervescence of ideas,
puns, witty and fantastic inflections of plot, character and
argument, generated by the dramatists' friendly rivalry.
Shaw, who started later, finished his play ahead of Barker
and nudged him on by writing a travesty ending for *The
Madras House*. Under such pressure, Barker hurriedly
completed his work in his own way. Dissatisfied, he rewrote
the last scene, as part of a total revision of the play, before
directing it at the Ambassadors' Theatre in 1925. The
present volume gives this revised text which has long been
out of print.

Writing in 1910, P. P. Howe acknowledged the difficulty
first-night critics must have experienced in grasping the
range and complexity of the play before their midnight
deadline. He himself, given greater leisure, was in full
agreement with Max Beerbohm's verdict: 'It is a tremendous
synthesis'. Every detail matches up with others: the hat
which the maid catches on the door handle at the opening of
the play, and the hat on the Board Room table in Act Three;
the social rituals of the Huxtable household and the gyra-
tions of the mannequins; variations on the living-in system;
the missionary interests of the Huxtable sisters and their
uncle's conversion to Islam. The 1925 text seizes further
opportunities: State's involvement with canned peaches and
the ready-made skirt is as far from the 'virgin forest' he

dreams of as the 'cockpit of haphazard love-making' and the 'farmyard world of sex' are from Rousseau's noble savage; and the fairytale quality of the Crystal Palace presides ironically over State's threat to freeze out competition. Beerbohm found 'deeper and nimbler thought' and 'richer humour' in Act Three than in any other scene of modern drama known to him. Yet both he and P. P. Howe were aware of excited audiences failing to adjust to the meticulous naturalism of the final Act.

Desmond MacCarthy, reviewing the 1925 production, began by stressing the necessity for listening hard. (It is a necessity that applies to all Barker's drama and is a particular challenge to our more visually oriented day: yet we relegate the plays to radio to our own serious loss.) He found the effort rewarded at many levels, and this time there was general critical agreement. The superlatives abounded. James Agate found the first two Acts 'enthrallingly interesting and put together with a sympathy in which there is nothing maudlin' and was prepared to hazard that the ensemble playing was the finest ever to have been seen on the stage. By this time, comparisons with Chekhov were readily made. MacCarthy applauded the fact that Barker allowed his carefully observed monsters to keep their human dignity instead of simply ridiculing them. The ability to provoke in the audience, and hold in balance, contradictory reactions is characteristic of Barker's drama: in *The Madras House*, a high proportion of the characters simultaneously amuse, appal, even embarrass us, yet claim some human kinship with us; 'the awful thing is that one feels that these people really did exist,' said Agate. This penetrating, curiously empathetic naturalism is perhaps the hallmark of an actor writing brilliantly for actors who wanted to portray human beings. Certainly, in this production, player after player, right down the cast list, collected notices of the absolute truthfulness of their art.

The play was revived by the National Theatre in 1977, under the direction of William Gaskill, and again, in a production by Peter James, at Edinburgh's Lyceum Theatre during the 1992 Festival. (It later transferred to the Lyric

Theatre, Hammersmith.) The first of these followed Barker's text in loving detail and let the characters unfold at leisure: truthfulness was the keynote. The equilibrium of the whole play, ranging as it does from precise realism to fantastic extravagance, was held through the contrast between the impressive Disraelian figure of Constantine (Paul Scofield) and a finely sensitive Philip (Ronald Pickup). The more recent production sharpened and narrowed the play's focus, making it a more specifically feminist work by using as scene-changers a bevy of corsetted young women who spat contemptuous defiance as they worked. Within this frame Constantine dwindled, and the successive Acts became mirror-images of Philip's growing awareness: the actor (Roger Allam) as Wildean young-man-about-town, treated Thomas as Jack to his Algy, but progressed towards the intimate final scene with ever-deepening thoughtfulness.

In *Farewell to the Theatre*, the short piece Barker wrote before going into the Army in the First World War, he broaches the subject of a kind of altruism which may be the supreme attainment of an actor's maturity (turning the mirrors to the wall), but which audiences of the early twentieth century were slow to appreciate. He especially wanted such actors for roles like Philip Madras, which involve being more than doing. First published in the *Fortnightly Review* in 1916, *Farewell to the Theatre* seems never to have been performed publicly in London. It was probably intended as a contribution to a bill of three short plays, such as he liked to include at intervals in the repertory of his company. This example is also a showcase for a leading actress. There is something of Ellen Terry in Dorothy, a hint of young Cathleen Nesbitt, who had played Perdita in Granville Barker's 1912 production of *A Winter's Tale* and had been celebrated by Rupert Brooke. The incidents Dorothy recalls – of begging for theatrical sponsorship from millionaires – had actual counterparts in Lillah McCarthy's efforts to raise finance in support of her work, as actress and joint manager with her husband. She does not seem to have acted in this piece, though it might have been written expressly for her. 1916 was a year when opportunities for serious work in the theatre had run out; there was no reason to suppose that Granville Barker, as dramatist or director, was saying farewell to his art for ever. It was an appropriate juncture for a declaration of faith in the imaginative power of theatre and, more specifically, in truthfulness as its supreme virtue.

By the time he had finished *His Majesty*, in 1928, Granville Barker's relationship with the theatre had changed radically. He was not less devoted to the future of theatre in society, but it was clear that he would never again work regularly and full time on the stage. He had become an elder statesman of the theatre and was about to make Paris his home. Nicholas Hannen, who had played Philip Madras in 1925, was anxious to play the King in the new play, and there were discussions with Harcourt Williams who wanted to put it on at the Old Vic. Finding the right actress for Queen Rosamund proved difficult. No one interested had both the degree of determination and the means to realise the project. The text was published, but not kept in print for very long. Except for a radio adaptation on the BBC Third Programme in 1950, oblivion took over until the Orange Tree Theatre of Richmond gave the first stage performance at St Bride's Centre, Edinburgh, as part of the 1992 Granville Barker retrospective. It was an intelligent, and generally well-cast, arena production by Sam Walters, which made an easy transition to in-the-round conditions back at the home theatre in the following weeks. The performance began with the rolling-up of the map of Europe which covered the boards. The play was unfamiliar to most people who saw it, including the critics. Although more explicit and exciting in more usual ways than Granville Barker's other plays, it is not a drama for the weary to doze through. Audiences tended to find it gripping and entertaining, but long; reviewers' reactions varied from a forthright assertion that this was the finest play of the century to expressions of disappointment at this evidence of the decline of Granville Barker's talent after his second marriage and retirement into wealth. The most favourable reviews seem to have come from critics who already knew the play, and who were less likely to associate it literally with current debates over the British monarchy.

The central paradox on which *His Majesty* rests is perfectly articulated by Carnaby in *The Marrying of Ann Leete*: 'What is more useful in the world than honour?' The theatrical symbols of honour wielded in Barker's last play would be found in any theatrical property box: a sword, and a pearl necklace. (Awareness of theatricality is carefully preserved throughout, keeping realism at bay.) Monarchy itself is another key symbol, less tangible: most useful when most useless, a symbol divested of power, like an obsolete currency.

Though there is continuity of thought from the earlier plays, the dramatist was extending his range in new ways: setting his play on a world stage and tackling an epic drama of action and suspense with thriller qualities. He had been working on Shakespeare's texts for years, practically on the stage and in the study, preparing what would be widely known as his *Prefaces to Shakespeare*. Much of what he learned in the process contributed to what was now an unrivalled mastery of dramatic techniques for the exploration of themes such as authority and government, which are as crucial to the modern world as they were in Shakespeare's day.

At the centre of *His Majesty* is a figure comparable to Philip in *The Madras House*, with a clear intelligence of the situation yet disabled from action – this time through principle as well as temperament. The playwright sets King Henry, the exiled, hereditary ruler of Carpathia, back on his native soil, jostled on all sides by the forces of a de-stabilised Europe, following the First World War. The Romanovs have met their fate; the Hapsburgs tenuously survive, and the western democracies look on, ready to do what they can to contain anarchy in the Balkans. The precise events on which the plot and characters of *His Majesty* rest have been narrated quite recently by Gordon Brook-Shepherd in *The Last Empress* (1991), his biography of Archduchess Zita, consort of the last crowned ruler of Austria-Hungary. Much of the detail in the play, as well as the main events, has a factual origin, though there has been some changing around of identities and relationships. Barker's King and Queen reflect the contrasted qualities of their historical models, though Henry comes across as an abler man than his actual peace-loving prototype. In the imaginative scheme of the play, the historical Admiral Horthy is replaced by the two figures of Madrassy and Horvath; as Colonel Strutt, Archduke Charles's English adviser, an intriguer probably in love with Zita, has had his role divided into Captain Roger Dod and Guastalla, secretary and quick-change artist 'warranted to look well in uniform'. Shades of Rudolph Rassendyll of *The Prisoner of Zenda*! (The casting of Michael Hordern, a master of humane comedy, as Guastalla in the 1950 broadcast picked up the qualities the character needs as solvent for the play's diverse elements.) Even Archduchess Zita's famous pearls came ready to the dramatist's purpose. Brook-Shepherd himself notes the ironic confluence of life and comic opera in that Colonel Anton Léhar, who sent the invitation bringing Archduke Charles back, was brother to the composer of *The Merry Widow*. With various deft touches the playwright confirms the undertones of myth in the royal couple's actual descent from the skies and eventual departure – to some island of the blessed.

Perhaps the main challenge the play offers to our imaginations lies in the combination of elements of Ruritanian romance, a make-believe world which we cannot take seriously, with a confrontation of the dark universe of *realpolitik*, ruthless and pessimistic. ('There's one way to govern a country . . . just one,' says Bruckner. 'Find where its real power is . . . and give that play . . .') Bruckner himself is prophetic of Adolf Hitler as surely as he is a shadow of Bela Kun, the communist leader who had briefly held power in Hungary, and represents a European proletariat educated in brutality by the experience of war and its aftermath and grimly ready to pulverise the old order. ('We lucky ones have been borrowing prosperity for these few hundred years' was taken by Auriol Smith as a key line for her interpretation of Countess Czernyak.) Always a deeply ironic writer, holding emotional turbulence at bay with a cool and steady rationality, Granville Barker was attracted to forms of tragi-comedy (though *Waste* had been a deliberate essay in tragic form). It was the obvious answer to his problem of maintaining a thoughtful response to the material he was handling in *His Majesty*. He could rely on both Shaw and Shakespeare as guides. One of Shaw's early and best-known plays, *Arms and the Man*, had attached its thoughts on war to a previous Balkan conflict and dared to take comedy to the bounds of farce in keeping horror at a distance. Stephen Czernyak is Barker's counterpart to Sergius Saranoff, while Queen Rosamund is a Raina of riper years and more chastened emotion. Comedy is an essential part of the fabric of Shakespearian tragedy. The comic scene with the Countryman, which delays Cleopatra's ritual suicide, in *Antony and Cleopatra*, is forcibly recalled by Farmer Jakab's interview with the Queen in the last Act of *His Majesty*.

King Henry was played by Sam Dastor, at Edinburgh and Richmond, as an engaging saint of right thinking, an authorial voice that abides no question. Yet, as with Philip Madras, other elements in the play trouble the effect: Queen Rosamund is dangerously silly and ignorant – as was Nora Helmer in her doll's house, and as queens with little experience of ordinary life must be – but the actress (Caroline John, in this production) carries some audience sympathy with her as she dashes herself in exasperation at the King's steadfast moderation and genius for doing nothing. The passionate authenticity of her own faith and hunger for commitment give her, against reason, something like 'the right of it'.

The old dialogue Shaw and Barker had conducted through their work was to continue, although they were personally estranged by 1928. *The Apple Cart* (1929) is testimony that Shaw had grasped Barker's meanings in *His Majesty* – though the Shaw play, in its turn, has suffered from over-literal reading as a plea for monarchy rather than an assertion of the primacy of individual responsibility in politics against mass rule through trade unions and party machines. It remains a narrower statement than Barker's exposition of the integrity which gives moral authority to government, and his distinction between ideal democracy and the games of *mauvaise foi*, the public appearances of righteousness whereby most politicians contrive to exercise power.

The status of a play in print is always problematic. It becomes what we make of it. The custom whereby plays are not reviewed on publication, but only when they are performed (and in a new production, not a new edition), rests on an understanding that the script is incomplete except when it is realised on stage. Yet the opposite, though not irreconcilable, assumption is also widespread: that performances are interpretations of what resides, authentic and absolute, in the script. The plays collected in this volume force such considerations on our attention. Reading *The Marrying of Ann Leete* is a very different experience from what is involved in reading the others. There is a minimal compromise with readers: the scene of each Act is specified and characters are introduced with brief and general indications of type, and then we are plunged into elliptical dialogue, left to find and keep our own bearings, forced to do at least some of the work a director and actors would more normally undertake. *The Madras House*, on the other hand, opens with a leisurely, novelistic commentary, witty and entertaining in itself, in which the author communes with the reader over the heads, as it were, of the characters and the plot in which they are enmeshed. This is sharply distinct from the autonomy of a staged play in progress. Thomas Hardy remarked to Granville Barker that he always read his plays as if they were novels and commented on *Waste*: 'It holds you to the end – just as a good novel does'. Indeed, he tried to persuade the younger man to change direction and write novels, on the grounds that the stage was not capable of presenting such subtle and thoughtful insights into life and human beings as Granville Barker had to offer; but this commonly prevailing view of stage and actors was among the assumptions the latter, as actor, director and dramatist, had set himself to challenge, and had challenged with considerable success.

After the banning of *Waste* from public performance,

Barker was persuaded to publish the text in a first collection of plays (*Three Plays*, Sidgwick & Jackson, 1909). Shaw urged him to follow his own example in appealing to public opinion through a medium not subject to advance censorship by a public official. Shaw himself had decided in 1898 to publish the body of plays he had been unable to get produced, disguising the volumes with prefatory essays and lengthy notes on scenes and characters to which the misnomer, 'stage directions', soon became attached. Barker resisted Shaw's prompting that he should write a lengthy preface for his plays, but otherwise followed his example, as many later playwrights have done. The experiment of reading only the dialogue of *The Madras House*, Act One, will quickly reveal the problem he had to solve. It is too easy to slip over the repeated nothings on the page and feel cheated of substance. How potent and expressive they can be in performance may be inferred from the fact that an entire week was taken to rehearse the comings and goings, greetings and farewells, for the 1925 production. William Archer, a close colleague of Barker's in the campaign for a National Theatre, had urged the author of *The Marrying of Ann Leete* to be more explicit, to make things clearer to his audience, in effect to write more conventionally. Setting *His Majesty* alongside *Ann Leete* may suggest that Archer's persuasions had had their effect on Barker's later plays. Of course, the enigmatic dialogue manner of *Ann Leete* corresponds to dominant themes in the play; but similar themes of conspiracy and doublespeak are more explicitly demonstrated in *His Majesty*. In publishing his early play, the author let the lines stand without interpretation, relying on deliberate patterning of dialogue to suggest dramatic rhythms, and indicating pauses as precisely as Beckett and Pinter were later to do.

Margery Morgan, 1994

Note
This edition follows the printing convention of the original Granville Barker texts in reserving the use of italics for stage directions and employing letter spacing as an unobtrusive indication of particular emphasis within passages of dialogue.

The Marrying of Ann Leete

A Comedy

1899

The Marrying of Ann Leete was first presented by the Stage Society at the Royal Theatre on 26 January 1902, directed by the author.

The play was given a first full public production by the Royal Shakespeare Company at the Aldwych Theatre, 18 September 1975, with the following cast:

Carnaby Leete	Paul Rogers
Lady Cottesham (Sarah)	Estelle Kohler
George Leete	Mike Gwilym
Ann Leete	Mia Farrow
Sir George Leete Bt	John Boswall
Lady Leete	Judith Nelmes
Mrs Opie	Janet Whiteside
Dimmuck	Norman Tyrrell
John Abud	Oliver Cotton
Lord John Carp	Richard Pasco
Daniel Tatton	Martin Boddey
The Rev. Dr Remnant	Denis Holmes
Mr Tetgeen	Patrick Godfrey
Lord Arthur Carp	Jeffry Wickham
Mr Smallpeice	Doyne Byrd
Mr Crowe	Richard Mayes
Dolly Leete	Emma Williams
The Rev. Mr Tozer	Norman Ettlinger
Mr Prestige	Wilfred Grove
Mrs Prestige	Annette Badland

Directed by David Jones
Designed by Timothy O'Brien *and* Tazeena Firth

*The first three acts of the comedy pass in the garden at
Markswayde,* **Mr Carnaby Leete**'s *house near Reading,
during a summer day towards the close of the eighteenth
century: the first act at four in the morning, the second shortly
after mid-day, the third near to sunset. The fourth act takes
place one day in the following winter; the first scene in the hall
at Markswayde, the second scene in a cottage some ten miles
off.*

*This part of the Markswayde garden looks to have been laid
out during the seventeenth century. In the middle a fountain;
the centrepiece the figure of a nymph, now somewhat cracked,
and pouring nothing from the amphora; the rim of the fountain
is high enough and broad enough to be a comfortable seat.*

*The close turf around is in parts worn bare. This plot of
ground is surrounded by a terrace three feet higher. Three sides
of it are seen. From two corners broad steps lead down; stone
urns stand at the bottom and top of the stone balustrades. The
other two corners are rounded convexly into broad stone seats.*

*Along the edges of the terrace are growing rose trees, close
together; behind these, paths; behind those, shrubs and trees.
No landscape is to be seen. A big copper beech overshadows
the seat on the left. A silver birch droops over the seat on the
right. The trees far to the left indicate an orchard, the few to
the right are more of the garden sort. It is the height of
summer, and after a long drought the rose trees are
dilapidated.*

*It is very dark in the garden. Though there may be by now a
faint morning light in the sky it has not penetrated yet among
these trees. It is very still, too. Now and then the leaves of a
tree are stirred, as if in its sleep; that is all. Suddenly a shrill,*

frightened, but not tragical scream is heard. After a moment
Ann Leete *runs quickly down the steps and on to the*
fountain, where she stops, panting. **Lord John Carp** *follows*
her, but only to the top of the steps, evidently not knowing his
way. **Ann** *is a girl of twenty; he an English gentleman, nearer*
forty than thirty.

Lord John I apologise.

Ann Why is it so dark?

Lord John Can you hear what I'm saying?

Ann Yes.

Lord John I apologise for having kissed you . . . almost
unintentionally.

Ann Thank you. Mind the steps down.

Lord John I hope I'm sober, but the air . . .

Ann Shall we sit for a minute? There are several seats to
sit on somewhere.

Lord John This is a very dark garden.

There is a slight pause.

Ann You've won your bet.

Lord John So you did scream!

Ann But it wasn't fair.

Lord John Don't reproach me.

Ann Somebody's coming.

Lord John How d'you know?

Ann I can h e a r somebody coming.

Lord John We're not sitting down.

Ann's brother, **George Leete**, *comes to the top of the steps, and afterwards down them. Rather an old young man.*

George Ann!

Ann Yes.

George My lord!

Lord John Here.

George I can't see you. I'm sent to say we're all anxious to know what ghost or other bird of night or beast has frightened Ann to screaming point, and won you . . . the best in Tatton's stables – so he says now. He's quite annoyed.

Lord John The mare is a very good mare.

Ann He betted it because he wanted to bet it; I didn't want him to bet it.

George What frightened her?

Ann I had rather, my lord, that you did not tell my brother why I screamed.

Lord John I kissed her.

George Did you?

Ann I had rather, Lord John, that you had not told my brother why I screamed.

Lord John I misunderstood you.

George I've broke up the whist party. Ann, shall we return?

Lord John She's not here.

George Ann.

Lady Cottesham, **Ann**'s *sister and ten years older,* and **Mr Daniel Tatton**, *a well-living, middle-aged country*

gentleman, arrive together. **Tatton** *carries a double candlestick
. . . the lights out.*

Mr Tatton Three steps?

Sarah No . . . four.

Lord John Miss Leete.

Tatton *in the darkness finds himself close to* **George**.

Mr Tatton I am in a rage with you, my lord.

George He lives next door.

Mr Tatton My mistake. (*He passes on.*) Confess that she
did it to please you.

Lord John Screamed!

Mr Tatton Lost my bet. We'll say . . . won your bet . . .
to please you. Was skeered at the dark . . . oh, fie!

Lord John Miss Leete trod on a toad.

Mr Tatton I barred toads . . . here.

Lord John I don't think it.

Mr Tatton I barred toads. Did I forget to? Well . . . it's
better to be a sportsman.

Sarah And whereabout is she?

Ann (*from the corner she has slunk to*) Here I am, Sally.

Mr Tatton Miss Ann, I forgive you. I'm smiling, I assure
you, I'm smiling.

Sarah We all laughed when we heard you.

Mr Tatton Which reminds me, young George Leete, had
you the ace?

George King . . . knave . . . here are the cards, but I
can't see.

Mr Tatton I had the king.

Ann (*quietly to her sister*) He kissed me.

Sarah A man would.

George What were trumps?

Mr Tatton What were we playing . . . cricket?

Ann (*as quietly again*) D'you think I'm blushing?

Sarah It's probable.

Ann I am by the feel of me.

Sarah George, we left Papa sitting quite still.

Lord John Didn't he approve of the bet?

Mr Tatton He said nothing.

Sarah Why, who doesn't love sport!

Mr Tatton I'm the man to grumble. Back a woman's pluck again . . . never. My lord . . . you weren't the one to go with her as umpire.

George No . . . to be sure.

Mr Tatton How was it I let that pass? Playing two games at once. Haven't I cause of complaint? But a man must give and take.

The master of the house, father of **George** *and* **Sarah Cottesham** *and* **Ann,** *Mr Carnaby Leete, comes slowly down the steps, unnoticed by the others. A man over fifty – à la Lord Chesterfield.*

George (*to* **Lord John**) Are you sure you're quite comfortable there?

Lord John Whatever I'm sitting on hasn't given way yet.

Mr Tatton Don't forget that you're riding to Brighton with me.

Lord John Tomorrow.

George Today. Well . . . the hour before sunrise is no time at all.

Mr Tatton Sixty-five miles.

Lord John What are we all sitting here for?

Mr Tatton I say people ought to be in bed and asleep.

Carnaby But the morning air is delightful.

Mr Tatton (*jumping at the new voice*) Leete! Now, had you the ace?

Carnaby Of course.

Mr Tatton We should have lost that too, Lady Charlie.

Sarah Bear up, Mr Tat.

Mr Tatton Come, a game of whist is a game of whist.

Carnaby And so I strolled out after you all.

Mr Tatton She trod on a toad.

Carnaby (*carelessly*) Does she say so?

Mr Tatton (*with mock roguishness*) Ah!

George *is on the terrace, looking to the left through the trees.* **Tatton** *is sitting on the edge of the fountain.*

George Here's the sun . . . to show us ourselves.

Mr Tatton Leete, this pond is full of water!

Carnaby Ann, if you are there . . .

Ann Yes, Papa.

Carnaby Apologise profusely; it's your garden.

Ann Oh . . .

Carnaby Coat-tails, Tatton . . . or worse?

Mr Tatton (*ruefully discovering damp spots about him*) Nothing vastly to matter.

Lord John Hardy, well-preserved, country gentleman!

Mr Tatton I bet I'm a younger man than you, my lord.

Ann (*suddenly to the company generally*) I didn't tread upon any toad . . . I was kissed.

There is a pause of some discomfort.

Sarah Ann, come here to me.

Lord John I apologised.

George (*from the terrace*) Are we to be insulted?

Carnaby My dear Carp, say no more.

There is another short pause. By this it is twilight, faces can be plainly seen.

Sarah Listen . . . the first bird.

Mr Tatton Oh, dear no, they begin to sing long before this.

Carnaby What is it now . . . a lark?

Mr Tatton I don't know.

Ann (*quietly to* **Sarah**) That's a thrush.

Sarah (*capping her*) A thrush.

Carnaby Charming!

Mr Tatton (*To* **Lord John**) I don't see why you couldn't have told me how it was that she screamed.

Carnaby Our dear Tatton! (*Sotto voce to his son.*) Hold your tongue, George.

Mr Tatton I did bar toads and you said I didn't, and anyway I had a sort of right to know.

Lord John You know now.

Sarah I wonder if this seat is dry.

Lord John There's been no rain for weeks.

Sarah The roads will be dusty for you, Mr Tat.

Mr Tatton Just one moment. You don't mind me, Miss Ann, do you?

Ann I don't mind much.

Mr Tatton We said distinctly . . . To the orchard end of the garden and back and if frightened – that's the word – so much as to scream . . . ! Now, what I want to know is . . .

Lord John Consider the bet off.

Mr Tatton Certainly not. And we should have added . . . Alone.

Carnaby Tatton has persistence.

Sarah Mr Tat, do you know where people go who take things seriously?

Mr Tatton Miss Leete, were you frightened when Lord John kissed you?

George Damnation!

Carnaby My excellent Tatton, much as I admire your searchings after truth I must here parentally intervene, regretting, my dear Tatton, that my own carelessness of duennahood has permitted this – this . . . to occur.

After this, there is silence for a minute.

Lord John Can I borrow a horse of you, Mr Leete?

Carnaby My entire stable; and your Ronald shall be physicked.

Sarah Spartans that you are to be riding!

Lord John I prefer it to a jolting chaise.

Mr Tatton You will have my mare.

Lord John (*ignoring him*) This has been a most enjoyable three weeks.

Carnaby Four.

Lord John Is it four?

Carnaby We bow to the compliment. Our duty to his grace.

Lord John When I see him.

George To our dear cousin.

Mr Tatton (*to* **Lady Cottesham**) Sir Charles at Brighton?

Sarah (*not answering*) To be sure . . . we did discover . . . our mother was second cousin . . . once removed to you.

Carnaby If the prince will be there . . . he is in waiting.

Lord John Any message, Lady Cottesham? . . . since we speak out of session.

Sarah I won't trust you.

Carnaby Or trouble you while I still may frank a letter. But my son-in-law is a wretched correspondent. Do you admire men of small vices? They make admirable husbands though their wives will be grumbling – Silence, Sarah – but that's a good sign.

Sarah Papa is a connoisseur of humanity.

Ann (*to the company as before*) No, Mr Tatton, I wasn't frightened when Lord John . . . kissed me. I screamed because I was surprised, and I'm sorry I screamed.

Sarah (*quietly to* **Ann**) My dear Ann, you're a fool.

Ann (*quietly to* **Sarah**) I will speak sometimes.

Sarah Sit down again.

Again an uncomfortable silence, a ludicrous air about it this time.

Mr Tatton Now, we'll say no more about that bet, but I was right.

Lord John Do you know, Mr Tatton, that I have a temper to lose?

Mr Tatton What the devil does that matter to me, sir . . . my lord?

Lord John I owe you a saddle and bridle.

Mr Tatton You'll oblige me by taking the mare.

Lord John We'll discuss it tomorrow.

Mr Tatton I've said all I have to say.

George The whole matter's ridiculous!

Mr Tatton I see the joke. Goodnight, Lady Cottesham, and I kiss your hand.

Sarah Good morning, Mr Tat.

Mr Tatton Good morning, Miss Ann, I . . .

Sarah (*shielding her sister*) Good morrow is appropriate.

Mr Tatton I'll go by the fields. (*To* **Carnaby**.) Thank you for a pleasant evening. Good morrow, George. Do we start at mid-day, my lord?

Lord John Any time you please.

Mr Tatton Not at all. (*He hands the candlestick – of which he has never before left go – to* **George**.) I brought this for a link. Thank you.

Carnaby Mid-day will be midnight if you sleep at all now; make it two or later.

Mr Tatton We put up at Guildford. I've done so before. I haven't my hat. It's a day and a half's ride.

Tatton *goes quickly up the other steps and away. It is now quite light.* **George** *stands by the steps,* **Lord John** *is on one of the seats,* **Carnaby** *strolls round, now and then touching the rose trees,* **Sarah** *and* **Ann** *are on the other seat.*

George Morning! These candles still smell.

Sarah How lively one feels and isn't.

Carnaby The flowers are opening.

Ann (*in a whisper*) Couldn't we go in?

Sarah Never run away.

Ann Everything looks so odd.

Sarah What's o'clock . . . my lord?

Lord John Half after four.

Ann (*to* **Sarah**) My eyes are hot behind.

George What ghosts we seem!

Sarah What has made us spend such a night?

Carnaby Ann incited me to it. (*He takes snuff.*)

Sarah In a spirit of rebellion against good country habits . . .

Ann (*to her sister again*) Don't talk about me.

Sarah They can see that you're whispering.

Carnaby . . . Informing me now she was a woman and wanted excitement.

George There's a curse.

Carnaby How else d'ye conceive life for women?

Sarah George is naturally cruel. Excitement's our education. Please vary it, though.

Carnaby I have always held that to colour in the world-picture is the greatest privilege of the husband, Sarah.

Sarah (*not leaving* **Ann**'s *side*) Yes, Papa.

Carnaby Sarah, when Sir Charles leaves Brighton . . .

Sarah *rises but will not move further.*

Carnaby (*sweetly threatening*) Shall I come to you?

But she goes to him now.

Carnaby By a gossip letter from town . . .

Sarah (*tensely*) What is it?

Carnaby You mentioned to me something of his visiting Naples.

Sarah Very well. I detest Italy.

Carnaby Let's have George's opinion.

He leads her towards **George**.

George Yes?

Carnaby Upon Naples.

George I remember Naples.

Carnaby Sarah, admire those roses.

Sarah (*cynically echoing her father*) Let's have George's opinion.

Now **Carnaby** *has drawn them both away, upon the terrace, and, the coast being clear,* **Lord John** *walks towards* **Ann***, who looks at him very scaredly.*

Carnaby Emblem of secrecy among the ancients.

Sarah Look at this heavy head, won't it snap off?

The three move out of sight.

Lord John I'm sober now.

Ann I'm not.

Lord John Uncompromising young lady.

Ann And, excuse me, I don't want to . . . play.

Lord John Don't you wish me to apologise quietly to you?

Ann Good manners are all mockery, I'm sure.

Lord John I'm very much afraid you're a cynic.

Ann I'm not trying to be clever.

Lord John Do I tease you?

Ann Do I amuse you?

Lord John How dare I say so!

Ann (*after a moment*) I was not frightened.

Lord John You kissed me back.

Ann Not on purpose. What do two people mean by behaving so . . . in the dark?

Lord John I am exceedingly sorry that I hurt your feelings.

Ann Thank you, I like to feel.

Lord John And you must forgive me.

Ann Tell me, why did you do it?

Lord John Honestly I don't know. I should do it again.

Ann That's not quite true, is it?

Lord John I think so.

Ann What does it matter at all!

Lord John Nothing.

George, **Sarah** *and then* **Carnaby** *move into sight and along the terrace,* **Lord John** *turns to them.*

Lord John Has this place been long in your family, Mr Leete?

Carnaby Markswayde my wife brought us, through the Peters's . . . old Chiltern people . . . connections of yours, of course. There is no entail.

Lord John *walks back to* **Ann**.

Sarah George, you assume this republicanism as you would – no, would not – a coat of latest cut.

Carnaby Never argue with him . . . persist.

Sarah So does he.

The three pass along the terrace.

Ann (*to* **Lord John**) Will you sit down?

Lord John It's not worth while. Do you know I must be quite twice your age?

Ann A doubled responsibility, my lord.

Lord John I suppose it is.

Ann I don't say so. That's a phrase from a book . . . sounded well.

Lord John My dear Miss Ann . . . (*He stops.*)

Ann Go on being polite.

Lord John If you'll keep your head turned away.

Ann Why must I?

Lord John There's lightning in the glances of your eye.

Ann Do use vulgar words to me.

Lord John (*with a sudden fatherly kindness*) Go to bed . . . you're dead tired. And goodbye . . . I'll be gone before you wake.

Ann Goodbye.

She shakes hands with him, then walks towards her father who is coming down the steps.

Ann Papa, don't my roses want looking to?

Carnaby (*pats her cheek*) These?

Ann Those.

Carnaby Abud is under your thumb, horticulturally speaking.

Ann Where's Sally?

She goes on to **Sarah**, *who is standing with* **George** *at the top of the steps.* **Carnaby** *looks* **Lord John** *up and down.*

Lord John (*dusting his shoulder*) This cursed powder!

Carnaby Do we respect innocence enough . . . any of us?

George *comes down the steps and joins them.*

George Respectable politics will henceforth be useless to me.

Carnaby My lord, was his grace satisfied with the young man's work abroad or was he not?

Lord John My father used to curse everyone.

Carnaby That's a mere Downing Street custom.

Lord John And I seem to remember that a letter of yours from . . . where were you in those days?

George Paris . . . Naples . . . Vienna.

Lord John One place . . . once lightened a fit of gout.

Carnaby George, you have in you the makings of a minister.

George No.

Carnaby Remember the Age tends to the disreputable.

George *moves away,* **Sarah** *moves towards them.*

Carnaby George is something of a genius, stuffed with theories and possessed of a curious conscience. But I am fortunate in my children.

Lord John All the world knows it.

Carnaby (*to* **Sarah**) It's lucky that yours was a love match, too. I admire you. Ann is 'to come', so to speak.

Sarah (*to* **Lord John**) Were you discussing affairs?

Lord John Not I.

George Ann.

Ann Yes, George.

She goes to him; they stroll together up the steps and along the terrace.

Sarah I'm desperately fagged.

Lord John (*politely*) A seat.

Sarah Also tired of sitting.

Carnaby Let's have the Brighton news, Carp.

Lord John If there's any.

Carnaby Probably I still command abuse. Even my son-in-law must, by courtesy, join in the cry . . . ah, poor duty-torn Sarah! You can spread abroad that I am as a green bay tree.

Carnaby *paces slowly away from them.*

Lord John Your father's making a mistake.

Sarah D'you think so?

Lord John He's played the game once.

Sarah I was not then in the knowledge of things when he left you.

Lord John We remember it.

Sarah I should like to hear it.

Lord John I have avoided this subject.

Sarah With him, yes.

Lord John Oh! . . . why did I desert the army for politics?

Sarah Better fighting.

Lord John It sat so nobly upon him . . . the leaving us for conscience sake when we were strongly in power. Strange that six months later we should be turned out.

Sarah Papa was lucky.

Lord John But this second time . . . ?

Sarah Listen. This is very much a private quarrel with Mr Pitt, who hates Papa . . . gets rid of him.

Lord John Shall I betray a confidence?

Sarah Better not.

Lord John My father advised me to this visit.

Sarah Your useful visit. More than kind of his grace.

Lord John Yes . . . there's been a paragraph in the *Morning Chronicle*, 'The Whigs woo Mr Carnaby Leete.'

Sarah We saw to it.

Lord John My poor father seems anxious to discover whether the Leete episode will repeat itself entirely. He is chronically unhappy in opposition. Are your husband and his colleagues trembling in their seats?

Sarah I can't say.

Lord John Politics is a game for clever children, and women, and fools. Will you take a word of warning from a soldier? Your father is past his prime.

Carnaby *paces back towards them.*

Carnaby I'm getting to be old for these all-night sittings. I must be writing to your busy brother.

Lord John Arthur? . . . is at his home.

Sarah Pleasantly sounding phrase.

Carnaby His grace deserted?

Sarah Quite secretaryless!

Lord John Lady Arthur lately has been brought to bed. I heard yesterday.

Sarah The seventh, is it not? Children require living up to. My congratulations.

Lord John Won't you write them?

Sarah We are not intimate.

Lord John A good woman.

Sarah Evidently. Where's Ann? We'll go in.

Lord John You're a mother to your sister.

Sarah Not I.

Carnaby My wife went her ways into the next world; Sarah hers into this; and our little Ann was left with a most admirable governess. One must never reproach circumstances. Man educates woman in his own good time.

Lord John I suppose she, or any young girl, is all heart.

Carnaby What is it that you call heart . . . sentimentally speaking?

Sarah Any bud in the morning.

Lord John That man Tatton's jokes are in shocking taste.

Carnaby Tatton is honest.

Lord John I'm much to blame for having won that bet.

Carnaby Say no more.

Lord John What can Miss Ann think of me?

Sarah Don't ask her.

Carnaby Innocency's opinions are invariably entertaining.

Lord John Am I the first . . . ? I really beg your pardon.

George and **Ann** come down the steps together.

Carnaby Ann, what do you think . . . that is to say – and answer me truthfully . . . what at this moment is your inclination of mind towards my lord here?

Ann I suppose I love him.

Lord John I hope not.

Ann I suppose I love you.

Carnaby No . . no . . no . . no . . no . . no.

Sarah Hush, dear.

Ann I'm afraid, papa, there's something very ill-bred in me.

Down the steps and into the midst of them comes **John Abud**, *carrying his tools, among other things a twist of bass. A young gardener, honest, clean and common.*

Abud (*to* **Carnaby**) I ask pardon, sir.

Carnaby So early, Abud! . . . this is your territory. So late . . . Bed.

Ann *starts away up the steps,* **Sarah** *is following her.*

Lord John Goodbye, Lady Cottesham.

At this **Ann** *stops for a moment, but then goes straight on.*

Sarah A pleasant journey.

Sarah *departs too.*

George (*stretching himself*) I'm roused.

Carnaby (*to* **Abud**) Leave your tools here for a few moments.

Abud I will, sir.

Abud *leaves them, going along the terrace and out of sight.*

Carnaby My head is hot. Pardon me.

Carnaby *is sitting on the fountain rim; he dips his handkerchief in the water, and wrings it; then takes off his wig and binds the damp handkerchief round his head.*

Carnaby Wigs are most comfortable and old fashioned . . . unless you choose to be a cropped republican like my son.

George Nature!

Carnaby Nature grows a beard, sir.

Lord John I've seen Turks.

Carnaby Horrible . . . horrible! Sit down, Carp.

Lord John *sits on the fountain rim.* **George** *begins to pace restlessly; he has been nursing the candlestick ever since* **Tatton** *handed it to him.*

Carnaby George, you look damned ridiculous strutting arm-in-arm with that candlestick.

George I am ridiculous.

Carnaby If you're cogitating over your wife and her expectations . . .

George *paces up the steps and away. There is a pause.*

Carnaby D'ye tell stories . . . good ones?

Lord John Sometimes.

Carnaby There'll be this.

Lord John I shan't.

Carnaby Say no more. If I may so express myself, Carp, you have been taking us for granted.

Lord John How wide awake you are! I'm not.

Carnaby My head's cool. Shall I describe your conduct as an unpremeditated insult?

Lord John Don't think anything of the sort.

Carnaby There speaks your kind heart.

Lord John Are you trying to pick a quarrel with me?

Carnaby As may be.

Lord John Why?

Carnaby For the sake of appearances.

Lord John Damn all appearances.

Carnaby Now I'll lose my temper. Sir, you have compromised my daughter.

Lord John Nonsense!

Carnaby Villain! What's your next move?

For a moment **Lord John** *sits with knit brows.*

Lord John (*brutally*) Mr Leete, your name stinks.

Carnaby My point of dis-ad-vantage!

Lord John (*apologising*) Please say what you like. I might have put my remark better.

Carnaby I think not; the homely Saxon phrase is our literary dagger. Princelike, you ride away from Markswayde. Can I trust you not to stab a socially sick man? Why it's a duty you owe to society . . . to weed out . . . us.

Lord John I'm not a coward. How?

Carnaby A little laughter . . . in your exuberance of health.

Lord John You may trust me not to tell tales.

Carnaby Of what . . . of whom?

Lord John Of here.

Carnaby And what is there to tell of here?

Lord John Nothing.

Carnaby But how your promise betrays a capacity for good-natured invention!

Lord John If I lie call me out.

Carnaby I don't deal in sentiment. I can't afford to be talked about otherwise than as I choose to be. Already the Aunt Sally of the hour; having under pressure of circumstances resigned my office; dating my letters from the borders of the Chiltern Hundreds . . . I am a poor politician, sir, and I must live.

Lord John I can't see that your family's infected . . . affected.

Carnaby With a penniless girl you really should have been more circumspect.

Lord John I might ask to marry her.

Carnaby My lord!

In the pause that ensues he takes up the twist of bass to play with.

Lord John What should you say to that?

Carnaby The silly child supposed she loved you.

Lord John Yes.

Carnaby Is it a match?

Lord John (*full in the other's face*) What about the appearances of blackmail?

Carnaby (*compressing his thin lips*) Do you care for my daughter?

Lord John I could . . . at a pinch.

Carnaby Now, my lord, you are insolent.

Lord John Is this when we quarrel?

Carnaby I think I'll challenge you.

Lord John That will look well.

Carnaby You'll value that kiss when you've paid for it. Kindly choose Tatton as your second. I want his tongue to wag both ways.

Lord John I was forgetting how it all began.

Carnaby George will serve me . . . protesting. His principles are vile, but he has the education of a gentleman. Swords or . . . ? Swords. And at noon shall we say? There's shade behind a certain barn, midway between this and Tatton's.

Lord John (*not taking him seriously yet*) What if we both die horridly?

Carnaby You are at liberty to make me a written apology.

Lord John A joke's a joke.

Carnaby *deliberately strikes him in the face with the twist of bass.*

Lord John That's enough.

Carnaby (*in explanatory apology*) My friend, you are so obtuse. Abud!

Lord John Mr Leete, are you serious?

Carnaby Perfectly serious. Let's go to bed. Abud, you can get to your work.

Wig in hand, **Mr Leete** *courteously conducts his guest towards the house.* **Abud** *returns to his tools and his morning's work.*

Act Two

Shortly after mid-day, while the sun beats strongly upon the terrace, **Abud** *is working dexterously at the rose trees.* **Dr Remnant** *comes down the steps, hatted, and carrying a stick and a book. He is an elderly man with a kind manner; type of the eighteenth century casuistical parson. On his way he stops to say a word to the gardener.*

Dr Remnant Will it rain before nightfall?

Abud About then, sir, I should say.

Down the other steps comes **Mrs Opie**, *a prim, decorous, but well bred and unobjectionable woman. She is followed by* **Ann**.

Mrs Opie A good morning to you, Parson.

Dr Remnant And to you, Mrs Opie, and to Miss Ann.

Ann Good morning, Dr Remnant. (*To* **Abud**.) Have you been here ever since . . . ?

Abud I've had dinner, miss.

Abud's *work takes him gradually out of sight.*

Mrs Opie We are but just breakfasted.

Dr Remnant I surmise dissipation.

Ann (*to* **Mrs Opie**) Thank you for waiting five hours.

Mrs Opie It is my rule to breakfast with you.

Dr Remnant (*exhibiting the book*) I am come to return, and to borrow.

Ann Show me.

Dr Remnant Ballads by Robert Burns.

Ann (*taking it*) I'll put it back.

Mrs Opie (*taking it from her*) I've never heard of him.

Dr Remnant Oh, ma'am, a very vulgar poet!

George Leete *comes quickly down the steps.*

George (*to* **Remnant**) How are you?

Dr Remnant Yours, sir.

George Ann.

Ann Good morning, George.

George Did you sleep well?

Ann I always do . . . but I dreamt.

George I must sit down for a minute. (*Nodding.*) Mrs Opie.

Mrs Opie I wish you a good morning, sir.

George (*to* **Ann**) Don't look so solemn.

Lady Cottesham *comes quickly to the top of the steps.*

Sarah Is Papa badly hurt?

Ann (*jumping up*) Oh, what has happened?

George Not badly.

Sarah He won't see me.

His three children look at each other.

Dr Remnant (*tactfully*) May I go my ways to the library?

Sarah Please do, Doctor Remnant.

Dr Remnant I flatly contradicted all that was being said in the village.

Sarah Thoughtful of you.

Dr Remnant But tell me nothing.

Dr Remnant *bows formally and goes.* **George** *is about to speak when* **Sarah** *with a look at* **Mrs Opie** *says . . .*

Sarah George, hold your tongue.

Mrs Opie (*with much hauteur*) I am in the way.

At this moment **Dimmuck,** *an old but unbenevolent-looking butler, comes to the top of the steps.*

Dimmuck The master wants Mrs Opie.

Mrs Opie Thank you.

George Your triumph!

Mrs Opie *is departing radiant.*

Dimmuck How was I to know you was in the garden?

Mrs Opie I am sorry to have put you to the trouble of a search, Mr Dimmuck.

Dimmuck He's in his room.

And he follows her towards the house.

George Carp fought with him at twelve o'clock.

The other two cannot speak from amazement.

Sarah No!

George Why, they didn't tell me and I didn't ask. Carp was laughing. Tatton chuckled . . . afterwards.

Sarah What had he to do?

George Carp's second.

Sarah Unaccountable children!

George Feather parade . . . throw in . . . parry quarte: over the arm . . . put by: feint . . . flanconade and through his arm . . . damned easy. The father didn't wince or say a word. I bound it up . . . the sight of blood makes me sick.

After a moment, **Sarah** *turns to* **Ann**.

Sarah Yes, and you've been a silly child.

George Ah, give me a woman's guess and the most unlikely reason to account for anything!

Ann I hate that man. I'm glad Papa's not hurt. What about a surgeon?

George No, you shall kiss the place well, and there'll be poetic justice done.

Sarah How did you all part?

George With bows and without a word.

Sarah Coming home with him?

George Not a word.

Sarah Papa's very clever; but I'm puzzled.

George Something will happen next, no doubt.

Ann Isn't this done with?

Sarah So it seems.

Ann I should like to be told just what the game has been.

George Bravo, Ann.

Ann Tell me the rules . . . for next time.

Sarah It would have been most advantageous for us to have formed an alliance with Lord John Carp, who stood here for his father and his father's party . . . now in opposition.

George Look upon yourself – not too seriously – Ann, as the instrument of political destiny.

Ann I'm afraid I take in fresh ideas very slowly. Why has Papa given up the Stamp Office?

Sarah His colleagues wouldn't support him.

Ann Why was that?

Sarah They disapproved of what he did.

Ann Did he do right . . . giving it up?

Sarah Yes.

George We hope so. Time will tell. An irreverent quipster once named him Carnaby Leech.

Sarah I know.

George I wonder if his true enemies think him wise to have dropped off the Stamp Office?

Ann Has he quarrelled with Sir Charles?

Sarah Politically.

Ann Isn't that awkward for you?

Sarah Not a bit.

George Hear a statement that includes our lives. Markswayde goes at his death . . . see reversionary mortgage. The income's an annuity now. The cash in the house will be ours. The debts are paid . . . at last.

Ann And there remains me.

George Bad grammar. Meanwhile our father is a tongue, which is worth buying; but I don't think he ought to go over to the enemy . . . for the second time.

Sarah One party is as good as another; each works for the same end, I should hope.

George I won't argue about it.

Ann I suppose that a woman's profession is marriage.

George My lord has departed.

Ann There'll be others to come. I'm not afraid of being married.

Sarah What did Papa want Mrs Opie for?

Ann There'll be a great many things I shall want to know about men now.

George Wisdom cometh with sorrow . . . oh, my sister.

Sarah I believe you two are both about as selfish as you can be.

George I am an egoist . . . with attachments.

Ann Make use of me.

George Ann, you marry – when you marry – to please yourself.

Ann There's much in life that I don't like, Sally.

Sarah There's much more that you will.

George I think we three have never talked together before.

Abud, *who has been in sight on the terrace for a few moments, now comes down the steps.*

Abud May I make so bold, sir, as to ask how is Mrs George Leete?

George She was well when I last heard.

Abud Thank you, sir. (*And he returns to his work.*)

Ann I wonder will it be a boy or a girl.

George Poor weak woman.

Sarah Be grateful to her.

Ann A baby is a wonderful thing.

Sarah Babyhood in the abstract . . . beautiful.

Ann Even kittens . . . (*She stops, and then in rather childish embarrassment, moves away from them.*)

Sarah Don't shudder, George.

George I have no wish to be a father. Why?

Sarah It's a vulgar responsibility.

George My wayside flower!

Sarah Why pick it?

George Sarah, I love my wife.

Sarah That's easily said.

George She should be here.

Sarah George, you married to please yourself.

George By custom her rank is my own.

Sarah Does she still drop her aitches?

George Dolly . . .

Sarah Pretty name.

George Dolly aspires to be one of us.

Sarah Child-bearing makes these women blowzy.

George Oh heaven!

Ann (*calling to* **Abud** *on the terrace*) Finish today, Abud. If it rains . . .

She stops, seeing **Mr Tetgeen** *standing at the top of the steps leading from the house. This is an intensely respectable, selfcontained-looking lawyer, but a man of the world too.*

Mr Tetgeen Lady Cottesham.

Sarah Sir?

Mr Tetgeen My name is Tetgeen.

Sarah Mr Tetgeen. How do you do?

Mr Tetgeen The household appeared to be in some confusion and I took the liberty to be my own messenger. I am anxious to speak with you.

Sarah Ann, dear, ask if Papa will see you now.

Dimmuck *appears.*

Dimmuck The master wants you, Miss Ann.

Sarah Ask papa if he'll see me soon.

Ann *goes towards the house.*

Sarah Dimmuck, Mr Tetgeen has been left to find his own way here.

Dimmuck I couldn't help it, my lady. (*And he follows* **Ann**.)

Sarah Our father is confined to his room.

George By your leave.

Then **George** *takes himself off up the steps, and out of sight. The old lawyer bows to* **Lady Cottesham**, *who regards him steadily.*

Mr Tetgeen From Sir Charles . . . a talking machine.

Sarah Please sit.

He sits carefully upon the rim of the fountain, she upon the seat opposite.

Sarah (*glancing over her shoulder*) Will you talk nonsense until the gardener is out of hearing? He is on his way away. You have had a tiring journey?

Mr Tetgeen Thank you, no . . . by the night coach to Reading and thence I have walked.

Sarah The country is pretty, is it not?

Mr Tetgeen It compares favourably with other parts.

Sarah Do you travel much, Mr Tetgeen? He has gone.

Mr Tetgeen (*deliberately and sharpening his tone ever so little*) Sir Charles does not wish to petition for a divorce.

Sarah (*controlling even her sense of humour*) I have no desire to jump over the moon.

Mr Tetgeen His scruples are religious. The case would be weak upon some important points, and there has been no public scandal . . . at the worst, very little.

Sarah My good manners are, I trust, irreproachable, and you may tell Sir Charles that my conscience is my own.

Mr Tetgeen Your husband's in the matter of . . .

Sarah Please say the word.

Mr Tetgeen Pardon me . . . not upon mere suspicion.

Sarah Now, is it good policy to suspect what is incapable of proof?

Mr Tetgeen I advise Sir Charles, that, should you come to an open fight, he can afford to lose.

Sarah And have I no right to suspicions?

Mr Tetgeen Certainly. Are they of use to you?

Sarah I have been a tolerant wife, expecting toleration.

Mr Tetgeen Sir Charles is anxious to take into consideration any complaints you may have to make against him.

Sarah I complain if he complains of me.

Mr Tetgeen For the first time, I think . . . formally.

Sarah Why not have come to me?

Mr Tetgeen Sir Charles is busy.

Sarah (*disguising a little spasm of pain*) Shall we get to business?

Mr Tetgeen *now takes a moment to find his phrase.*

Mr Tetgeen I don't know the man's name.

Sarah This, surely, is how you might address a seduced housemaid.

Mr Tetgeen But Sir Charles and he, I understand, have talked the matter over.

The shock of this brings **Sarah** *to her feet, white with anger.*

Sarah Divorce me.

Mr Tetgeen (*sharply*) Is there ground for it?

Sarah (*with a magnificent recovery of self control*) I won't tell you that.

Mr Tetgeen I have said we have no case . . . that is to say, we don't want one; but any information is a weapon in store.

Sarah You did quite right to insult me.

Mr Tetgeen As a rule I despise such methods.

Sarah It's a lie that they met . . . those two men?

Mr Tetgeen It may be.

Sarah It must be.

Mr Tetgeen I have Sir Charles's word. (*Now he takes from his pocket some notes, putting on his spectacles to read them.*)

Sarah What's this . . . a written lecture?

Mr Tetgeen We propose . . . first: that the present complete severance of conjugal relations shall continue. Secondly: that Lady Cottesham shall be at liberty to remove from South Audley Street and Ringham Castle all personal and private effects, excepting those family jewels which have merely been considered her property. Thirdly: Lady Cottesham shall undertake, formally and in writing, not to molest – a legal term – Sir Charles Cottesham. (*Her handkerchief has dropped, here he picks it up and restores it to her.*) Allow me, my lady.

Sarah I thank you.

Mr Tetgeen (*continuing*) Fourthly: Lady Cottesham shall undertake . . . etc. . . . not to inhabit or frequent the city and towns of London, Brighthelmstone, Bath, The Tunbridge Wells, and York. Fifthly: Sir Charles Cottesham will, in acknowledgement of the maintenance of this agreement, allow Lady C. the sum of two hundred and fifty pounds per annum, which sum he considers sufficient for the upkeep of a small genteel establishment; use of the house known as Pater House, situate some seventeen miles from the Manor of Barton-le-Street, Yorkshire; coals from the mine adjoining; and from the home farm, milk, butter and eggs. (*Then he finds a further note.*) Lady Cottesham is not to play cards.

Sarah I am a little fond of play.

Mr Tetgeen There is no question of jointure.

Sarah None. Mr Tetgeen . . . I love my husband.

Mr Tetgeen My lady . . . I will mention it.

Sarah Such a humorous answer to this. No . . . don't. What is important? Bread and butter . . . and eggs. Do I take this?

Mr Tetgeen (*handing her the paper*) Please.

Sarah (*with the ghost of a smile*) I take it badly.

Mr Tetgeen (*courteously capping her jest*) I take my leave.

Sarah This doesn't call for serious notice? I've done nothing legal by accepting?

Mr Tetgeen There's no law in the matter; it's one of policy.

Sarah I might bargain for a bigger income. (**Mr Tetgeen** *bows.*) On the whole I'd rather be divorced.

Mr Tetgeen Sir Charles detests scandal.

Sarah Besides there's no case . . . is there?

Mr Tetgeen Sir Charles congratulates himself.

Sarah Sir Charles had best not bully me so politely . . . tell him.

Mr Tetgeen My lady!

Sarah I will not discuss this impertinence. Did those two men meet and talk . . . chat together? What d'you think of that?

Mr Tetgeen 'Twas very practical. I know that the woman is somehow the outcast.

Sarah A bad woman . . . an idle woman! But I've tried to do so much that lay to my hands without ever questioning . . . ! Thank you, I don't want this retailed to my husband. You'll take a glass of wine before you go?

Mr Tetgeen Port is grateful.

She takes from her dress two sealed letters.

Sarah Will you give that to Sir Charles . . . a letter he wrote me which I did not open. This, my answer, which I did not send.

He takes the one letter courteously, the other she puts back.

Sarah I'm such a coward, Mr Tetgeen.

Mr Tetgeen May I say how sorry . . . ?

Sarah Thank you.

Mr Tetgeen And let me apologise for having expressed one opinion of my own.

Sarah He wants to get rid of me. He's a bit afraid of me, you know, because I fight . . . and my weapons are all my own. This'll blow over.

Mr Tetgeen (*with a shake of the head*) You are to take this offer as final.

Sarah Beyond this?

Mr Tetgeen As I hinted, I am prepared to advise legal measures.

Sarah I could blow it over . . . but I won't perhaps. I must smile at my husband's consideration in suppressing even to you . . . the man's name. Butter and eggs . . . and milk. I should grow fat.

Ann *appears suddenly.*

Ann We go to Brighton tomorrow! (*And she comes excitedly to her sister.*)

Sarah Was that duel a stroke of genius?

Ann All sorts of things are to happen.

Sarah (*turning from her to* **Mr Tetgeen**) And you'll walk as far as Reading?

Mr Tetgeen Dear me, yes.

Sarah (*to* **Ann**) I'll come back.

Sarah *takes* **Mr Tetgeen** *towards the house.* **Ann** *seats herself. After a moment* **Lord John Carp**, *his clothes dusty with some riding, appears from the other quarter. She looks up to find him gazing at her.*

Lord John Ann, I've ridden back to see you.

Ann (*after a moment*) We're coming to Brighton tomorrow.

Lord John Good.

Ann Papa's not dead.

Lord John (*with equal cheerfulness*) That's good.

Ann And he said we should be seeing more of you.

Lord John Here I am. I love you, Ann. (*He goes on his knees.*)

Ann D'you want to marry me?

Lord John Yes.

Ann Thank you very much; it'll be very convenient for us all. Won't you get up?

Lord John At your feet.

Ann I like it.

Lord John Give me your hand.

Ann No.

Lord John You're beautiful.

Ann I don't think so. You don't think so.

Lord John I do think so.

Ann I should like to say I don't love you.

Lord John Last night you kissed me.

Ann Do get up, please.

Lord John As you wish. (*Now he sits by her.*)

Ann Last night you were nobody in particular . . . to me.

Lord John I love you.

Ann Please don't; I can't think clearly.

Lord John Look at me.

Ann I'm sure I don't love you because you're making me feel very uncomfortable and that wouldn't be so.

Lord John Then we'll think.

Ann Papa . . . perhaps you'd rather not talk about Papa.

Lord John Give yourself to me.

Ann (*drawing away from him*) Four words! There ought to be more in such a sentence . . . it's ridiculous. I want a year to think about its meaning. Don't speak.

Lord John Papa joins our party.

Ann That's what we're after . . . thank you.

Lord John I loathe politics.

Ann Tell me something against them.

Lord John In my opinion your father's not a much bigger blackguard – I beg your pardon – than the rest of us.

Ann . . . Miserable sinners.

Lord John Your father turns his coat. Well . . . ?

Ann I see nothing at all in that.

Lord John What's right and what's wrong?

Ann Papa's right . . . for the present.

Ann When shall we be married?

Lord John Tomorrow?

Ann (*startled*) If you knew that it isn't easy for me to be practical you wouldn't make fun.

Lord John Why not tomorrow?

Ann Papa –

Lord John Papa says yes . . . suppose.

Ann I'm very young . . . not to speak of clothes. I must have lots of new dresses.

Lord John Ask me for them.

Ann Why do you want to marry me?

Lord John I love you.

Ann It suddenly occurs to me that sounds unpleasant.

Lord John I love you.

Ann Out of place.

Lord John I love you.

Ann What if Papa were to die?

Lord John I want you.

Ann I'm nothing . . . I'm nobody . . . I'm part of my family.

Lord John I want you.

Ann Won't you please forget last night?

Lord John I want you. Look straight at me.

She looks, and stays fascinated.

Lord John If I say now that I love you –

Ann I know it.

Lord John And love me?

Ann I suppose so.

Lord John Make sure.

Ann But I hate you too . . . I know that.

Lord John Shall I kiss you?

Ann (*helplessly*) Yes.

He kisses her full on the lips.

Ann I can't hate you enough.

Lord John (*triumphantly*) Speak the truth now.

Ann I feel very degraded.

Lord John Nonsense.

Ann (*wretchedly*) This is one of the things which don't matter.

Lord John Ain't you to be mine?

Ann You want the right to behave like that as well as the power.

Lord John You shall command me.

Ann (*with a poor laugh*) I rather like this in a way.

Lord John Little coquette!

Ann It does tickle my vanity.

For a moment he sits looking at her, then shakes himself to his feet.

Lord John Now I must go.

Ann Yes . . . I want to think.

Lord John For Heaven's sake . . . no!

Ann I came this morning straight to where we were last night.

Lord John As I hung about the garden my heart was beating.

Ann I shall like you better when you're not here.

Lord John We're to meet in Brighton?

Ann I'm afraid so.

Lord John Goodbye.

Ann There's just a silly sort of attraction between certain people, I believe.

Lord John Can you look me in the eyes and say you don't love me?

Ann If I looked you in the eyes you'd frighten me again. I can say anything.

Lord John You're a deep child.

George Leete *appears on the terrace.*

George My lord!

Lord John (*cordially*) My dear Leete.

George No . . . I am not surprised to see you.

Ann George, things are happening.

Lord John Shake hands.

George I will not.

Ann Lord John asks me to be married to him. Shake hands.

George Why did you fight?

Ann Why d i d you fight?

Lord John (*shrugging*) Your father struck me.

Ann Now you've hurt him . . . that's fair.

Then the two men do shake hands, not heartily.

George We've trapped you, my lord.

Lord John I know what I want. I love your sister.

Ann I don't like you . . . but if you're good and I'm good we shall get on.

George Why shouldn't one marry politically?

Lord John (*in Ann's ear*) I love you.

Ann No . . . no . . . no . . . no . . . no . . . (*Discovering in this an echo of her father, she stops short.*)

George We're a cold-blooded family.

Lord John I don't think so.

George I married for love.

Lord John Who doesn't? But, of course there should be other reasons.

George You won't receive my wife.

Lord John Here's your sister.

Lady Cottesham *comes from the direction of the house.*

Sarah Back again?

Lord John You see.

From the other side appears **Mr Tatton**.

Mr Tatton As you all seem to be here I don't mind interrupting.

George (*hailing him*) Well . . . neighbour?

Mr Tatton Come . . . come . . . what's a little fighting more or less!

George Bravo, English sentiment . . . relieves a deal of awkwardness.

The two shake hands.

Sarah (*who by this has reached* **Lord John**) . . . And back so soon?

Ann Lord John asks to marry me.

Lord John Yes.

Mr Tatton I guessed so . . . give me a bit of romance!

Sarah (*suavely*) This is perhaps a little sudden, my dear Lord John. Papa may naturally be a little shocked.

George Not at all, Sarah.

Mr Tatton How's the wound?

George Not serious . . . nothing's serious.

Sarah You are very masterful, wooing sword in hand.

Ann George and I have explained to Lord John that we are all most anxious to marry me to him and he doesn't mind –

Lord John Being made a fool of. I love –

Ann I will like you.

George Charming cynicism, my dear Sarah.

Mr Tatton Oh, Lord!

Ann (*to her affianced*) Goodbye now.

Lord John When do I see you?

Ann Papa says soon.

Lord John Very soon, please. Tatton, my friend, Brighton's no nearer.

Mr Tatton Lady Cottesham . . . Miss Leete . . . I kiss your hands.

Lord John (*ebulliently clapping* **George** *on the back*) Look more pleased. (*Then he bends over* **Lady Cottesham's** *hand.*) Lady Charlie . . . my service to you . . . all. Ann. (*And he takes* **Ann's** *hand to kiss.*)

Ann If I can think better of all this, I shall. Goodbye.

She turns away from him. He stands for a moment considering her, but follows **Tatton** *away through the orchard.* **George** *and* **Sarah** *are watching their sister, who then comments on her little affair with life.*

Ann I'm growing up. (*Then with a sudden tremor.*) Sally, don't let me be forced to marry.

George Force of circumstances, my dear Ann.

Ann Outside things. Why couldn't I run away from this garden and over the hills . . . I suppose there's something on the other side of the hills.

Sarah You'd find yourself there . . . and circumstances.

Ann So I'm trapped as well as that Lord John.

Sarah What's the injury?

Ann I'm taken by surprise and I know I'm ignorant and I think I'm learning things backwards.

George You must cheer up and say: John's not a bad sort.

Sarah A man of his age is a young man.

Ann I wish you wouldn't recommend him to me.

Sarah Let's think of Brighton. What about your gowns?

Ann I've nothing to wear.

Sarah We'll talk to Papa.

George The war-purse is always a long one.

Sarah George . . . be one of us for a minute.

George But I want to look on too, and laugh.

Sarah (*caustically*) Yes . . . that's your privilege . . . except occasionally. (*Then to her sister.*) I wish you all the happiness of courtship days.

George Arcadian expression!

Ann I believe it means being kissed . . . often.

Sarah Have you not a touch of romance in you, little girl?

Ann Am I not like Mr Dan Tatton? He kisses dairy-maids and servants and all the farmer's daughters . . . I beg your pardon, George.

George (*nettled*) I'll say to you, Ann, that – in all essentials – one woman is as good as another.

Sarah That is not so in the polite world.

George When you consider it no one l i v e s in the polite world.

Ann Do they come outside for air sooner or later?

Sarah (*briskly*) Three best dresses you must have and something very gay if you're to go near the Pavilion.

Ann You're coming to Brighton, Sally?

Sarah No.

Ann Why not?

Sarah I don't wish to meet my husband.

George That man was his lawyer.

Ann The political difference, Sally?

Sarah Just that. (*Then with a deft turn of the subject.*) I don't say that yours is a pretty face, but I should think you would have charm.

George For fashion's sake cultivate sweetness.

Sarah You dance as well as they know how in Reading.

Ann Yes . . . I can twiddle my feet.

Sarah Do you like dancing?

Ann I'd sooner walk.

George What . . . and get somewhere!

Ann Here's George laughing.

Sarah He's out of it.

Ann Are you happy, George?

George Alas . . . Dolly's disgraceful ignorance of etiquette damns us both from the beautiful drawing-room.

Sarah That laugh is forced. But how can you . . . look on?

There is a slight pause in their talk. Then . . .

Ann He'll bully me with love.

Sarah Your husband will give you just what you ask for.

Ann I hate myself too. I want to take people mentally.

George You want a new world . . . you new woman.

Ann And I'm a good bit frightened of myself.

Sarah We have our places to fill in this. My dear child, leave futile questions alone.

George Neither have I any good advice to give you.

Ann I think happiness is a thing one talks too much about.

Dimmuck *appears. And by now* **Abud**'s *work has brought him back to the terrace.*

Dimmuck The master would like to see your ladyship now.

Sarah I'll say we've had a visitor . . . Guess.

George And you've had a visitor, Sarah.

Ann Papa will know.

Sarah Is he in a questioning mood?

Ann I always tell everything.

Sarah It saves time. (*She departs towards the house.*)

Dimmuck Mr George.

George What is it?

Dimmuck He said No to a doctor when I haven't even mentioned the matter. Had I better send . . . ?

George Do . . . if you care to waste the doctor's time.

Dimmuck *gives an offended sniff and follows* **Lady Cottesham**.

Ann I could sit here for days. George, I don't think I quite believe in anything I've been told yet.

George What's that man's name?

Ann John – John is a common name – John Abud.

George Abud!

Abud Sir?

George Come here.

Abud *obediently walks towards his young master and stands before him.*

George Why did you ask after the health of Mrs George Leete?

Abud We courted once.

George (*after a moment*) Listen, Ann. Do you hate me, John Abud?

Abud No, sir.

George You're a fine-looking fellow. How old are you?

Abud Twenty-seven, sir.

George Is 'once' long ago?

Abud Two years gone.

George Did Mrs Leete quarrel with you?

Abud No, sir.

George Pray tell me more.

Abud I was beneath her.

George But you're a fine-looking fellow.

Abud Farmer Crowe wouldn't risk his daughter being unhappy.

George But she was beneath me.

Abud That was another matter, sir.

George I don't think you intend to be sarcastic.

Abud And . . . being near her time for the first time, sir . . . I wanted to know if she is in danger of dying yet.

George Every precaution has been taken . . . a nurse . . . there is a physician near. I need not tell you . . . but I do tell you.

Abud Thank you, sir.

George I take great interest in my wife.

Abud We all do, sir.

George Was it ambition that you courted her?

Abud I thought to start housekeeping.

George Did you aspire to rise socially?

Abud I wanted a wife to keep house, sir.

George Are you content?

Abud I think so, sir.

George With your humble position?

Abud I'm a gardener, and there'll always be gardens.

George Frustrated affections . . . I beg your pardon . . . To have been crossed in love should make you bitter and ambitious.

Abud My father was a gardener and my son will be a gardener if he's no worse a man than I and no better.

George Are you married?

Abud No, sir.

George Are you going to be married?

Abud Not especially, sir.

George Yes . . . you must marry . . . some decent woman; we want gardeners.

Abud Do you want me any more now, sir?

George You have interested me. You can go back to your work.

Abud *obeys.*

George (*almost to himself*) I am hardly human. (*He slowly moves away and out of sight.*)

Ann John Abud.

He comes back and stands before her too.

Ann I am very sorry for you.

Abud I am very much obliged to you, miss.

Ann Both those sayings are quite meaningless. Say something true about yourself.

Abud I'm not sorry for myself.

Ann I won't tell. It's very clear you ought to be in a despairing state. Don't stand in the sun with your hat off.

Abud (*putting on his hat*) Thank you, miss.

Ann Have you nearly finished the rose trees?

Abud I must work till late this evening.

Ann Weren't you ambitious for Dolly's sake?

Abud She thought me good enough.

Ann I'd have married her.

Abud She was ambitious for me.

Ann And are you frightened of the big world?

Abud Fine things dazzle me sometimes.

Ann But gardening is all that you're fit for?

Abud I'm afraid so, miss.

Ann But it's great to be a gardener . . . to sow seeds and to watch flowers grow and to cut away dead things.

Abud Yes, miss.

Ann And you're in the fresh air all day.

Abud That's very healthy.

Ann Are you very poor?

Abud I get my meals in the house.

Ann Rough clothes last a long time.

Abud I've saved money.

Ann Where do you sleep?

Abud At Mrs Hart's . . . at a cottage . . . it's a mile off.

Ann And you want no more than food and clothes and a bed and you earn all that with your hands.

Abud The less a man wants, miss, the better.

Ann But you mean to marry?

Abud Yes . . . I've saved money.

Ann Whom will you marry? Would you rather not say? Perhaps you don't know yet?

Abud It's all luck what sort of a maid a man gets fond of. It won't be a widow.

Ann Be careful, John Abud.

Abud No . . . I shan't be careful.

Ann You'll do very wrong to be made a fool of.

Abud I'm safe, miss; I've no eye for a pretty face.

Dimmuck *arrives asthmatically at the top of the steps.*

Dimmuck Where's Mr George? Here's a messenger come post.

Ann Find him, Abud.

Abud (*to* **Dimmuck**) From Dolly?

Dimmuck Speak respectful.

Abud Is it from his wife?

Dimmuck Go find him.

Ann (*as* **Abud** *is immovable*) Dimmuck . . . tell me about Mrs George.

Dimmuck She's doing well, miss.

Abud (*shouting joyfully now*) Mr George! Mr George!

Ann A boy or a girl, Dimmuck?

Dimmuck Yes, miss.

Abud Mr George! Mr George!

Dimmuck Ecod . . . is he somewhere else?

Dimmuck, *somewhat excited himself, returns to the house.*

Ann George!

Abud Mr George! Mr George!

George *comes slowly along the terrace, in his hand an open book, which some people might suppose he was reading. He speaks with studied calm.*

George You are very excited, my good man.

Abud She's brought you a child, sir.

Ann Your child!

George Certainly.

Abud Thank God, sir!

George I will if I please.

Ann And she's doing well.

Abud There's a messenger come post.

George To be sure . . . it might have been bad news.

And slowly he crosses the garden towards the house.

Abud (*suddenly, beyond all patience*) Run . . . damn you!

George *makes one supreme effort to maintain his dignity, but fails utterly. He gasps out . . .*

George Yes, I will. (*And runs off as hard as he can.*)

Abud (*in an ecstasy*) This is good. Oh, Dolly and God . . . this is good!

Ann (*round-eyed*) I wonder that you can be pleased.

Abud (*apologising . . . without apology*) It's life.

Ann (*struck*) Yes, it is.

And she goes towards the house, thinking this over.

Act Three

It is near to sunset. The garden is shadier than before.

Abud *is still working.* **Carnaby Leete** *comes from the house followed by* **Dr Remnant**. *He wears his right arm in a sling. His face is flushed, his speech rapid.*

Carnaby Parson, you didn't drink enough wine . . . damme, the wine was good.

Dr Remnant I am very grateful for an excellent dinner.

Carnaby A good dinner, sir, is the crown to a good day's work.

Dr Remnant It may also be a comfort in affliction. Our philosophy does ill, Mr Leete, when it despises the more simple means of contentment.

Carnaby And which will be the better lover of a woman, a hungry or a well-fed man?

Dr Remnant A good meal digests love with it; for what is love but a food to live by . . . but a hungry love will ofttimes devour its owner.

Carnaby Admirable! Give me a man in love to deal with. Vous l'avez vu?

Dr Remnant Speak Latin, Greek or Hebrew to me, Mr Leete.

Carnaby French is the language of little things. My poor France! Ours is a little world, Parson . . . a man may hold it here. (*His open hand.*) Lord John Carp's a fine fellow.

Dr Remnant Son of a duke.

Carnaby And I commend to you the originality of his return. At twelve we fight . . . at one-thirty he proposes marriage to my daughter. D'ye see him humbly on his knees? Will there be rain, I wonder?

Dr Remnant We need rain . . . Abud?

Abud Badly, sir.

Carnaby Do we want a wet journey tomorrow! Where's Sarah?

Dr Remnant Lady Cottesham's taking tea.

Carnaby (*to* **Abud** *with a sudden start*) And why the devil didn't you marry my daughter-in-law . . . my own gardener?

George *appears dressed for riding.*

George Goodbye, sir, for the present.

Carnaby Boots and breeches!

George You shouldn't be about in the evening air with a green wound in your arm. You drank wine at dinner. Be careful, sir.

Carnaby Off to your wife and the expected?

George Yes, sir.

Carnaby Riding to Watford?

George From there alongside the North Coach, if I'm in time.

Carnaby Don't founder my horse. Will ye leave the glorious news with your grandfather at Wycombe?

George I won't fail to. (*Then to* **Abud**.) We've been speaking of you.

Abud It was never any secret, sir.

George Don't apologise.

Soon after this **Abud** *passes out of sight.*

Carnaby Nature's an encumbrance to us, Parson.

Dr Remnant One disapproves of flesh uninspired.

Carnaby She allows you no amusing hobbies . . . always takes you seriously.

George Goodbye, Parson.

Dr Remnant (*as he bows*) Your most obedient.

Carnaby And you trifle with damnable democracy, with pretty theories of the respect due to womanhood and now the result . . . hark to it squalling.

Dr Remnant Being fifty miles off might not one say: The cry of the new-born?

Carnaby Ill-bred babies squall. There's no poetic glamour in the world will beautify an undesired infant . . . George says so.

George I did say so.

Carnaby I feel the whole matter deeply.

George *half laughs*.

Carnaby George, after days of irritability, brought to bed of a smile. That's a home thrust of a metaphor.

George *laughs again*.

Carnaby Twins!

George Yes, a boy and a girl . . . I'm the father of a boy and a girl.

Carnaby (*in dignified, indignant horror*) No one of you dared tell me that much!

Sarah and **Ann** *come from the house.*

George You could have asked me for news of your grandchildren.

Carnaby Twins is an insult.

Sarah But you look very cheerful, George.

George I am content.

Sarah I'm surprised.

George I am surprised.

Sarah Now what names for them?

Carnaby No family names, please.

George We'll wait for a dozen years or so and let them choose their own.

Dr Remnant But, sir, christening will demand –

Carnaby Your son should have had my name, sir.

George I know the rule . . . as I have my grandfather's which I take no pride in.

Sarah George!

George Not to say that it sounds his, not mine.

Carnaby Our hopes of you were high once.

George Sarah, may I kiss you? (*He kisses her cheek.*) Let me hear what you decide to do.

Carnaby The begetting you, sir, was a waste of time.

George (*quite pleasantly*) Don't say that.

At the top of the steps **Ann** *is waiting for him.*

Ann I'll see you into the saddle.

George Thank you, sister Ann.

Ann Why didn't you leave us weeks ago?

George Why!

They pace away, arm-in-arm.

Carnaby (*bitterly*) Glad to go! Brighton, Sarah.

Sarah No, I shall not come, Papa.

Carnaby Coward. (*Then to* **Remnant**.) Goodnight.

Dr Remnant (*covering the insolent dismissal*) With your kind permission I will take my leave. (*Then he bows to* **Sarah**.) Lady Cottesham.

Sarah (*curtseying*) Doctor Remnant, I am yours.

Carnaby (*sitting by the fountain, stamping his foot*) Oh, this cracked earth! Will it rain . . . will it rain?

Dr Remnant I doubt now. That cloud has passed.

Carnaby Soft, pellucid rain! There's a good word and I'm not at all sure what it means.

Dr Remnant Per . . . lucere . . . letting light through.

Remnant *leaves them.*

Carnaby Soft, pellucid rain! . . . thank you. Brighton, Sarah.

Sarah Ann needs new clothes.

Carnaby See to it.

Sarah I shall not be there. (*She turns from him.*)

Carnaby Pretty climax to a quarrel!

Sarah Not a quarrel.

Carnaby A political difference.

Sarah Don't look so ferocious.

Carnaby My arm is in great pain and the wine's in my head.

Sarah Won't you go to bed?

Carnaby I'm well enough . . . to travel. This marriage makes us safe, Sarah . . . an anchor in each camp . . . There's a mixed metaphor.

Sarah If you'll have my advice, Papa, you'll keep those plans clear from Ann's mind.

Carnaby John Carp is so much clay . . . a man of forty ignorant of himself.

Sarah But if the Duke will not . . .

Carnaby The Duke hates a scandal.

Sarah Does he detest scandal!

Carnaby The girl is well-bred and harmless . . . why publicly quarrel with John and incense her old brute of a father? There's the Duke in a score of words. He'll take a little time to think it out so.

Sarah And I say: Do you get on the right side of the Duke once again – that's what we've worked for – and leave these two alone.

Carnaby Am I to lose my daughter?

Sarah Papa . . . your food's intrigue.

Carnaby Scold at Society . . . and what's the use?

Sarah We're over-civilised.

Ann *rejoins them now. The twilight is gathering.*

Carnaby My mother's very old . . . your grandfather's younger and seventy-nine . . . he swears I'll never come into the title. There's little else.

Sarah You're feverish . . . why are you saying this?

Carnaby Ann . . . George . . . George via Wycombe . . . Wycombe Court . . . Sir George Leete baronet, Justice of the Peace, Deputy Lieutenant . . . the thought's tumbled. Ann, I first saw your mother in this garden . . . there.

Ann Was she like me?

Sarah My age when she married.

Carnaby She was not beautiful . . . then she died.

Ann Mr Tatton thinks it a romantic garden.

Carnaby (*pause*) D'ye hear the wind sighing through that tree?

Ann The air's quite still.

Carnaby I hear myself sighing . . . when I first saw your mother in this garden . . . that's how it was done.

Sarah For a woman must marry.

Carnaby (*rises*) You all take to it as ducks to water . . . but apple sauce is quite correct . . . I must not mix metaphors.

Mrs Opie *comes from the house.*

Sarah Your supper done, Mrs Opie?

Mrs Opie I eat little in the evening.

Sarah I believe that saves digestion.

Mrs Opie Ann, do you need me more tonight?

Ann Not any more.

Mrs Opie Ann, there is gossip among the servants about a wager . . .

Ann Mrs Opie, that was . . . yesterday.

Mrs Opie Ann, I should be glad to be able to contradict a reported . . . embrace.

Ann I was kissed.

Mrs Opie I am shocked.

Carnaby Mrs Opie, is it possible that all these years I have been nourishing a prude in my . . . back drawing-room?

Mrs Opie I presume I am discharged of Ann's education; but as the salaried mistress of your household, Mr Leete, I am grieved not to be able to deny such a rumour to your servants. (*She sails back, righteously indignant.*)

Carnaby Call out that you're marrying the wicked man . . . comfort her.

Sarah Mrs Opie!

Carnaby Consider that existence. An old maid . . . so far as we know. Brevet rank . . . missis. Not pleasant.

Ann She wants nothing better . . . at her age.

Sarah How forgetful!

Carnaby (*the force of the phrase growing*) Brighton, Sarah.

Sarah Now you've both read the love letter which Tetgeen brought me.

Carnaby Come to Brighton.

Ann Come to Brighton, Sally.

Sarah No. I have been thinking. I think I will accept the income, the house, coals, butter and eggs.

Carnaby I give you a fortnight to bring your husband to his knees . . . to your feet.

Sarah I'm not sure that I could. My marriage has come naturally to an end.

Carnaby Sarah, don't annoy me.

Sarah Papa, you joined my bridegroom's political party . . . now you see fit to leave it. (*She glances at* **Ann**, *who gives no sign, however.*)

Carnaby What have you been doing in ten years?

Sarah Waiting for this to happen . . . now I come to think.

Carnaby Have ye the impudence to tell me that ye've never cared for your husband?

Sarah I was caught by the first few kisses; but he . . .

Carnaby Has he ever been unkind to you?

Sarah Never. He's a gentleman through and through . . . quite charming to live with.

Carnaby I see what more you expect. And he neither drinks nor . . . nor . . . no one even could suppose your leaving him.

Sarah No. I'm disgraced.

Carnaby Fight for your honour.

Sarah You surprise me sometimes, by breaking out into cant phrases.

Carnaby What is more useful in the world than honour?

Sarah I think we never had any . . . we!

Carnaby Give me more details. Tell me, who is this man?

Sarah I'm innocent . . . if that were all.

Ann Sally, what do they say you've done?

Sarah I cry out like any poor girl.

Carnaby There must be no doubt that you're innocent. Why not go for to force Charles into court?

Sarah My innocence is not of the sort which shows up well.

Carnaby Hold publicity in reserve. No fear of the two men arranging to meet, is there?

Sarah They've met . . . and they chatted about me.

Carnaby (*after a moment*) There's sound humour in that.

Sarah I shall feel able to laugh at them both from Yorkshire.

Carnaby God forbid! Come to Brighton . . . we'll rally Charles no end.

Sarah Papa. I know there's nothing to be done.

Carnaby Coward!

Sarah Besides I don't think I want to go back to my happiness.

They are silent for a little.

Carnaby How still! Look . . . leaves falling already. Can that man hear what we're saying?

Sarah (*to Ann*) Can Abud overhear?

Ann I've never talked secrets in the garden before today. (*Raising her voice but a very little.*) Can you hear me, Abud?

No reply comes.

Carnaby Evidently not. There's brains shown in a trifle.

Sarah Does your arm pain you so much?

Ann Sarah, this man that you're fond of and that's not your husband is not by any chance Lord John Carp?

Sarah No.

Ann Nothing would surprise me.

Sarah You are witty . . . but a little young to be so hard.

Carnaby Keep to your innocent thoughts.

Ann I must study politics.

Sarah We'll stop talking of this.

Ann No . . . let me listen . . . quite quietly.

Carnaby Let her listen . . . she's going to be married.

Sarah Good luck, Ann.

Carnaby I have great hopes of Ann.

Sarah I hope she may be heartless. To be heartless is to be quite safe.

Carnaby Now we detect a taste of sour grapes in your mouth.

Sarah Butter and eggs.

Carnaby We must all start early in the morning. Sarah will take you, Ann, round the Brighton shops . . . fine shops. You shall have the money . . .

Sarah I will not come with you.

Carnaby (*vexedly*) How absurd . . . how ridiculous . . . to persist in your silly sentiment.

Sarah (*her voice rising*) I'm tired of that world . . . which goes on and on, and there's no dying . . . one grows into a ghost . . . visible . . . then invisible. I'm glad paint has gone out of fashion . . . the painted ghosts were very ill to see.

Carnaby D'ye scoff at civilisation?

Sarah Look ahead for me.

Carnaby Banished to a hole in the damned provinces! But you're young yet, you're charming . . . you're the wife . . . and the honest wife of one of the country's best men. My head aches. D'ye despise good fortune's gifts? Keep as straight in your place in the world as you can. A monthly packet of books to Yorkshire . . . no . . . you never were fond of reading. Ye'd play patience . . . cultivate chess problems . . . kill yourself!

Sarah When one world fails take another.

Carnaby You have no more right to commit suicide than to desert the society you were born into. My head aches.

Sarah George is happy.

Carnaby D'ye dare to think so?

Sarah No . . . it's a horrible marriage.

Carnaby He's losing refinement . . . mark me . . . he no longer polishes his nails.

Sarah But there are the children now.

Carnaby You never have wanted children.

Sarah I don't want a little child.

Carnaby She to be Lady Leete . . . some day . . . soon! What has he done for his family?

Sarah I'll come with you. You are clever, Papa. And I know just what to say to Charles.

Carnaby (*with a curious change of tone*) If you study anatomy you'll find that the brain, as it works, pressing forward the eyes . . . thought is painful. Never be defeated. Chapter the latest . . . the tickling of the Carp. And my throat is dry . . . shall I drink that water?

Sarah No, I wouldn't.

Carnaby Not out of my hand?

Ann (*speaking in a strange quiet voice, after her long silence*) I will not come to Brighton with you.

Carnaby Very dry!

Ann You must go back, Sally.

Carnaby (*as he looks at her, standing stiffly*) Now what is Ann's height . . . five feet . . . ?

Ann Sally must go back, for she belongs to it . . . but I'll stay here where I belong.

Carnaby You've spoken three times and the words are jumbling in at my ears meaninglessly. I certainly took too much wine at dinner . . . or else . . . Yes . . . Sally goes back . . . and you'll go forward. Who stays here? Don't burlesque your sister. What's in the air . . . what disease is this?

Ann I mean to disobey you . . . to stay here . . . never to be unhappy.

Carnaby So pleased!

Ann I want to be an ordinary woman . . . not clever . . . not fortunate.

Carnaby I can't hear.

Ann Not clever. I don't believe in you, Papa.

Carnaby I exist . . . I'm very sorry.

Ann I won't be married to any man. I refuse to be tempted . . . I won't see him again.

Carnaby Yes. It's raining.

Sarah Raining!

Carnaby Don't you stop it raining.

Ann (*in the same level tones, to her sister now, who otherwise would turn, alarmed, to their father*) And I curse you . . . because, we being sisters, I suppose I am much what you were, about to be married; and I think, Sally, you'd have cursed your present self. I could become all that you are and more . . . but I don't choose.

Sarah Ann, what is to become of you?

Carnaby Big drops . . . big drops!

At this moment **Abud** *is passing towards the house, his work finished.*

Ann John Abud . . . you mean to marry. When you marry . . . will you marry me?

A blank silence, into which breaks **Carnaby**'s *sick voice.*

Carnaby Take me indoors. I heard you ask the gardener to marry you.

Ann I asked him.

Carnaby I heard you say that you asked him. Take me in . . . but not out of the rain.

Ann Look . . . he's straight-limbed and clear eyed . . . and I'm a woman.

Sarah Ann, are you mad?

Ann If we two were alone here in this garden and everyone else in the world were dead . . . what would you answer?

Abud (*still amazed*) Why . . . yes.

Carnaby Then that's settled . . . pellucid.

He attempts to rise, but staggers backwards and forwards.
Sarah *goes to him alarmed.*

Sarah Papa! . . . there's no rain yet.

Carnaby Hush, I'm dead.

Ann (*her nerves failing her*) Oh . . . oh . . . oh . . . !

Sarah Abud, don't ever speak of this.

Abud No, my lady.

Ann (*with a final effort*) I mean it all. Wait three months.

Carnaby Help me up steps . . . son-in-law. (**Carnaby** *has
started to grope his way indoors. But he reels and falls
helpless.*)

Abud I'll carry him.

Throwing down his tools **Abud** *lifts the frail sick man and
carries him towards the house.* **Sarah** *follows.*

Ann (*sobbing a little, and weary*) Such a long day it has
been . . . now ending.

She follows too.

Act Four

The hall at Markswayde is square; in decoration strictly
eighteenth century. The floor polished. Then comes six feet of
soberly painted wainscot and above the greenish blue and
yellowish green wall painted into panels. At intervals are low
relief pilasters; the capitals of these are gilded. The ceiling is
white and in the centre of it there is a frosted glass dome
through which a dull light struggles. Two sides only of the hall
are seen.

In the corner is a hat stand and on it are many cloaks and hats
and beneath it several pairs of very muddy boots.

In the middle of the left hand wall are the double doors of the
dining-room led up to by three or four stairs with balusters,
and on either side standing against the wall long, formal,
straight backed sofas.

In the middle of the right hand wall is the front door; glass
double doors can be seen and there is evidently a porch beyond.
On the left of the front door a small window. On the right a
large fireplace, in which a large fire is roaring. Over the front
door, a clock (the hands pointing to half-past one). Over the
fireplace a family portrait (temp. Queen Anne), below this a
blunderbuss and several horse-pistols. Above the sofa full-
length family portraits (temp. George I). Before the front door
a wooden screen, of lighter wood than the wainscot, and in the
middle of it a small glass panel. Before this a heavy square
table on which are whips and sticks, a hat or two and brushes;
by the table a wooden chair. On either side the fire stand tall
closed-in armchairs, and between the fireplace and the door a
smaller red-baize screen.

When the dining-room doors are thrown open another wooden
screen is to be seen.

There are a few rugs on the floor, formally arranged.

Mrs Opie *stands in the middle of the hall, holding out a woman's brown cloak: she drops one side to fetch out her handkerchief and apply it to her eye.* **Dimmuck** *comes in by the front door, which he carefully closes behind him. He is wrapped in a hooded cloak and carries a pair of boots and a newspaper. The boots he arranges to warm before the fire. Then he spreads the* Chronicle *newspaper upon the arm of a chair, then takes off his cloak and hangs it upon a peg close to the door.*

Dimmuck Mrs Opie . . . will you look to its not scorching?

Mrs Opie *still mops her eyes.* **Dimmuck** *goes towards the dining-room door, but turns.*

Dimmuck Will you kindly see that the *Chronicle* newspaper does not burn?

Mrs Opie I was crying.

Dimmuck I leave this tomorrow sennight . . . thankful, ma'am, to have given notice in a dignified manner.

Mrs Opie I understand . . . Those persons at table . . .

Dimmuck You give notice.

Mrs Opie Mr Dimmuck, this is my home.

Lord Arthur Carp *comes out of the dining-room. He is a thinner and more earnest-looking edition of his brother.* **Mrs Opie** *turns a chair and hangs the cloak to warm before the fire, and then goes into the dining-room.*

Lord Arthur My chaise round?

Dimmuck I've but just ordered it, my lord. Your lordship's man has give me your boots.

Lord Arthur Does it snow?

Dimmuck Rather rain than snow.

Lord Arthur *takes up the newspaper.*

Dimmuck Yesterday's, my lord.

Lord Arthur I've seen it. The mails don't hurry hereabouts. Can I be in London by the morning?

Dimmuck I should say you might be, my lord.

Lord Arthur *sits by the fire, while* **Dimmuck** *takes off his pumps and starts to put on his boots.*

Lord Arthur Is this a horse called 'Ronald'?

Dimmuck Which horse, my lord?

Lord Arthur Which I'm to take back with me . . . my brother left here. I brought the mare he borrowed.

Dimmuck I remember, my lord. I'll enquire.

Lord Arthur Tell Parker . . .

Dimmuck Your lordship's man?

Lord Arthur . . . he'd better ride the beast.

Sarah *comes out of the dining-room. He stands up; one boot, one shoe.*

Sarah Please put on the other.

Lord Arthur Thank you . . . I a m in haste.

Sarah To depart before the bride's departure.

Lord Arthur Does the bride go with the bridegroom?

Sarah She goes away.

Lord Arthur I shall never see such a thing again.

Sarah I think this entertainment is unique.

Lord Arthur Any commissions in town?

Sarah Why can't you stay to travel with us tomorrow and talk business to Papa by the way?

Dimmuck *carrying the pumps and after putting on his cloak goes out through the front door. When it is closed, her voice changes.*

Sarah Why . . . Arthur?

He does not answer. Then **Mrs Opie** *comes out of the dining-room to fetch the cloak. The two, with an effort, reconstruct their casual disjointed conversation.*

Sarah . . . Before the bride's departure?

Lord Arthur Does the bride go away with the bridegroom?

Sarah She goes.

Lord Arthur I shall never see such an entertainment again.

Sarah We are quite unique.

Lord Arthur Any commissions in town?

Sarah Is she to go soon too, Mrs Opie?

Mrs Opie It is arranged they are to walk . . . in this weather . . . ten miles . . . to the house.

Sarah Cottage.

Mrs Opie Hut.

Mrs Opie *takes the cloak into the dining-room. Then* **Sarah** *comes a little towards* **Lord Arthur**, *but waits for him to speak.*

Lord Arthur (*a little awkwardly*) You are not looking well.

Sarah To our memory . . . and beyond your little chat with my husband about me . . . I want to speak an epitaph.

Lord Arthur Charlie Cottesham behaved most honourably.

Sarah And I think you did. Why have you not let me tell you so in your ear till now, today?

Lord Arthur Sarah . . . we had a narrow escape from . . .

Sarah How's your wife?

Lord Arthur Well . . . thank you.

Sarah Nervous, surely, at your travelling in winter?

Lord Arthur I was so glad to receive a casual invitation from you and to come . . . casually.

Sarah Fifty miles.

Lord Arthur Your father has been ill?

Sarah Very ill through the autumn.

Lord Arthur Do you think he suspects us?

Sarah I shouldn't care to peep into Papa's innermost mind. You are to be very useful to him.

Lord Arthur No.

Sarah Then he'll go back to the government.

Lord Arthur If he pleases . . . if they please . . . if you please.

Sarah I am not going back to my husband. Arthur . . . be useful to him.

Lord Arthur No . . . you are not coming to me. Always your father! (*After a moment.*) It was my little home in the country somehow said aloud you didn't care for me.

Sarah I fooled you to small purpose.

Lord Arthur I wish you had once made friends with my wife.

Sarah If we . . . this house I'm speaking of . . . had made friends where we've only made tools and fools we shouldn't now be cursed as we are . . . all. George, who is a cork, trying to sink socially. Ann is mad . . . and a runaway.

Lord Arthur Sarah, I've been devilish fond of you.

Sarah Be useful to Papa. (*He shakes his head, obstinately.*) Praise me a little. Haven't I worked my best for my family?

Lord Arthur Suppose I could be useful to him now, would you, in spite of all, come to me . . . no half measures?

Sarah Arthur . . . (*He makes a little passionate movement towards her, but she is cold.*) It's time for me to vanish from this world, because I've nothing left to sell.

Lord Arthur I can't help him. I don't want you. (*He turns away.*)

Sarah I feel I've done my best.

Lord Arthur Keep your father quiet.

Sarah I mean to leave him.

Lord Arthur What does he say to that?

Sarah I've not yet told him.

Lord Arthur What happens?

Sarah To sell my jewels . . . spoils of a ten years' war. Three thousand pound . . . how much a year?

Lord Arthur I'll buy them.

Sarah And return them? You have almost the right to make such a suggestion.

Lord Arthur Stick to your father. He'll care for you?

Sarah No . . . we all pride ourselves on our lack of sentiment.

Lord Arthur You must take money from your husband.

Sarah I have earned that and spent it.

Lord Arthur (*yielding once again to temptation*) I'm devilish fond of you . . .

At that moment **Abud** *comes out of the dining-room. He is dressed in his best.* **Sarah** *responds readily to the interruption.*

Sarah And you must give my kindest compliments to Lady Arthur and my . . . affectionately . . . to the children and I'll let Papa know that you're going.

Lord Arthur Letters under cover to your father?

Sarah Papa will stay in town through the session of course . . . but they all tell me that seventy-five pounds a year is a comfortable income in . . . Timbuctoo.

She goes into the dining-room. **Abud** *has selected his boots from the corner and now stands with them in his hand looking rather helpless. After a moment –*

Lord Arthur I congratulate you, Mr Abud.

Abud My lord . . . I can't speak of myself.

Carnaby *comes out of the dining-room. He is evidently by no means recovered from his illness. He stands for a moment with an ironical eye on* **John Abud.**

Carnaby Son-in-law.

Abud I'm told to get on my boots, sir.

Carnaby Allow me to assist you?

Abud I couldn't, sir.

Carnaby Désolé!

Then he passes on. **Abud** *sits on the sofa, furtively puts on his boots and afterwards puts his shoes in his pockets.*

Lord Arthur You were so busy drinking health to the two fat farmers that I wouldn't interrupt you.

Carnaby Goodbye. Describe all this to your brother John.

Lord Arthur So confirmed a bachelor!

Carnaby Please say that we missed him.

Lord Arthur *hands him the newspaper.*

Lord Arthur I've out-raced your *Chronicle* from London by some hours. There's a paragraph . . . second column . . . near the bottom.

Carnaby (*looking at it blindly*) They print villainously nowadays.

Lord Arthur Inspired.

Carnaby I trust his grace is well?

Lord Arthur Gouty.

Carnaby Now doesn't the social aspect of this case interest you?

Lord Arthur I object to feeding with the lower classes.

Carnaby There's pride! How useful to note their simple manners! From the meeting of extremes new ideas spring . . . new life.

Lord Arthur Take that for a new social-political creed, Mr Leete.

Carnaby Do I lack one?

Lord Arthur Please make my adieux to the bride.

Carnaby Appropriate . . . 'à Dieu' . . . she enters Nature's cloister. My epigram.

Lord Arthur But . . . good heavens . . . are we to choose to be toiling animals?

Carnaby To be such is my daughter's ambition.

Lord Arthur You have not read that.

Carnaby (*giving back the paper, vexedly*) I can't see.

Lord Arthur 'The Right Honourable Carnaby Leete is, we are glad to hear, completely recovered and will return to town for the opening of Session.'

Carnaby I mentioned it.

Lord Arthur 'We understand that although there has been no reconciliation with the Government it is quite untrue that this gentleman will in any way resume his connection with the Opposition.'

Carnaby Inspired?

Lord Arthur I am here from my father to answer any questions.

Carnaby (*with some dignity and the touch of a threat*) Not now, my lord.

Dimmuck *comes in at the front door.*

Dimmuck The chaise, my lord.

Carnaby I will conduct you.

Lord Arthur Please don't risk exposure.

Carnaby Nay, I insist.

Lord Arthur Health and happiness to you both, Mr Abud.

Lord Arthur *goes out, followed by* **Carnaby**, *followed by* **Dimmuck**. *At that moment* **Mr Smallpeice** *skips excitedly out of the dining-room. A ferret-like little lawyer.*

Mr Smallpeice Oh . . . where is Mr Leete?

Not seeing him **Mr Smallpeice** *skips as excitedly back into the dining-room.* **Dimmuck** *returns and hangs up his cloak then goes towards* **Abud**, *whom he surveys.*

Dimmuck Sir!

With which insult he starts for the dining-room reaching the door just in time to hold it open for **Sir George Leete** *who comes out. He surveys* **Abud** *for a moment, then explodes.*

Sir George Leete Damn you . . . stand in the presence of your grandfather-in-law.

Abud *stands up.* **Carnaby** *returns coughing, and* **Sir George** *looks him up and down.*

Sir George Leete I shall attend your funeral.

Carnaby My daughter Sarah still needs me.

Sir George Leete I wonder at you, my son.

Carnaby Have you any money to spare?

Sir George Leete No.

Carnaby For Sarah, my housekeeper; I foresee a busy session.

Abud *is now gingerly walking up the stairs.*

Sir George Leete Carnaby . . . look at that.

Carnaby Sound in wind and limb. Tread boldly, son-in-law.

Abud *turns, stands awkwardly for a moment and then goes into the dining-room.*

Sir George Leete (*relapsing into a pinch of snuff*) I'm calm.

Carnaby Regard this marriage with a wise eye . . . as an amusing little episode.

Sir George Leete Do you?

Carnaby And forget its oddity. Now that the humiliation is irrevocable, is it a personal grievance to you?

Sir George Leete Give me a dinner a day for the rest of my life and I'll be content.

Carnaby Lately, one by one, opinions and desires have been failing me . . . a flicker and then extinction. I shall shortly attain to being a most able critic upon life.

Sir George Leete Shall I tell you again? You came into this world without a conscience. That explains you and it's all that does. That such a damnable coupling as this should be permitted by God Almighty . . . or that the law shouldn't interfere! I've said my say.

Mr Smallpeice *again comes out of the dining-room.*

Mr Smallpeice Mr Leete.

Carnaby (*ironically polite*) Mr Smallpeice.

Mr Smallpeice Mr Crowe is proposing your health.

Mr Crowe *comes out. A crop-headed beefy-looking farmer of sixty.*

Mr Crowe Was.

Carnaby There's a good enemy!

Mr Crowe Get out of my road . . . lawyer Smallpeice.

Carnaby Leave enough of him living to attend to my business.

Mr Smallpeice (*wriggling a bow at* **Carnaby**) Oh . . . , dear sir!

Sir George Leete (*disgustedly to* **Mr Smallpeice**) You!

Mr Smallpeice Employed in a small matter . . . as yet.

Carnaby (*to* **Crowe**) I hope you spoke your mind of me.

Mr Crowe Not behind your back, sir.

Mrs George Leete *leads* **Lady Leete** *from the dining-room.* **Lady Leete** *is a very old, blind and decrepit woman.* **Dolly** *is a buxom young mother whose attire borders on the gaudy.*

Carnaby (*with some tenderness*) Well . . . Mother . . . dear?

Mr Crowe (*bumptiously to* **Sir George Leete**) Did my speech offend you, my lord?

Sir George Leete (*sulkily*) I'm a baronet.

Lady Leete Who's this here?

Carnaby Carnaby.

Dolly Step down . . . grandmother.

Lady Leete Who did ye say you were?

Dolly Mrs George Leete.

Lady Leete Take me to the fire-side.

So **Carnaby** *and* **Dolly** *lead her slowly to a chair by the fire where they carefully bestow her.*

Mr Smallpeice (*to* **Farmer Crowe**) He's leaving Marks的wayde, you know . . . and me agent.

Lady Leete (*suddenly bethinking her*) Grace was not said. Fetch my chaplain . . . at once.

Mr Smallpeice I will run. (*He runs into the dining-room.*)

Dolly (*calling after with her country accent*) Not Parson Remnant . . . t'other one.

Lady Leete (*demanding*) Snuff.

Carnaby (*to his father*) Sir . . . my hand is a little unsteady.

Sir George *and* **Carnaby** *between them give* **Lady Leete** *her snuff.*

Mr Crowe Dolly . . . ought those children to be left so long?

Dolly All right, Father . . . I have a maid.

Lady Leete *sneezes.*

Sir George Leete She'll do that once too often altogether.

Lady Leete I'm cold.

Dolly I'm cold . . . I lack my shawl.

Mr Crowe Call out to your man for it.

Dolly (*going to the dining-room door*) Will a gentleman please ask Mr George Leete for my Cache-y-mire shawl?

Mr Crowe (*to* **Carnaby**) And I drank to the health of our grandson.

Carnaby Now suppose George were to assume your name, Mr Crowe?

Mr Tozer *comes out of the dining-room. Of the worst type of eighteenth century parson, for which one may see Hogarth's 'Harlot's Progress'. He is very drunk.*

Sir George Leete (*in his wife's ear*) Tozer!

Lady Leete When . . . why!

Sir George Leete To say grace.

Lady Leete *folds her withered hands.*

Mr Tozer (*through his hiccoughs*) Damn you all.

Lady Leete (*reverently, thinking it is said*) Amen.

Mr Tozer Only my joke.

Carnaby (*rising to the height of the occasion*) Mr Tozer, I am indeed glad to see you, upon this occasion so delightfully drunk.

Mr Tozer Always a gen'elman . . . by nature.

Sir George Leete Lie down . . . you dog.

George *comes out carrying the cashmere shawl.*

George (*to his father*) Dolly wants her father to rent Markswayde, sir.

Mr Crowe Not me, my son. You're to be a farmer-baronet.

Sir George Leete Curse your impudence!

Carnaby My one regret in dying would be to miss seeing him so.

George *goes back into the dining-room.*

Mr Crowe I am tickled to think that the man marrying your daughter wasn't good enough for mine.

Carnaby And yet at fisticuffs, I'd back John Abud against our son George.

Dr Remnant *has come out of the dining-room.* **Tozer** *has stumbled towards him and is wagging an argumentative finger.*

Mr Tozer . . . Marriage means enjoyment!

Dr Remnant (*controlling his indignation*) I repeat that I have found in my own copy of the prayer book no insistence upon a romantic passion.

Mr Tozer My 'terpretation of God's word is 'bove criticism.

Mr Tozer *reaches the door and falls into the dining-room.*

Carnaby (*weakly to* **Dr Remnant**) Give me your arm for a moment.

Dr Remnant I think Lady Cottesham has Mrs John Abud prepared to start, sir.

Carnaby I trust Ann will take no chill walking through the mud.

Dr Remnant Won't you sit down, sir?

Carnaby No.

For some moments **Crowe** *has been staring indignantly at* **Sir George**. *Now he breaks out.*

Mr Crowe The front door of this mansion is opened to a common gardener and only then to me and mine!

Sir George Leete (*virulently*) Damn you and yours and damn them . . . and damn you again for the worse disgrace.

Mr Crowe Damn *you*, sir . . . have you paid him to marry the girl?

He turns away, purple faced and **Sir George** *chokes impotently.* **Abud** *and* **Mr Prestige** *come out talking. He is younger and less assertive than* **Farmer Crowe**.

Mr Prestige (*pathetically*) All our family always has got drunk at weddings.

Abud (*in remonstrance*) Please, uncle.

Carnaby Mr Crowe . . . I have been much to blame for not seeking you sooner.

Mr Crowe (*mollified*) Shake hands.

Carnaby (*offering his with some difficulty*) My arm is stiff . . . from an accident. This is a maid's marriage, I assure you.

Mr Prestige (*open mouthed to* **Dr Remnant**) One c o u l d hang bacon here!

Dolly (*very high and mighty*) The family don't.

Carnaby (*to his father*) And won't you apologise for your remarks to Mr Crowe, sir?

Lady Leete (*demanding*) Snuff!

Carnaby And your box to my mother, sir.

Sir George *attends to his wife.*

Dolly (*anxiously to* **Dr Remnant**) Can a gentleman change his name?

Mr Crowe Parson . . . once noble always noble, I take it.

Dr Remnant Certainly . . . but I hope you have money to leave them, Mr Crowe.

Dolly (*to* **Abud**) John.

Abud Dorothy.

Dolly You've not seen my babies yet.

Lady Leete *sneezes.*

Sir George Leete Carnaby . . . d'ye intend to murder that Crowe fellow . . . or must I?

Mr Smallpeice *skips from the dining-room.*

Mr Smallpeice Mr John Abud . . .

Mr Crowe (*to* **Dr Remnant** *as he nods towards* **Carnaby**) Don't tell me he's got over that fever yet.

Mr Smallpeice . . . The ladies say . . . are you ready or are you not?

Mr Prestige I'll get thy cloak, John.

Mr Prestige goes for the cloak. Carnaby has taken a pistol from the mantelpiece and now points it at Abud.

Carnaby He's fit for heaven!

George Leete comes from the dining-room and noticing his father's action says sharply . . .

George I suppose you know that pistol's loaded. (*Which calls everyone's attention. Dolly shrieks.*)

Carnaby What if there had been an accident!

And he puts back the pistol. Abud takes his cloak from Prestige.

Abud Thank you, uncle.

Mr Prestige I'm a proud man. Mr Crowe . . .

Carnaby Pride!

George (*has a sudden inspiration and strides up to* **Abud**) Here ends the joke, my good fellow. Be off without your wife.

Abud stares, as do the others. Only Carnaby suddenly catches Remnant's arm.

Mr Prestige (*solemnly*) But it's illegal to separate them.

George (*giving up*) Mr Prestige . . . you are the backbone of England.

Carnaby (*to* **Remnant**) Where are your miracles?

Mrs Prestige *comes out. A motherly farmer's wife, a mountain of a woman.*

Mrs Prestige John . . . kiss your aunt.

Abud *goes to her, and she obliterates him in an embrace.*

George (*to his father*) Sense of humour . . . Sense of humour!

Lady Leete Snuff. (*But no one heeds her this time.*)

Carnaby It doesn't matter.

George Smile. Let's be helpless gracefully.

Carnaby There are moments when I'm not sure –

George It's her own life.

Tozer *staggers from the dining-room drunker than ever. He falls against the baluster and waves his arms.*

Mr Tozer Silence there for the corpse!

Mr Crowe You beast!

Mr Tozer Respect my cloth . . . Mr Prestige.

Mr Crowe That's not my name.

Mr Tozer I'll have you to know that I'm Sir George Leete's baronet's most boon companion and her la'ship never goes nowhere without me. (*He subsides into a chair.*)

Lady Leete (*tearfully*) Snuff.

From the dining-room comes **Ann**; *her head bent. She is crossing the hall when* **Sarah** *follows, calling her.*

Sarah Ann!

Ann *turns back to kiss her. The rest of the company stand gazing.* **Sir George** *gives snuff to* **Lady Leete**.

Ann Goodbye, Sally.

Sarah (*in a whisper*) Forget us.

George (*relieving his feelings*) Goodbye, everybody . . . goodbye, everything.

Abud *goes to the front door and opening it stands waiting for her. She goes coldly, but timidly to her father, to whom she puts her face up to be kissed.*

Ann Goodbye, Papa.

Carnaby (*quietly, as he kisses her cheek*) I can do without you.

Sir George Leete (*raging at the draught*) Shut that door.

Ann I'm gone.

She goes with her husband. **Mrs Opie** *comes hurriedly out of the dining-room, too late.*

Mrs Opie Oh!

Dr Remnant Run . . . Mrs Opie.

Carnaby There has started the new century!

Mrs Opie *opens the front door to look after them.*

Sir George Leete (*with double energy*) Shut that door.

Lady Leete *sneezes and then chokes. There is much commotion in her neighbourhood.*

Sir George Leete Now she's hurt again.

Dolly Water!

Mr Crowe Brandy!

Sarah (*going*) I'll fetch both.

George We must all die . . . some day.

Mr Tozer (*who has struggled up to see what is the matter*) And go to –

Dr Remnant Hell. You do believe in that, Mr Toper.

Mrs Opie (*fanning the poor old lady*) She's better.

Carnaby (*to his guests*) Gentlemen . . . punch.

Prestige *and* **Smallpeice**; **Mrs Prestige**, **George** *and* **Dolly** *move towards the dining-room.*

Mr Prestige (*to* **Smallpeice**) You owe all this to me.

Mr Crowe Dolly . . . I'm going.

Mrs Prestige (*to her husband as she nods towards* **Carnaby**) Nathaniel . . . look at 'im.

George (*to his father-in-law*) Must we come too?

Mrs Prestige (*as before*) I can't help it . . . a sneerin' carpin' cavillin' devil!

Mrs Opie Markswayde is to let . . . as I hear . . . Mr Leete?

Carnaby Markswayde is to let.

He goes on his way to the dining-room meeting **Sarah** *who comes out carrying a glass of water and a decanter of brandy.* **Sir George Leete** *is comfortably warming himself at the fire.*

* * *

The living room of **John Abud**'s *new cottage has bare plaster walls and its ceilings and floor are of red brick; all fresh-looking but not new. In the middle of the middle wall there is a latticed window, dimity curtained; upon the plain shelf in front are several flower pots.*

To the right of this, a door, cross-beamed and with a large lock to it besides the latch.

Against the right hand wall, is a dresser, furnished with dishes and plates: below it is a common-looking grandfather clock; below this a small door which when opened shows winding stairs leading to the room above. In the left hand wall there is a door which is almost hidden by the fireplace which juts out below it. In the fireplace a wood fire is laid but not lit. At right angles to this stands a heavy oak settle opposite a plain deal table; just beyond which is a little bench. On either side of the window is a Windsor armchair. Between the window and the door hangs a framed sampler.

In the darkness the sound of the unlocking of a door and of
Abud *entering is heard. He walks to the table, strikes a light
upon a tinder-box and lights a candle which he finds there.*
Ann *is standing in the doorway.* **Abud** *is in stocking feet.*

Abud Don't come further. Here are your slippers.

*He places one of the Windsor chairs for her on which she sits
while he takes off her wet shoes and puts on her slippers which
he found on the table. Then he takes her wet shoes to the
fireplace. She sits still. Then he goes to the door and brings in
his own boots from the little porch and puts them in the
fireplace too. Then he locks the door and hangs up the key
beside it. Then he stands looking at her; but she does not
speak, so he takes the candle, lifts it above his head and walks
to the dresser.*

Abud (*encouragingly*) Our dresser . . . Thomas Jupp made
that. Plates and dishes. Here's Uncle Prestige's clock.

Ann Past seven.

Abud That's upstairs. Table and bench, deal. Oak settle
. . . solid.

Ann Charming.

Abud Windsor chairs . . . Mother's sampler.

Ann Home.

Abud Is it as you wish? I have been glad at your not
seeing it until tonight.

Ann I'm sinking into the strangeness of the place.

Abud Very weary? It's been a long nine miles.

*She does not answer. He goes and considers the flowerpots in
the window.*

Ann I still have on my cloak.

Abud Hang it behind the door there . . . no matter if the wet drips.

Ann . . . I can wipe up the puddle.

She hangs up her cloak. He selects a flowerpot and brings it to her.

Abud Hyacinth bulbs for the spring.

Ann (*after a glance*) I don't want to hold them.

He puts back the pot, a little disappointed.

Abud Out there's the scullery.

Ann It's very cold.

Abud If we light the fire now that means more trouble in the morning.

She sits on the settle.

Ann Yes, I am very weary.

Abud Go to bed.

Ann Not yet. (*After a moment.*) How much light one candle gives! Sit where I may see you.

He sits on the bench. She studies him curiously.

Ann Well . . . this is an experiment.

Abud (*with reverence*) God help us both.

Ann Amen. Some people are so careful of their lives. If we fail miserably we'll hold our tongues . . . won't we?

Abud I don't know . . . I can't speak of this.

Ann These impossible things which are done mustn't be talked of . . . that spoils them. We don't want to boast of this, do we?

Abud I fancy nobody quite believes that we are married.

Ann Here's my ring . . . real gold.

Abud (*with a sudden fierce throw up of his head*) Never you remind me of the difference between us.

Ann Don't speak to me so.

Abud Now I'm your better.

Ann My master . . . The door's locked.

Abud (*nodding*) I know that I must be . . . or be a fool.

Ann (*after a moment*) Be kind to me.

Abud (*with remorse*) Always I will.

Ann You are master here.

Abud And I've angered you?

Ann And if I fail . . . I'll never tell you . . . to make a fool of you. And you're trembling. (*She sees his hand, which is on the table, shake.*)

Abud Look at that now.

Ann (*lifting her own*) My white hands must redden. No more dainty appetite . . . no more pretty books.

Abud Have you learned to scrub?

Ann Not this floor.

Abud Mother always did bricks with a mop. Tomorrow I go to work. You'll be left for all day.

Ann I must make friends with the other women around.

Abud My friends are very curious about you.

Ann I'll wait to begin till I'm seasoned.

Abud Four o'clock's the hour for getting up.

Ann Early rising always was a vice of mine.

Abud Breakfast quickly . . . and I take my dinner with me.

Ann In a handkerchief.

Abud Hot supper, please.

Ann It shall be ready for you.

There is silence between them for a little. Then he says timidly.

Abud May I come near to you?

Ann (*in a low voice*) Come.

He sits beside her, gazing.

Abud Wife . . . I never have kissed you.

Ann Shut your eyes.

Abud Are you afraid of me?

Ann We're not to play such games at love.

Abud I can't help wanting to feel very tender towards you.

Ann Think of me . . . not as a wife . . . but as a mother of your children . . . if it's to be so. Treat me so.

Abud You are a part of me.

Ann We must try and understand it . . . as a simple thing.

Abud But shall I kiss you?

Ann (*lowering her head*) Kiss me.

But when he puts his arms round her she shrinks.

Ann No.

Abud But I will. It's my right.

Almost by force he kisses her. Afterwards she clenches her hands and seems to suffer.

Abud Have I hurt you?

She gives him her hand with a strange little smile.

Ann I forgive you.

Abud (*encouraged*) Ann . . . we're beginning life together.

Ann Remember . . . work's enough . . . no stopping to talk.

Abud I'll work for you.

Ann I'll do my part . . . something will come of it.

For a moment they sit together hand in hand. Then she leaves him and paces across the room. There is a slight pause.

Ann Papa . . . I said . . . we've all been in too great a hurry getting civilised. False dawn. I mean to go back.

Abud He laughed.

Ann So he saw I was of no use to him and he's penniless and he let me go. When my father dies what will he take with him? . . . for you do take your works with you into heaven or hell, I believe. Much wit. Sally is afraid to die. Don't you aspire like George's wife. I was afraid to live . . . and now . . . I am content. (*She walks slowly to the window and from there to the door against which she places her ear. Then she looks round at her husband.*) I can hear them chattering.

Then she goes to the little door and opens it. **Abud** *takes up the candle.*

Abud I'll hold the light . . . the stairs are steep.

He lights her up the stairs.

The Madras House

(Revised 1925)

1909
revised 1925

The Madras House was first produced at the Duke of York's Theatre (Mr Charles Frohman's Repertory Theatre) on 9 March 1910, under the direction of the author.

The play was revived at the Ambassadors Theatre in a revised version (that of the present edition), on 30 November 1925, under the direction of the author, with the following cast:

Henry Huxtable	Aubrey Mather
Katherine Huxtable	Frances Ivor
Laura Huxtable	Christine Jensen
Minnie Huxtable	Winifred Oughton
Clara Huxtable	Valerie Wyngate
Julia Huxtable	Ann Codrington
Emma Huxtable	Marie Ney
Jane Huxtable	Lois Heatherley
Major Hippisley Thomas	David Hawthorne
Philip Madras	Nicholas Hannen
Jessica Madras	Cathleen Nesbitt
Constantine Madras	Allan Jeayes
Amelia Madras	Irene Rooke
Eustace Perrin State	Claude Rains
Marion Yates	Doris Lytton
Mr Brigstock	Stafford Hilliard
Mrs Brigstock	Mary Barton
Miss Chancellor	Agnes Thomas
Mr Windlesham	Ernest Milton
Mr Belhaven	Robert Burnard
Three Mannequins	⎰ Winifred Ashford ⎱ Helene Barr ⎰ Elyse King
Maid at Denmark Hill	
Maid at Dorset Square	Gladys Gaynor

Scenery designed by Norman Wilkinson

Act One

The **Huxtables** *live at Denmark Hill, for* **Mr Huxtable** *is the surviving partner in the well-known Peckham drapery establishment of Roberts & Huxtable, and the situation besides being salubrious is therefore convenient. It is a new house;* **Mr Huxtable** *bought it half finished so that the interior might be to his liking; its exterior the builder said one might describe as of a Free Queen Anne Treatment; to which* **Mr Huxtable** *rejoined, after blinking at the red brick spotted with stone ornament, that After all it was inside they were going to live, you know.*

Through the stained, grained front door, rattling with coloured glass, one reaches the hall, needlessly narrow, needlessly dark, but with its black and white tessellated pavement making for cleanliness. On the left is the stained and grained staircase with its Brussels carpet and twisted brass stair-rods, on the right the drawing-room. The drawing-room can hardly be said to express the personality of **Mr Huxtable.** *The foundations of its furnishing are in the taste of* **Mrs Huxtable.** *For fifteen years or so additions to this family museum have been disputed into their place by the six* **Miss Huxtables:** **Laura** *(aged thirty-nine),* **Minnie, Clara, Julia, Emma, Jane** *(aged twenty-six). The rosewood cabinets, the picture from some Academy of the early seventies entitled 'In Ye Olden Time' (this was a wedding present most likely), the gilt clock, which is a Shakespeare, narrow-headed, but with a masterly pair of legs, propped pensively against a dial and enshrined beneath a dome of glass, another wedding present. These were the treasures of* **Mrs Huxtable's** *first drawing-room, her solace in the dull post-honeymoon days. She was the daughter of a city merchant, wholesale as against her husband's retail; but even in the seventies retail was lifting its head. It was considered* *though that* **Katherine Tombs** *conferred some distinction upon young* **Harry Huxtable** *by marrying him, and even now, as a portly lady nearing sixty, she figures by the rustle of her dress, the measure of her mellow voice with its carefully chosen phrases, for the dignity of the household.*

The difference between one **Miss Huxtable** *and another is to a casual eye the difference between one lead pencil and another, as these lie upon one's table after some weeks' use; a matter of length, of sharpening, of wear.* **Laura's** *distinction lies in her being the housekeeper; it is a solid power, that of ordering the dinner. She is very silent. While her sisters are silent with strangers, she is silent with her sisters. She doesn't seem to read much either; one hopes she dreams, if only of wild adventures with a new carpet-sweeper. When there was some family bitterness as to whether the fireplace in summer should hold ferns or a Chinese umbrella, it was* **Laura's** *opinion that an umbrella gathers less dust, which carried the day.* **Minnie** *and* **Clara** *are inclined to religion; not sentimentally; works are a good second with them to faith. They have veered, though, lately, from district visiting to an interest in Missions – missions to Poplar or China (one is almost as far as the other); good works, the results of which they cannot see. Happily they forbear to ask why this proves the more soul-satisfying sort.*

Julia *started life – that is to say, left school – as a genius. The headmistress had had two or three years of such dull girls that really she could not resist this excitement. Watercolour sketches were the medium. So* **Julia** *was dressed in brown velveteen and sent to an art school, where they wouldn't let her do watercolour drawing at all. And in two years she learnt enough about the trade of an artist not ever to want to do those watercolour drawings again.* **Julia** *is now over thirty and very unhappy. Three of her watercolours (early masterpieces) hang on the drawing-room wall. They shame her, but her mother won't have them taken down. On a holiday she'll be off now and then for a solitary day's sketching, and as she tears up the vain attempt to put on paper the things she has learnt to see, she sometimes cries. It was* **Julia**, **Emma** *and* **Jane** *who, some years ago, conspired to present their mother with that intensely* *conspicuous cosy corner. A cosy corner is apparently a device for making a corner just what the very nature of a corner should forbid it to be. They beggared themselves; but one wishes that* **Mr Huxtable** *were more lavish with his dress allowances, then they might at least have afforded something not quite so hideous.*

Emma, *having* **Julia** *in mind, has run rather to coats and skirts and common sense. She would have been a success in an office and worth perhaps thirty shillings a week. But the* **Huxtables** *don't want another thirty shillings a week and this gift, such as it is, has been wasted, so that* **Emma** *runs also to a brusque temper.*

Jane *is meekly enough a little wild.* **Mrs Huxtable**'s *power of applying the brake of good breeding, strong enough over five daughters, waned at the sixth attempt in twelve years, and* **Jane** *has actually got herself proposed to twice by not quite desirable young men. Now the fact that she was old enough to be proposed to at all came as something of a shock to the family. Birthdays pass, their celebration growing less emphatic. No one likes to believe that the years are passing; even the birthday's owner, least able to escape its significance, laughs and then changes the subject. So the* **Miss Huxtables** *never openly asked each other what the marriage of the youngest of them might imply; perhaps they never even asked themselves. Besides,* **Jane** *didn't marry. But if she does, unless perhaps she runs away to do it, there will be heart-searchings at least.* **Mr Huxtable** *asked though, and* **Mrs Huxtable**'s *answer – given early one morning before the hot water came – scarcely satisfied him. 'For,' said* **Mr Huxtable**, *'if the girls don't marry some day what are they to do? It's not as if they had to go into the shop.' 'No, thank Heaven!' said* **Mrs Huxtable**.

Since his illness **Mr Huxtable** *has taken to asking questions – of anybody and about anything; of himself oftenest of all. But for that illness he would have been a conventional enough type of successful shopkeeper, coarsely fed, whiskered, podgy. But eighteen months' nursing and dieting and removal from the*

*world seem to have brought a gentleness to his voice, a spark
of humour to his eye, a childishness to his little bursts of temper
– they have added, in fact, a wistfulness which makes him
rather a lovable old buffer on the whole.*

*This is a Sunday morning, a bright day in October. The
family are still at church and the drawing-room is empty. The
door opens and the parlour-maid – much becapped and
aproned – shows in* **Philip Madras** *and his friend* **Major
Hippisly Thomas**. **Thomas**, *long-legged and deliberate,
moves across the room to the big French windows which open
on to a balcony and look down on the garden and to many
gardens beyond.* **Thomas** *is a good fellow.*

Philip Madras *is more complex than that. To begin with, it is
obvious he is not wholly English. A certain litheness of figure,
the keenness and colour of his voice, and a liking for
metaphysical turns of speech show an Eastern origin perhaps.
He is kind in manner but rather cold, capable of that least
English of dispositions – intellectual passion. He is about
forty, a year or two younger than his friend. The parlour-maid
has secured* **Major Thomas***'s hat and stands clutching it. As*
Philip *passes her into the room he asks . . .*

Philip About how long?

Maid In just a few minutes now, I should say, sir. Oh, I
beg pardon, does it appen to be the third Sunday in the
month?

Philip I don't know. Does it, Tommy?

Thomas (*from the window*) I can tell you. (*And he vaguely
fishes for his diary.*)

Maid I don't think it does, sir. Because then some of them
stop for the Oly Communion and that may make them late
for dinner, but I don't think it is, sir. (*She backs through
the door, entangling the hat in the handle.*)

Philip Is my mother still staying here?

Maid Mrs Madras, sir. Yes, sir.

Then having disentangled the hat, the parlour-maid vanishes.
Philip *thereupon plunges swiftly into what must be an
interrupted argument.*

Philip Very well then, my dear Tommy . . . what are the
two master tests of a man's character? His attitude towards
money and his attitude towards women.

Thomas By all means stand for the L.C.C. if you can
afford it . . .

Philip Can any decent man walk from Dorset Square to
Denmark Hill with his eyes open on a Sunday morning
and not beg me on his knees to stand for the County
Council?

Thomas But you've got what I call the Reformer's Mind
. . . and got it badly, Phil. Not that you'll make this
country any different by making it tidier, you know.

Philip I'm very interested in England, Tommy.

Thomas So am I . . . even if I don't talk quite so much
about it . . . even if I've had to chuck the army, to earn
bread and treacle for a wife and a family . . . which ain't a
bad thing for me either. What good will it do y o u,
though, to chuck a thousand a year and a directorship if
State wants you to keep 'em?

Philip The Madras House is Woman Incarnate and I
loathe it. Your Mr State may buy the place and do
whatever he likes with it.

Thomas You're sick of the dressmaking business. Right!
But you'd think a lot clearer, Phil, if you didn't spell
everything with a capital letter.

Philip Tommy, that is a sound observation. I like a good
talk with you. Sooner or later you always say one sensible
thing.

Thomas Thank you.

*Julia and Laura arrive. They are the first from church.
Sunday frocks, Sunday hats, best gloves, umbrellas and prayer
books.*

Julia Oh, what a surprise!

Philip We walked over. Ah, you don't know . . . Major
Hippisly Thomas . . . my cousin, Miss Julia Huxtable . . .
and Miss Huxtable.

Julia How do you do?

Thomas How do you do?

Laura How do you do?

Julia Have you come to see Aunt Amy?

Philip No, your father.

Julia He's walking back with her. So they'll be last, I'm
afraid.

Laura Will you stay to dinner?

Philip No, I think not.

Laura I'd better tell them. They'll be laying for you.

*Laura goes out, decorously avoiding a collision with Emma,
who, panoplied as the others, comes in at the same moment.*

Philip Hullo, Emma!

Emma Well, what a surprise!

Philip You don't know . . . Major Hippisly Thomas . . .
Miss Emma Huxtable.

Thomas How do you do?

Emma How do you do? Will you stay to dinner?

Philip No, we can't. (*That formula again completed, he
varies his explanation.*) I've just brought Thomas a Sunday

morning walk to help me tell Uncle Henry a bit of news.
My father will be back again in England tomorrow.

Emma (*with a round mouth*) Oh!

Julia It's a beautiful morning for a walk, isn't it?

Thomas Wonderful for October.

These two look first at each other, and then out of the window.
Emma *gazes quizzically at* **Philip**.

Emma I think he knows.

Philip He sort of knows.

Emma Why are you being odd, Philip?

Philip *is more hail-fellow-well-met with* **Emma** *than with the
others.*

Philip Emma . . . I have enticed a comparative stranger to
be present so that your father and mother cannot in
decency begin to fight the family battle over again with
me. Very cunning, but we did want a walk. And there's
the meeting tomorrow . . .

Jane *peeps through the door.*

Jane You? Mother!

She has turned to the hall, and from the hall comes **Mrs
Huxtable**'s *rotund voice, 'Yes, Jane?'*

Jane Cousin Philip!

Mrs Huxtable *sails in and superbly compresses every family
greeting into one.*

Mrs Huxtable What a surprise! Will you stay to dinner?

Emma (*alive to a certain redundancy*) No, Mother, they
can't.

Philip May I introduce my friend . . . Major Hippisly
Thomas . . . my aunt, Mrs Huxtable.

Mrs Huxtable (*stately and gracious*) How do you do, Major Thomas?

Philip Thomas is Mr Eustace State's London manager.

Thomas How do you do?

Mrs Huxtable *takes an armchair with the air of one mounting a throne, and from that vantage point begins polite conversation. Her daughters distribute themselves, so do* **Philip** *and* **Hippisly Thomas.**

Mrs Huxtable Not in the Army, then, Major Thomas?

Thomas I was in the Army.

Emma Jessica quite well, Philip?

Philip Yes, thanks.

Emma And Mildred?

Philip I think so. She's back at school.

Mrs Huxtable A wonderfully warm autumn, is it not?

Thomas Quite.

Mrs Huxtable Do you know Denmark Hill well?

Thomas Not well.

Mrs Huxtable We have always lived here. I consider it healthy. But London is a healthy place, I think. Oh, I beg your pardon . . . my daughter Jane.

Jane How do you do?

They shake hands with ceremony. **Emma,** *in a mind to liven things up, goes to the window.*

Emma We've quite a good garden, that's one thing.

Thomas (*not wholly innocent of an attempt to escape from his hostess, makes for the window too*) I noticed it. I am keen on gardens.

Mrs Huxtable (*her attention distracted by* **Julia**'s *making for the door*) Julia, where are you going?

Julia To take my things off, Mother.

Julia *departs. When they were quite little girls* **Mrs Huxtable** *always did ask her daughters where they were going when they left the room and where they had been when they entered it, and she has never dropped the habit. They resent it only by the extreme patience of their replies.*

Emma (*entertainingly*) That's the Crystal Palace.

Thomas Is it?

They both peer appreciatively at that famous landmark . . . In the Crystal Palace and the sunset the inhabitants of Denmark Hill have acquired almost proprietary interest. Then **Mrs Huxtable** *speaks to her nephew with a sudden severity.*

Mrs Huxtable Philip, I don't consider your mother's health is at all the thing!

Philip (*amicably*) It never is, Aunt Kate.

Mrs Huxtable (*admitting the justice of the retort*) That's true.

Philip Uncle Henry keeps better, I think.

Mrs Huxtable He's well enough now. I have had a slight cold. Is it true that your father may appear in England again?

Philip Yes, he has only been on the Continent, doing cures. He arrives tomorrow.

Mrs Huxtable I'm sorry.

Jane Mother!

Mrs Huxtable *has launched this with such redoubled severity that* **Jane** *had to protest. However, at this moment arrives* **Mr Huxtable** *himself; one glad smile.*

Mr Huxtable Ah, Phil . . . I ad an idea you might come over. You'll stay to dinner. Jane, tell your aunt . . . she's taking er bonnet off.

Jane *obeys. He sights on the balcony* **Major Thomas**'*s back.*

Mr Huxtable Who's that outside?

Philip Hippisly Thomas. We wanted a walk; we can't stay.

Mr Huxtable Oh.

Mrs Huxtable Have you come on business?

Philip Well . . .

Mrs Huxtable On Sunday?

Philip Not exactly.

She shakes her head, gravely deprecating. **Thomas** *comes from the balcony.*

Mr Huxtable Ow are you?

Thomas How are y o u ?

Mr Huxtable Fine morning, isn't it? Nice prospect this . . . see the Crystal Palace?

While **Thomas** *turns with perfect politeness to view again this phenomenon,* **Philip** *pacifies his aunt.*

Philip You see, Aunt Katherine, tomorrow afternoon we definitely confer with this Mr State about his buying up the two firms, and my father is passing through England again to attend.

Mrs Huxtable Of course, Philip, if it's business I know nothing about it. But is it suggested that your uncle should attend too?

Her voice has found a new gravity. **Philip** *becomes very airy; so does* **Mr Huxtable**, *who comes back to rejoin the conversation.*

Philip My dear aunt, naturally.

Mr Huxtable What's this?

Mrs Huxtable (*the one word expressing volumes*)
Constantine.

Mr Huxtable (*with elaborate innocence*) That's definite
now, is it?

Mrs Huxtable You dropped a hint last night, Henry.

Mr Huxtable I dessay. I dessay I did. (*His eye shifts
guiltily.*)

Mrs Huxtable Quite out of the question, I should say.

Jane *comes back.*

Jane Aunt Mary's coming.

Mr Huxtable (*genial again*) Oh. My daughter Jane . . .
Major Thomas, Major Hippisly Thomas.

Jane (*with discretion*) Yes, Father.

Mrs Huxtable (*tactfully*) You are naturally not aware,
Major Thomas, that for family reasons into which we need
not go, Mr Huxtable has not spoken to his brother-in-law
for a number of years.

Philip's *eye meets* **Thomas**'s *in comic agony. But* **Mr
Huxtable** *too plunges delightedly into the forbidden subject.*

Mr Huxtable Thirty years very near. Wonderful, isn't it?
Interested in the same business. Wasn't easy to keep it up.

Thomas I had heard.

Mr Huxtable Oh yes, notorious.

Mrs Huxtable (*in reprobation*) And well it may be, Henry.

Mrs Madras *comes in. It is evident that* **Philip** *is his father's
son. He would seem so wholly, but for that touch of 'self-
worship which is often self-mistrust'; his mother's gift,
appearing nowadays less lovably in her as a sort of querulous
assertion of her rights and wrongs against the troubles which
have been too strong for her. She is a pale old lady, shrunk a
little, the life gone out of her.*

Mrs Huxtable (*some severity remaining*) Amy, your
husband is in England again.

Philip *presents a filial cheek. It is kissed.*

Philip How are you, Mother?

Mr Huxtable (*sotto voce*) Oh, tact, Katherine, tact!

Philip Perhaps you remember Reggie Thomas?

Thomas I was at Marlborough with Philip, Mrs Madras.

Mrs Madras Yes. Is he, Katherine?

Having given **Thomas** *a limp hand and her sister this coldest
of responses, she finds her way to a sofa, where she sits silent,
thinking to herself.* **Mrs Huxtable** *keeps majestic hold upon
her subject.*

Mrs Huxtable I am unable to see, Philip, why your uncle
should break through his rule now.

Mr Huxtable There you are, Phil!

Philip Of course it is for Uncle Henry to decide.

Mr Huxtable Naturally . . . naturally. (*Still he has an
appealing eye on* **Philip**, *who obliges him.*)

Philip But since Mr State's offer may not be only for the
Madras House but for Roberts & Huxtable into the
bargain . . . if the two principal proprietors can't meet
him round a table to settle the matter . . .

Thomas (*ponderously diplomatic*) Yes . . . a little awkward
. . . if I may say so . . . as Mr State's representative, Mrs
Huxtable.

Mrs Huxtable Do you think, Major Thomas, that
awkwardness should make us overlook wicked conduct?

This reduces the assembly to such a shamed silence that poor
Mr Huxtable *can only add* –

Mr Huxtable Oh, talk of something else . . . talk of
something else.

After a moment **Mrs Madras***'s pale voice steals in, as she turns to her son.*

Mrs Madras When did you hear from your father?

Philip A letter from Marienbad two or three days ago and a telegram yesterday morning.

Mrs Huxtable, *with a hostess's authority, now restores a polite and easy tone to the conversation.*

Mrs Huxtable And have you left the Army long, Major Thomas?

Thomas Four years.

Mrs Huxtable Now what made you take to the Drapery Trade?

Philip (*very explanatory*) Mr State is an American financier, Aunt Kitty, who bought up Burrow's, the big mantle place in the city, three years ago, and now wants to buy us up too.

Mrs Huxtable We are not in difficulties, I hope.

Philip Oh no.

Mrs Huxtable No. No doubt Henry would have told me if we had been.

As she thus gracefully dismisses the subject there appear up the steps and along the balcony the last arrivals from church, **Minnie** *and* **Clara***. The male part of the company unsettles itself.*

Mr Huxtable Ullo! Where have you been?

Minnie We went for a walk.

Mrs Huxtable (*in apparently deep surprise*) A walk, Minnie! Where to?

Minnie Just the long way home. We thought we'd have time.

Clara Did you notice what a short sermon?

Mr Huxtable Oh, may I . . . My daughter Clara . . .
Major Ippisly Thomas. My daughter Minnie . . . Major
Thomas.

The conventional chant begins.

Minnie How d' you do?

Thomas How d' you do?

Clara How d' you do?

Minnie How d' you do, Philip?

Philip How d' you do?

Clara How d' you do?

Philip How d' you do?

The chant over, the company re-settles; **Mr Huxtable**
buttonholing **Philip** *in the process with an air of some mystery.*

Mr Huxtable By the way, Phil, remind me to ask you
something before you go . . . rather important.

Philip I shall be at your place in the morning. Thomas is
coming to go through some figures.

Mr Huxtable (*with a regular snap*) Yes . . . I shan't.

Philip The State meeting is in Bond Street, three o'clock.

Mr Huxtable I know, I know. (*Then, finding himself
prominent, he captures the conversation.*) I'm slacking off,
Major Thomas, slacking off. Ever since I was ill I've been
slacking off.

Mrs Huxtable You are perfectly well again now, Henry.

Mr Huxtable Not the point. I want leisure, you know,
leisure. Time for reading . . . time to think a bit.

Mrs Huxtable Nonsense! (*She adds, with correctness.*)
Major Thomas will excuse me.

Mr Huxtable (*on his hobby*) Oh, well . . . a man must . . . some portion of his life . . .

Thomas Quite. I got most of my reading done early.

Mrs Huxtable The natural time for it.

Mr Huxtable Ah, lucky feller! Educated, I suppose. Well, I wasn't. I've been getting the books for years – good editions. I'd like you to see my library. But these geniuses want settling down to . . . if a man's to keep pace with the thought of the world, y' know. Macaulay, Erbert Spencer, Grote's *Istory of Greece*! I've got em all there.

He finds no further response; **Mrs Huxtable** *fills the gap.*

Mrs Huxtable I thought the sermon dull this morning, Amy, didn't you?

Mrs Madras (*unexpectedly*) No, I didn't.

Minnie (*to do her share of the entertaining*) Mother, somebody ought to speak about those boys . . . it's disgraceful. Mr Vivian had actually to turn round from the organ at them during the last hymn.

Julia, *her things taken off, reappears.* **Mr Huxtable** *is on the spot.*

Mr Huxtable Ah, my daughter Julia . . . Major –

Julia We've been introduced, Father.

She says this with a hauteur which really is pure nervousness, but **Mr Huxtable** *is sufficiently crushed.*

Mr Huxtable Oh, I beg pardon.

But **Mrs Huxtable** *disapproves of any self-assertion and descends upon the culprit; who is for some obscure reason (or for none) more often disapproved of than the others.*

Mrs Huxtable Close the door, please, Julia.

Julia I'm sorry, Mother.

Philip *closes the offending door.* **Julia** *obliterates herself in a chair, and the conversation, hardly encouraged by this little affray, comes to an intolerable standstill. At last* **Clara** *makes an effort.*

Clara Is Jessica quite well, Philip?

Philip Yes, thank you, Clara.

Mrs Huxtable And dear little Mildred?

Philip Yes, thank you, Aunt Kate.

Further standstill. Then **Minnie** *contrives a remark.*

Minnie Do you still like that school for her?

Philip (*with finesse*) It seems to provide every accomplishment that money can buy.

Mrs Huxtable *discovers a sure opening.*

Mrs Huxtable Have you been away for the summer, Major Thomas?

Thomas (*vaguely – he is getting sympathetically tongue-tied*) Oh . . . yes . . .

Philip Tommy and Jessica and I took a holiday motoring round Munich and into it for the operas.

Mrs Huxtable Was that pleasant?

Philip Very.

Mrs Huxtable And where was dear Mildred?

Philip With her aunt most of the time . . . Jessica's sister-in-law, you know.

Minnie Lady Ames?

Philip Yes.

Mrs Huxtable (*innocently snobbish*) Very nice for her.

Mr Huxtable We take a ouse at Weymouth as a rule.

Mrs Huxtable Do you know Weymouth, Major Thomas?

Thomas No, I don't.

Mrs Huxtable George III used to stay there, but that is a hotel now.

Mr Huxtable Keep your spare money in the country, y' know.

Mrs Huxtable Oh, and there is everything one wants at Weymouth.

But even this subject flags.

Mrs Huxtable You think more of Bognor, Amy, I know.

Mrs Madras Only to live in, Katherine.

They have made their last effort. The conversation is dead.
Mr Huxtable's discomfort suddenly becomes physical.

Mr Huxtable I'm going to change my coat.

Philip I think perhaps we ought to be off.

Mr Huxtable No, no, no, no, no, I shan't be a minute. Don't go, Phil; there's a good fellow.

And he has left them all to it. The **Huxtable** *conversation, it will be noticed, consists mainly of asking questions. Visitors after a time fall into the habit too.*

Philip Do you like this house better than the old one, Clara?

Clara It has more rooms, you know.

Mrs Huxtable Do you live in London, Major Thomas?

Thomas No, I live at Woking. I come up and down every day as a rule. I think the country's better for the children.

Mrs Huxtable Not a cheerful place, is it?

Thomas Oh, very cheerful!

Mrs Huxtable I had thought not for some reason.

Emma The cemetery, Mother.

Mrs Huxtable (*accepting the suggestion with dignity*) Perhaps.

Clara And of course there's a much larger garden. We have the garden of the next house as well.

Jane Not all the garden of the next house.

Clara Well, most of it.

This stimulating difference of opinion takes them to the balcony. **Philip** *follows.* **Julia** *follows* **Philip**. **Minnie** *departs to take her things off.*

Julia Do you notice how near the Crystal Palace seems? That means rain.

Philip Of course . . . you can see the Crystal Palace.

Mrs Huxtable Julia, won't you catch cold on the balcony without a hat?

Julia (*meek, but before the visitor, determined*) I don't think so, Mother.

Mrs Huxtable *turns, with added politeness, to* **Major Thomas**.

Mrs Huxtable Yes, we used to live not so far along the hill; it certainly was a smaller house.

Philip *is now on the balcony receiving more information.*

Philip That's Ruskin's house, is it? Yes, I see the chimney pots.

Mrs Huxtable I should not have moved, myself, but I was overruled.

Emma Mother, we had grown out of Hollybank.

Mrs Huxtable I was overruled. Things are done on a larger scale than they used to be. Not that I approve of that.

Thomas One's family will grow up.

Mrs Huxtable People spend their money nowadays. My father's practice was to live on half his income. However, he lost the greater part of his money by unwise investments . . . in lead, I think it was. I was at school at the time in Brighton. And he educated me above my station in life.

At this moment **Clara** *breaks out of the conservatory. Something has happened.*

Clara Jane, that Cineraria's out.

Jane Oh!

They crowd in to see it. **Philip** *crowds in too.* **Mrs Huxtable** *is unmoved.*

Mrs Huxtable We are told that riches are a snare, Major Thomas.

Thomas It is one I've always found easy to avoid.

Mrs Huxtable (*oblivious of the joke, which indeed she would not have expected on such a subject*) And I have noticed that their acquisition seldom improves the character of people in my station of life. I am of course ignorant of my husband's affairs . . . that is to say, I keep myself as ignorant as possible . . . but I think we should not try to be anything but what we are.

Thomas (*forestalling a yawn*) Quite so.

Mrs Huxtable *takes a breath.*

Mrs Huxtable And with a family of daughters, Major Thomas . . .

Emma (*a little agonised*) Mother!

Mrs Huxtable What is it, Emma?

But **Emma** *thinks better of it and goes to join the cineraria party, saying –*

Emma Nothing, Mother, I beg your pardon.

Mrs Huxtable *retakes her breath.*

Mrs Huxtable What were we saying?

Thomas (*with resigned politeness*) A family of daughters.

Mrs Huxtable Yes. You fought in the war, I suppose?

The inexplicable but characteristic suddenness of this rouses the **Major** *a little.*

Thomas I was in it. I just missed South Africa.

Mrs Huxtable Still I find people look differently at life nowadays. A man no longer seems prepared to marry and support a wife and family by his unaided exertions. I consider that a pity.

Thomas (*near another yawn*) Quite . . . quite so.

Mrs Huxtable I have always determined that my daughters should be sought after for themselves alone. That should ensure their happiness. Any eligible gentleman who visits here constantly is given to understand, delicately, that little need be expected from Mr Huxtable beyond his approval. You a r e married, I think you said, Major Thomas.

This quite wakes him up, though **Mrs Huxtable** *is really innocent of the implication.*

Thomas Yes, oh, dear me, yes.

Mrs Huxtable And a family?

Thomas Four children . . . my youngest is three.

Mrs Huxtable Pretty dear!

Thomas No, ugly little beggar, but has character.

Mrs Huxtable I must take off my things before dinner. You'll excuse me. If one is not punctual oneself . . .

Thomas Quite.

Mrs Huxtable We cannot induce you to join us?

Thomas Many thanks, but we have to meet Mrs Phil for lunch in town at two.

Mrs Huxtable I am sorry.

Thomas *opens the door for her with his best bow and she graciously departs, conscious of having properly impressed him.*

Clara, *who has now her things to take off, crosses the room, saying to* **Philip**, *who follows her from the balcony —*

Clara Yes, I'll tell father, Philip. I'm going upstairs.

Thomas *opens the door for her, but only with his second best bow, and then turns to* **Philip** *with a sigh.*

Thomas Phil, we ought to be going.

Philip Wait till we've seen my uncle again.

Thomas All right.

He heaves another sigh and sits down. All this time there has been **Mrs Madras** *upon her sofa, silent, as forgotten as any other piece of furniture for which there is no immediate use.* **Philip** *now goes to her. When she does speak it is unresponsively.*

Philip How long do you stay in town, Mother?

Mrs Madras I have been here a fortnight. I generally stay three weeks.

Philip Jessica has been meaning to ask you to Dorset Square again.

Mrs Madras Has she?

Philip (*a little guiltily*) She's very busy just now . . . with one thing and another.

Suddenly **Mrs Madras** *rouses herself.*

Mrs Madras I wish to see your father, Philip.

Philip (*in doubt*) He won't be here long, Mother.

Mrs Madras No, I am sure he won't.

With three delicate strides **Thomas** *lands himself on to the balcony.*

Philip Well, I'll tell him you want to see him.

Mrs Madras Please don't. Tell him I think he ought to come and see me.

Philip He won't, Mother.

Mrs Madras I know he won't. He came to England in
May, didn't he? He was here till July, wasn't he? Did he
so much as send me a message?

Philip (*with unkind patience*) No, Mother.

Mrs Madras What was he doing all the while, Philip?

Philip I didn't see much of him. I really don't know why
he's back again now at all. We could have done this
business without him. There's not much to be gained by
your seeing him, you know.

Mrs Madras You are very heartless, Philip.

This is true enough for **Philip** *to resent it rather.*

Philip My dear mother, you and he have been separated
for . . . how long?

Mrs Madras (*with withered force*) I am his wife still, I
should hope. I have never forgotten my duty. He is an old
man now and past such sin, and I am an old woman. And
I am ready to be a comfort to his declining years, and it's
right I should be allowed to tell him so. And you should
not let your wife put you against your own mother, Philip.

Philip (*bewildered*) Really!

Mrs Madras I know what Jessica thinks of me. Jessica is
very clever and has no patience with people who can only
do their best to be good . . . I understand that. Well, it
isn't her duty to love me . . . at least it may not be her
duty to love her husband's mother, or it may be, I don't
say. But it is your duty. I sometimes think, Philip, you
don't love me any longer, though you're afraid to say so.

The appeal ends so pathetically that **Philip** *is very gently
equivocal.*

Philip If I didn't love you, my dear mother, I should be
afraid to say so.

Mrs Madras When are you to see your father?

Philip We've asked him to dinner tomorrow.

At this moment **Emma** *comes in with a briskness so jarring to poor* **Mrs Madras's** *already wrought nerves, that she turns on her.*

Mrs Madras Emma, why do you come bouncing in like that when I'm trying to get a quiet word with Philip?

Emma Really, Aunt Amy, the drawing-room belongs to every one.

Mrs Madras I'm sure I don't know why I come and stay here at all. I dislike your mother extremely.

Emma Then kindly don't tell me so. I've no wish not to be polite to you.

Philip (*pacifically*) Emma, I think Uncle Henry ought to attend this meeting tomorrow.

Mrs Madras (*beginning to cry*) Of course he ought. Who is he to go on like this about Constantine! My handkerchief's upstairs.

Emma (*contritely*) Shall I fetch it for you, Aunt Amy?

Mrs Madras No, I'll be a trouble to no one.

She retires, injured. **Philip** *continues, purposely placid.*

Philip What's more, he really wants to attend it.

Emma I'm sorry I was rude . . . but she does get on our nerves, you know.

Philip Why do you invite her?

Emma (*quite jolly with him*) Oh, we're all very fond of Aunt Amy, and anyhow mother would think it our duty. I don't see how she can enjoy coming though. She never goes out . . . never joins in the conversation . . . just sits nursing herself.

Philip (*quizzically*) You're all too good, Emma.

Emma Yes. I heard you making fun of Julia in the conservatory. But if one stopped doing one's duty what would happen to the world? (*Her voice now takes that tone which is the well-bred substitute for a wink.*) I say . . . I suppose I oughtn't to tell you about Julia, but it is rather a joke. You know Julia gets hysterical when her headaches last too long.

Philip Does she?

Emma Well, a collar marked Owen Nares came back from the wash in mistake for one of father's. I don't think he lives near here, but it's one of these big steam laundries. And Morgan the cook got it and she gave it to Julia . . . and Julia kept it. And when mother found out she cried for a whole day. She said it showed a wanton mind.

Philip's mocking face becomes grave.

Philip I don't think that's at all amusing, Emma.

Emma (*in genuine surprise*) Don't you?

Philip How old is Julia?

Emma She's thirty-four. (*Her face falls too.*) No . . . it is rather dreadful, isn't it? (*Then wrinkling her forehead as at a puzzle.*) It isn't exactly that one wants to get married. I daresay mother is right about that.

Philip About what?

Emma Well, some time ago, a gentleman proposed to Jane. And mother said it would have been more honourable if he had spoken to father first, and that Jane was the youngest and too young anyhow to know her own mind. Well, you know, she's twenty-six. And then they heard of something he'd once done and it was put a stop to. And Jane was very rebellious and mother cried . . .

Philip Does she always cry?

Emma Yes, she does cry if she's upset about us. And I think she was right. One ought not to risk being unhappy for life, ought one?

Philip Are you all so happy now, then?

Emma Oh, deep down, I think we are. It would be ungrateful not to be. When one has a good home and. . . ! But of course living together and going away together and being together all the time, one does get a little irritable now and then. We sit as mum as maggots when people are here . . . I suppose we're afraid of squabbling.

Philip Do you squabble?

Emma Not like we used. You know till we moved into this house we had only two bedrooms between us, the nursery and the old night nursery. Laura and Minnie have one each now and there's one we take by turns, year and year about. There wasn't a bigger house to be got here or I suppose we could have had it. They hated the idea of moving far. And it's odd, you know, father's afraid of spending money, though he must have got lots. He says if he gave u s any more we shouldn't know what to do with it . . . and of course that's true.

Philip But what do you girls d o?

Emma We keep busy. There's lots to be done about the house and there's the Parish . . . and of course we've our friends . . . and tennis. Julia used to sketch quite well. D'you think novels and newspapers tell you the truth about things, Philip?

Philip Some novels may. Why?

Emma Because you'd think from them there wasn't any one else in England like us. But I know lots. You mustn't think I'm grumbling. I talk too much. They tell me so.

Philip's *comment is the question, half serious* . . .

Philip Why don't you go away, all six of you, or say five of you?

Emma (*wide-eyed*) Go away!

Philip (*comprehensively*) Out of it.

Emma (*wider-eyed*) Where to?

Philip (*with a sigh – for her*) Ah, that's just it.

Emma How could one! And it would upset everything so. Father and mother don't know one feels like this at times . . . they would be grieved.

Philip *turns to her with kindly irony.*

Philip Emma, they're telling your father at the shop that he'll have to abolish the living-in system. He might as well do it at home for a start.

Mr Huxtable *returns, at ease in a jacket. He pats his daughter kindly on the shoulder.*

Mr Huxtable Now run along, Jane . . . I mean Emma . . . I want a word with your cousin.

Emma Yes, Father.

Emma – *or* **Jane** – *obediently disappears.* **Philip** *then looks sideways at his uncle.*

Philip I've come over, as you asked me.

Mr Huxtable I didn't ask you.

Philip You dropped a hint.

Mr Huxtable (*almost with a blush*) Did I? I dessay I did.

Philip But you must hurry up and decide about the meeting tomorrow. Thomas and I have to go.

Mr Huxtable Phil, I suppose you're set on selling.

Philip Quite.

Mr Huxtable You young men! The Madras Ouse means nothing to you.

Philip (*anti-sentimental*) Nothing unsaleable.

Mr Huxtable Well, well well! (*Then in a furtive fuss.*) Well, just a minute, my boy, before your aunt comes down . . . she's been on at me upstairs . . . I tell you! Something you must do for me tomorrow, like a good feller, at the shop in the morning. (*He suddenly becomes portentous.*) Have you heard this yet about Miss Yates?

Philip No.

Mr Huxtable Disgraceful! Disgraceful!!

Philip She did very well in Bond Street . . . learnt a good deal. She has only been back a few weeks.

Mr Huxtable (*snorting derisively*) Learnt a good deal! (*Then he sights* **Thomas** *on the balcony and hails him.*) Oh, come in, Major Thomas. (*And dropping his voice again ominously.*) Shut the window if you don't mind; we don't want the ladies to hear this.

Thomas *shuts the window and* **Mr Huxtable** *spreads himself to the awful enjoyment of imparting scandal.*

Mr Huxtable I tell you, my boy, up at your place, got hold of she's been by some feller . . . some West End club feller, I dessay . . . and he's put her in the . . . well, I tell you!! Major Thomas will excuse me. Not a chit of a girl, mind you, but first hand in our Costume room. Buyer we were going to make her! Thought we'd get her taught a bit of style! Style!!

Philip *frowns, both at the news and at his uncle's manner of giving it.*

Philip What do you want me to do?

Mr Huxtable (*more portentous than ever*) You wait, that's not what's the worst of it. You know Brigstock.

Philip Do I?

Mr Huxtable Oh, yes, third man in the Osiery.

Philip True.

Mr Huxtable Well . . . it seems that more than a week ago Miss Chancellor caught them kissing.

Philip (*his impatience of the display growing*) Caught w h o kissing?

Mr Huxtable I know it ain't clear. Let's go back to the beginning . . . Major Thomas will excuse me.

Thomas (*showing the properest feeling*) Not at all.

Mr Huxtable Wednesday afternoon, Willoughby, that's our doctor, comes up as usual. Miss Yates goes in to see him. Miss Chancellor – that's our housekeeper, Major Thomas – over'ears something, quite by accident, so she says, and afterwards taxes her with it.

Philip Unwise.

Mr Huxtable No, no, her plain duty . . . she knows my principle about such things. But then she remembers the kissing and that gets about among our young ladies. Somebody stupid there, I grant you, but you know what these things are. And then it gets about about Miss Yates . . . all over the shop. And then it turns out that Brigstock's a married man . . . been married two years . . . secret from us, you know, because he's living in and on promotion and all the rest. And yesterday morning his wife turns up in my office and has hysterics and says her husband's been slandered.

Philip I don't see why Miss Yates should have come to any particular harm at our place. What she does out of hours is her own business, of course . . .

Mr Huxtable No, it ain't . . . oh no, it ain't! (*Still instinctively spreading himself, but with that wistful look creeping on him now.*) Anyhow . . . I had er up the day before yesterday. And I don't know what's coming over me. I scolded her well. I was in the right in all I said . . . but. . . ! Have you ever suddenly eard your own voice as it might be a gramophone? If she'd only have answered back! But she just sat looking at me . . . and I went funny all over. So I told her to leave the room quick. (*He grows distressed and appealing.*) And you must take the job on,

Phil . . . it ought all to be settled tomorrow. Miss Yates must have the sack and I'm not sure Brigstock hadn't better have the sack. We don't want to lose Miss Chancellor, but really if she can't hold er tongue at her age . . . well, she'd better have . . .

Philip (*out of patience*) Oh, nonsense.

Mr Huxtable (*his old unquestioning self asserted for a moment*) No, I will not have scandals in the shop. We've always been free of em . . . almost always. I don't want to be hard on the girl. If the man is in our employ and you can find im out . . . punish the guilty as well as the innocent . . . I'm for all that. (*That breath exhausted, he continues quite pathetically to* **Thomas**.) But I do not know what's coming over me. Before I got ill I'd have tackled this business like winking. But when you're a long time in bed . . . I'd never been ill like that before . . . I dunno how it is . . . you get thinking . . . and things which used to be clear don't seem so clear . . . and then after, when you start to do and say the things that used to come natural . . . they don't come natural . . . and that puts you off something . . .

This is interrupted by the reappearance of **Mrs Huxtable**, *lace-capped and ready for dinner. She is at the pitch to which the upstairs dispute with her husband evidently brought her. It would seem he bolted in the middle of it.*

Mrs Huxtable Is it the fact, Philip, that if your uncle does not attend the meeting tomorrow this business transaction with Mr – I forget his name – the American gentleman . . . and which I of course know nothing about, will be seriously upset?

Mr Huxtable (*joining battle*) Kitty, why shouldn't I go? If Constantine chooses to turn up . . . that is his business. I needn't speak directly to him . . . so to say.

Mrs Huxtable (*hurling this choice bolt from her vocabulary*) A quibble, Henry.

Mr Huxtable If he's really leaving England now for good . . .

Mrs Huxtable But you do as you wish, of course.

Mr Huxtable (*wistful again*) I should like you to be convinced.

Mrs Huxtable Don't prevaricate, Henry. And your sister is just coming into the room. We had better drop the subject.

And in **Mrs Madras** *does come, but what with one thing and another* **Mr Huxtable** *is now getting what he would call thoroughly put out.*

Mr Huxtable Now if Amelia here was to propose seeing im –

Mr Huxtable Henry . . . a little consideration!

Mr Huxtable (*goaded to the truth*) Well, I want to go, Kitty, and that's all about it. And I dropped a int, I did, to Phil to come over and help me through it with you. I thought he'd make it seem as if it was most pressing business . . . only he hasn't . . . so as to hurt your feelings less. Because I'd been bound to have told you afterwards or it might have slipped out somehow. Goodness gracious me, here's the Madras House, which I've sunk enough money in these last ten years to have paid our Peckham rates and taxes pretty nearly . . . it's to be sold because Phil won't stand by me and his father don't care a straw now. Not but what that's Constantine all over! Marries you, Amelia, acts like a prince in a fairy tale for eighteen months and then –

Mrs Huxtable (*scandalised 'Before visitors too!'*) Henry!

Mr Huxtable All right, all right. And I'm not to attend this meeting, if you please!

The little storm subsides.

Mrs Madras It's to be sold now, is it?

Philip Yes, Mother.

Mrs Madras (*at her brother*) It was started with my money as well as yours.

Mr Huxtable *is recovering and takes no notice.*

Philip Yes, Mother, we know.

Mrs Madras And if that's all you've lost by Constantine, I don't see you've a right to be so bitter against him.

She is still ignored. **Mr Huxtable**, *quite cheery again, goes on affably.*

Mr Huxtable D'you know, Major Thomas, that thirty years ago when that shop was the talk of London . . . yes, and Paris houses poorparleying for a partnership too . . . why, duchesses have been known to go to all intents and purposes on their knees to him to design them a dress. Wouldn't do it unless he pleased – not unless he approved their figures and thought they'd do him credit. Ad Society under his thumb.

Mrs Huxtable (*from the height of respectability*) No doubt he knew his business.

Mr Huxtable (*in an ecstasy*) Knew his business! Knew his business!! And in Society too . . . asked everywhere like one of themselves very nearly! It's my belief that if we'd ad a Prime Minister in those days with a wife who cared a button what she looked like, he could have had a knighthood. And a knighthood was a knighthood then!

Mrs Huxtable (*explicitly*) He was untrue to his wife, Henry.

At this **Mr Huxtable** *is the moral man again. These sudden changes are so like him. They are genuine; he is just half conscious of their suddenness.*

Mr Huxtable I know, and Amy did what she should have done. You see it wasn't even an ordinary case, Major Thomas. It was girls in the shop. And even though he took em out of the shop . . . that's a slur on the whole trade. A man in his position . . . you can't overlook that.

Mrs Madras (*palely asserting herself*) I could have overlooked it if I had chosen.

Philip (*to whom this is all so futile and foolish*) My dear mother, you were unhappy with my father and you left him . . . the matter is very simple.

Mrs Madras I beg your pardon, Philip . . . I was not unhappy with him.

Mrs Huxtable Amy, how could you be happy with a man who was unfaithful to you? What nonsense!

Jane *and* **Julia**, *from the balcony, finding the window locked, tap with their fingernails upon the pane. The very sharpness of the sound begins to put out* **Mr Huxtable** *again.*

Mr Huxtable No, no, they can't come in. (*He mouths at them through the window.*) You can't come in.

Jane *mouths back.*

Mr Huxtable What? (*Then the sense of it coming to him, he looks at his watch.*) No, it isn't . . . two minutes yet.

And he turns away, having excluded the innocent mind from this unseemly discussion. But at the very moment **Laura** *comes in by the door. His patience flies.*

Mr Huxtable Oh, damn! Well, I beg pardon. (*Then in desperate politeness.*) Let me introduce . . . my daughter Laura . . . Major Thomas.

Laura (*collectedly*) We have met, Father.

Mr Huxtable (*giving it all up*) Well . . . how can I tell . . . there are so many of you!

Mrs Huxtable (*severely*) Henry, you had better go to this meeting tomorrow.

Mr Huxtable (*wistful for a moment*) You think I ought?

Mrs Huxtable You know you ought not.

Mr Huxtable (*disputing it manfully*) No . . . I don't know I ought not. It isn't so easy to know what ought and ought not to be done as you always make out, Kitty. Suppose I just do something wrong for once and see what happens.

Mrs Huxtable Henry, don't say such things.

Mr Huxtable (*very reasonably to* **Major Thomas**) Well, since I've been ill –

But **Emma** *and* **Minnie** *have come in now, and* **Jane** *and* **Julia**, *finding their exile a little unreasonable, rattle hard at the window.* **Mr Huxtable** *gives it all up again.*

Mr Huxtable Oh, let em in, Phil . . . there's a good feller.

Thomas Allow me. (*And he does so.*)

Emma (*crisply*) Oh, what's it all been about?

Mrs Huxtable Never mind, Emma.

She says this to **Emma** *as she would have said it to her at the age of four. Meanwhile* **Mr Huxtable** *has recovered.*

Mr Huxtable You know, Major Thomas, Constantine could always get the better of me in little things.

Jane *has sighted* **Minnie** *and, callously, across the breadth of the room, imparts a tragedy.*

Jane Minnie, your frog's dead . . . in the conservatory.

Minnie *pales.*

Minnie Oh, dear.

Mr Huxtable . . . After the difference, of course, I began to write to him as Dear Sir. To this day he'll send me letters beginning Dear Arry.

Minnie *is hurrying to the glass house of death.*

Jane We've been burying it.

Mr Huxtable . . . Always at his ease, you know.

Thomas *escapes from him.* **Philip** *is bending over his mother – a little kindlier.*

Philip I'll try to see you again before you go back to Bognor, Mother.

At this moment the gong rings. A tremendous gong, beloved of the English middle class, which makes any house seem small. A hollow sound: the dinner hour striking its own empty stomach. **Jane,** *whose things are not taken off, gives a mitigated yelp and dashes for the door, dashes into the returning, tidy* **Clara. Mrs Huxtable** *shakes a finger.*

Mrs Huxtable Late again, Jane.

Philip We'll be off, Aunt Katherine.

Mrs Huxtable (*with a common humanity she has not shown before*) Philip . . . never think I mean to be uncharitable about your father. But he made your mother most unhappy when you were too young to know of it . . . and there is the example to others, isn't there?

Philip Yes . . . of course. I know just how you feel about it . . . I don't much like him either.

Philip *must be a little mischievous with his aunt. She responds by returning at once to her own apparent self again.*

Mrs Huxtable My dear boy . . . your own father!

From the balcony one hears the tag of **Julia's** *entertaining of* **Major Thomas.** *They have been peering at the horizon.*

Julia Yes, it means rain . . . when you see it so clearly.

A general-post of leave-taking now begins.

Philip Well, see you tomorrow, Uncle Henry.

Mr Huxtable Yes, I suppose so. Oh, and about that other matter . . .

Philip What can I do?

Mr Huxtable I'll telephone you in the morning.

Philip Goodbye, Mother.

Thomas Goodbye, Mrs Huxtable.

Mrs Huxtable (*with a final flourish of politeness*) You will overlook this domestic dissension, I hope, Major Thomas . . . it will happen sometimes.

Thomas I've been most interested.

Minnie comes back sadly from the frog's grave.

Philip Goodbye, Clara.

Clara Goodbye, Philip.

Mr Huxtable You really won't stay to dinner?

Philip Goodbye, Laura.

Thomas Thanks, no. We meet tomorrow.

The general-post quickens, the chorus grows confused.

Laura Goodbye.

Thomas Goodbye.

Jane Goodbye.

Thomas Goodbye.

Philip Goodbye, Emma – oh, pardon.

There has been the confusion of crossed hands. Apologies, withdrawals, a treading on toes, more apologies.

Emma Goodbye, Major Thomas.

Philip Now goodbye, Emma.

Thomas Goodbye, Mrs Madras.

Philip Goodbye.

Thomas Goodbye.

The chorus and the general-post continue, until at last **Philip** *and* **Thomas** *escape to a tram and a tube and their lunch, while the* **Huxtables** *sit down in all ceremony to Sunday dinner: roast beef, horseradish, Yorkshire pudding, brown potatoes, Brussels sprouts, apple tart, custard and cream, Stilton cheese, dessert.*

Act Two

The business offices of Roberts & Huxtable are tucked away upon the first floor somewhere at the back of that large drapery establishment. The waiting-room — the one in which employee sits in shivering preparation for interviews with employer — besides thus having been the silent scene of more misery than most places on earth, is one of the very ugliest rooms that ever entered into the mind of a builder and decorator. Four plain walls of brick or plaster, with seats round them, would have left it a waiting-room pure and simple. But the ugly hand of the money-maker was upon it. In the person of a contractor he thrust upon the unfortunate room — as on all the others — everything that could excuse his price and disguise his profit. The walls, to start with, were distempered an unobjectionable green, but as that might seem too plain and cheap, a dado of a nice stone colour was added, topped with stencilling in dirty red of a pattern that once was Greek.

The fireplace is apparently designed to provide the maximum amount of work possible for the wretched boy who cleans it every morning, retiring from the contest well black-leaded himself. The mantelpiece above — only an expert in such abominations knows what it is made of; but it pretends, with the aid of worm-shaped dashes of paint, to be brown marble. It is too high for comfort, too low for dignity. It has to be dusted, and usually isn't.

The square lines of the two long windows, which look upon some sanitary brick airshaft, have been carefully spoilt by the ovaling of their top panes. The half-glazed door, that opens from the passage, is of the wrong shape; the green baize door, that admits to **Mr Philip**'s room, is of the wrong colour.

And then the furnishing! Those yellow chairs upholstered in red cotton goose-flesh plush; that plush-seated, plush-backed bench, placed draughtily between the windows! There is a reasonable office table in the middle of the room. On the walls are, firstly, photographs of **Roberts** *and* **Huxtable**. **Roberts** *was a Welshman and looks it. No prosperous drapery business in London but has its Welshman. There is also a photograph of the premises – actual; and an advertisement sketch of them – ideal. There is a ten-year-old fashion plate: twenty faultless ladies engaged in ladylike occupations or serene in the lack of any. There is an insurance almanac, the one thing of beauty in the room. On the mantelpiece lies a London Directory, the one piece of true colour.*

The hand of the money-maker that has wrenched awry the Greek pattern on the wall has been laid also on all the four people who sit waiting for **Mr Philip** *at noon on this Monday; and to the warping more or less of them all.*

Mrs Brigstock, *sitting stiffly on the plush bench, in brown quilled hat and coat and skirt, is, one would guess, a clerk of some sort. She lacks colour; she lacks repose; she lacks – one stops to consider that she might possibly be a beautiful woman were it not for the things she lacks. But she is the product of fifteen years or so of long hours and little lunch. Certainly at this moment she is not seen at her best. She sits twisting her gloved hands, pulling at a loose thread, now and then biting it. Otherwise she bites her lips; her face is drawn, and she stares in front of her with only a twist of the eye now and then towards her husband, who is uncomfortable upon a chair a few feet away.*

If one were asked to size up **Mr Brigstock**, *one would say: Nothing against him. The position of Third Man in the Hosiery does not require any special talents, and it doesn't get them; or if it does they don't stay there. And* **Mr Brigstock** *stays there – just stays there. It sums him up – sums up millions of him – to say that in their youth they have energy enough to get into a position; afterwards in their terror – or sometimes only because their employers have not the heart to* *dismiss them – they stay there. Sometimes, though, the employers have the heart and do. And then what happens? Considered as a man rather than a wage earner – not that it is usual for us so to consider him – he is one of those who happily for themselves get married by women whom apparently no other man much wants to marry. Subdued to what he works in, he is dressed as a Third Man in the Hosiery should be. He is, at the moment, as agitated as his wife, and as he has no nervous force to be agitated with, is in a state of greater wretchedness.*

On the other side of the room sits **Miss Chancellor**. *Every large living-in draper's should have as housekeeper a lady of a certain age, who can embody in her own person the virtues she will expect in the young ladies under her. Decorum, sobriety of thought, tidiness, respect of persons – these are the qualities generally necessary to a shop-assistant's salvation.* **Miss Chancellor** *radiates them. They are genuine in her, too. She is now planted squarely on her chair, as it might be in easy authority, but looking closely, one may see that it is a dignified resentment keeping her there unmovable.*

In the middle of the room by the table sits **Miss Yates**. *While they wait this long time the other three try hard to keep their eyes off her. It isn't easy; partly because she is in the middle of the room and they are not. But anyhow and anywhere* **Miss Yates** *is a person that you look at, though you may ignorantly wonder why. She is by no means pretty, nor does she try to attract you. But you look at her as you look at a fire or a light in an otherwise empty room. She is not a lady, nor is she well educated, and ten years' shop-assisting has left its mark on her. But there it is. To the seeing eye she glows in that room like a live coal. She has genius – she has life, to however low a use she – or the world for her – may put it. And commoner people are lustreless beside her.*

They wait silently and the tension increases. At last it is slightly relieved by **Philip***'s arrival. He comes in briskly, his hat on, a number of unopened letters in his hand. They get up*

*to receive him with varying degrees of respect and
apprehension.*

Philip Good morning, Miss Chancellor. Good morning
Miss Yates. Good morning, Mr Brigstock.

Mr Brigstock (*introducing her*) Mrs Brigstock.

Philip *nods pleasantly to* **Mrs Brigstock**, *who purses her lips
in a half-frightened, half-vengeful way, and sits down again.
Then he puts his hat on the mantelpiece and settles himself in
the master position at the table.*

Philip I'm afraid I've kept you waiting. Well, now –

There is a sharp knock at the door.

Philip Come.

It is **Belhaven**. **Belhaven** *is seventeen, perhaps, on the climb
from office boy to clerk, of the usual pattern.* **Philip** *greets him
pleasantly.*

Philip Oh, good morning, Belhaven.

Belhaven I've put Major Thomas in your room, sir, as the
papers were there, but Mr Huxtable's is empty if you'd
like . . .

Philip This'll do.

Belhaven Major Thomas said would you speak to him for
a minute when you'd time.

Philip I'll go in now.

Belhaven Thank you, sir.

Philip (*to the waiting four*) Excuse me one minute, please.

Belhaven *bolts back to his outer office by one door – his way
of opening and getting through it is a labour-saving invention;
and* **Philip** *goes to find* **Thomas** *through the other. There is
silence again, held by these four at a greater tension than ever.
At last* **Mrs Brigstock**, *least able to bear it, gives one*

desperate wriggle-fidget. **Brigstock** *looks at her deprecatingly and says* . . .

Mr Brigstock Will you sit here, Freda, if you feel the draught?

Mrs Brigstock (*just trusting herself to answer*) No, thank you.

Silence again, but soon broken by **Philip,** *who comes from the other room, throwing over his shoulder the last of his few words with* **Thomas,** '*All right, Tommy*'. **Tommy,** *even at the dullest business, always pleasantly amuses him. Then he settles himself at the table for the second time, conciliatory, kind.*

Philip Well . . . now . . .

Mrs Brigstock, *determined to be first heard, lets slip the torrent of her wrath.*

Mrs Brigstock It's slander, Mr Madras, and I request that it shall be retracted immediately . . . before everybody . . . in the public press . . . by advertisement.

Mr Brigstock (*in an agonised whisper*) Oh, Freda . . . not so eadstrong.

Philip *is elaborately cool and good-tempered.*

Philip Miss Chancellor.

Miss Chancellor *is even more elaborately cold and dignified.*

Miss Chancellor Yes, sir.

Philip I think we might tell Mrs Brigstock we're sorry the accusation became public . . . it has naturally caused her pain.

Mrs Brigstock (*ascending the scale*) I don't believe it . . . I didn't believe it . . . if I'd have believed it –

Mr Brigstock (*interposing*) Oh, Freda!

Miss Chancellor (*very definitely*) I saw them kissing. I didn't know Mr Brigstock was a married man. But if I had known it . . . I saw them kissing.

Miss Yates, *opening her mouth for the first time, shows an easy impatience of their anger and their attitudes too.*

Miss Yates Oh . . . what sort of a kiss?

Miss Chancellor Are there different sorts of kisses, Miss Yates?

Miss Yates Yes, there are!

Mrs Brigstock (*growing shrill now*) He owns he did that, and he knows he shouldn't have and he asked my pardon . . . and whose business is it but mine. . . ?

Mr Brigstock (*vainly interposing this time*) Oh, Freda!

Mrs Brigstock (*climbing to hysterics*) Hussy to make him though . . . hussy . . . hussy!

Philip *adds a little severity to his coolness.*

Philip Mrs Brigstock.

Miss Yates (*as pleasant as possible*) All right . . . Mr Madras, I don't mind.

Philip But I do. Mrs Brigstock, I shall not attempt to clear up this business unless we can all manage to keep our tempers.

Miss Yates *collectedly explains.*

Miss Yates I've been friends with Mr Brigstock these twelve years. We both came into the firm together . . . and I knew he was married . . . p'raps I'm the only one that did. And when I told him . . . all I chose to tell him as to what had happened . . . and I felt a bit below myself that morning . . . I asked him to kiss me just to show he didn't think so much the worse of me. I had the impulse. And he gave me a kiss . . . here (*She dabs with one finger* *the left top corner of her forehead*.) and that is the truth of that.

Philip You might have given this explanation to Miss Chancellor.

Miss Yates She wouldn't have believed it.

Miss Chancellor I don't believe it.

Mrs Brigstock (*with gathering force*) William! William!! William!!!

Brigstock *desperately musters a little authority.*

Mr Brigstock Freda, be quiet . . . haven't I sworn it to you on the Bible?

Miss Chancellor *now puts her case.*

Miss Chancellor I may say I have known other young ladies in trouble, and whether they behaved properly or improperly under the circumstances . . . and I've known them behave both . . . they did not confide in their gentlemen friends . . . without the best of reasons.

Philip There is no real reason they shouldn't, Miss Chancellor.

Miss Chancellor They didn't.

Miss Yates Well . . . I did.

Miss Chancellor I had no wish for the scandal to get about. I don't know how it happened.

Miss Yates Ask your little favourite, Miss Jordan, how it happened.

This shot tells. **Miss Chancellor**'s *voice sharpens.*

Miss Chancellor Mr Madras, if I am to be accused of favouritism –

Philip Yes, yes . . . we'll keep to the point, I think.

Miss Chancellor If Mr Brigstock is not her husband, and if he wasn't the man –

Mrs Brigstock (*the spring touched*) William!

Miss Chancellor Why shouldn't she tell me who it was?

Miss Yates Why should I?

Miss Chancellor Am I here to look after the morals of these young ladies or am I not?

Mrs Brigstock A set of hussies!

Mr Brigstock (*in agony*) Freda, you'll get me the sack.

Philip Brigstock, if I wished to give anyone the sack, I should not be taking the trouble to discuss this with you all in – I hope – a reasonable way.

Mrs Brigstock, *much resenting reasonableness, stands up now to give battle.*

Mrs Brigstock Oh, give him the sack, if you please, Mr Madras. It's time he had it for his own sake.

Mr Brigstock No, Freda!

Mrs Brigstock You've got your way to make in the world, haven't you? He's got to start on his own like other people, hasn't he?

Mr Brigstock (*feeling safety and his situation slipping*) In time, Freda.

Mrs Brigstock Now's the time. If you're not sick of the life you lead . . . seeing me once a week for an hour or two . . . then I am. And this libel and slander makes about the last straw, I should think.

Philip How long have you been married, Mrs Brigstock?

Mrs Brigstock Four years.

Philip Four years!

Mrs Brigstock (*a little quelled by his equable courtesy*) Four years!

Philip (*in amazed impatience*) My dear Brigstock, why not have come to the firm and told them? It could have been arranged for you to live out with your wife.

Mr Brigstock Well, I have been thinking of it lately, sir, but I never seemed to happen on a really likely moment. I'm afraid I'm not a favourite in my department.

Mrs Brigstock No fault of his!

Mr Brigstock And it's sometimes a very little thing makes the difference between a chap's going and staying . . . when all those that aren't wanted are cleared out after sale time, I mean, for instance. And of course the forty pound a year they allow you to live out on does not keep you . . . it's no use my saying it does. And when you're married . . .

Mrs Brigstock (*who has gathered her grievances again*) I agreed to it. I have my profession too. We've been saving quicker. It's three hundred pounds now, all but a bit . . . that's enough to start on. I've got my eye on the premises. It's near here, I don't mind telling you. Why shouldn't we do as well as others . . . and ride in our carriage when we're fifty!

Mr Brigstock (*deprecating such great optimism*) Well, I've asked advice . . .

Mrs Brigstock You think too much of advice. If you'd value yourself higher! Give him the sack, if you please, Mr Madras, and I'll say thank you.

She finishes, and suddenly **Miss Yates** *takes up this part of the tale quite otherwise.*

Miss Yates He asked my advice, and I told him to stay where he is.

Mrs Brigstock (*her breath leaving her*) Oh, indeed!

Miss Yates He's steady enough. But his appearance is against him . . . and he's too romantic.

Mrs Brigstock (*hardly recovering it*) Well, I never!

Mr Brigstock A chap does think of the future, Marion.

Miss Yates Oh . . . premises near here and three hundred pounds. Perfect foolery and William ought to know it. This firm'll undersell you and eat you up and a dozen more like you . . . and the place that's trusted you for your stock will sell up every stick and there you'll be in the gutter. I advised him to own up to y o u (*She nods at* **Mrs Brigstock**.) and live out and do the best he could.

Mrs Brigstock (*more drenched with the cold water than she'll own*) I'm much obliged, I'm sure . . . I've my own opinion . . .

Philip (*who has been studying her rather anxiously*) You've no children, Mrs Brigstock?

Mrs Brigstock *goes white.*

Mrs Brigstock No, I've no children. How can you save when you have children? But if it was his child this hussy was going to have and I thought God wouldn't strike him dead on the spot, I'd do it myself, so I would . . . and he knows I would.

Mr Brigstock Haven't I taken my oath to you, Freda?

Mrs Brigstock How can I tell if he's speaking the truth . . . I ask you how can I tell? I lie awake at night away from him till I could scream with thinking about it. And I do scream as loud as I dare . . . not to wake the house. And if somebody don't open that window, I shall go off.

Philip Open the window, please, Mr Brigstock.

Philip*'s voice is serious, though he says but a simple thing.* **Mr Brigstock** *opens the window as a man may do in a sick room, helpless, a little dazed. Then he turns back to his wife, who is sitting, head tilted against the sharp back of the plush bench,* *eyes shut, mouth open. Only* **Miss Yates** *is ready with her bit of practical comfort.*

Miss Yates Here, don't you worry. I could have married William if I'd wanted. That ought to prove it to you.

Mr Brigstock There, Freda!

Miss Yates Before he knew you, though.

Mrs Brigstock (*opening her eyes*) Did you ask her?

Miss Yates No, he never asked me . . . but you know what I mean.

Miss Yates *gives emphasis to this with what one fears must be described as a wink.* **Mrs Brigstock** *looks at the acquiescent* **Brigstock** *and acknowledges the implication.*

Mrs Brigstock Yes, I know. Oh, I don't believe it really.

Comforted, she discovers her handkerchief and blows her nose, after which **Miss Chancellor,** *who has been sitting all this while still, silent, and scornful, inquires in her politest voice.*

Miss Chancellor Do you wish me still to remain, Mr Madras?

Philip One moment.

Miss Yates Oh, you'll excuse my back, sir. (*And she turns to the table again.*)

Philip I don't think I need detain you any longer, Mr and Mrs Brigstock. Your character is now quite clear in the firm's eyes, Brigstock, and I shall see that arrangements are made for you to live out in the future. I apologise to you both for all this unpleasantness.

They have both risen at this, and now **Brigstock** *begins hesitatingly.*

Mr Brigstock Well . . . thank you . . . sir . . . and . . .

Mrs Brigstock No, William.

Mr Brigstock All right, Freda! (*He struggles into his prepared speech.*) We are very much obliged to you, sir, but I do not see how I can remain with the firm unless there has been, with regard to the accusation, some definite retractation.

Philip (*near the end of his patience*) My good man, it is retracted.

Mrs Brigstock Publicly.

Philip Nonsense, Mrs Brigstock.

Mrs Brigstock (*quite herself again*) Is it indeed . . . how would you like it? (*Then becoming self-conscious.*) Well, I beg pardon. I'm sure we're very sorry for Miss Yates and I wish she w e r e married.

Miss Yates (*with some gusto*) So do I!

Suddenly **Miss Chancellor** *bursts out.*

Miss Chancellor Then, you wicked girl, why didn't you say so before . . . when I wanted to be kind to you? And we shouldn't all be talking in this outrageous indecent way. I never did in all my life. I don't know how I manage to sit here. Didn't I try to be kind to you?

Miss Yates (*unconquerable*) Yes, and you tried to cry over me. Well, I don't wish I were married, then.

Mr Brigstock Of course it's not for me to say, Marion, but the way you're going on now won't ever stop the other young ladies tattling!

The tone of the dispute now sharpens rather dangerously.

Mrs Brigstock And how's Mr Brigstock to remain in the firm if Miss Chancellor does?

Philip That is my business, Mrs Brigstock.

Miss Chancellor What . . . when I saw him kissing her . . . kissing her. . . !

Mrs Brigstock William!

Philip That has been explained.

Miss Chancellor No, Mr Madras, while I'm housekeeper here I will not countenance loose behaviour. I don't believe one word of these excuses . . .

Philip This is just obstinacy, Miss Chancellor.

Miss Chancellor And I wish to reiterate every single thing I said.

And now it degenerates into a wrangle.

Mrs Brigstock Then the law shall deal with you.

Miss Chancellor Dismiss me if you wish to, Mr Madras.

Mrs Brigstock It's libel . . . it's slander. . . !

Mr Brigstock Oh, Freda, don't!

Mrs Brigstock She can be put in prison for it.

Miss Chancellor But if Miss Yates and Mr Brigstock stay with this firm, I go.

Mrs Brigstock And she shall be put in prison . . . the cat.

Mr Brigstock Don't, Freda!

Mrs Brigstock The heartless cat! Do you swear it isn't true, William?

Philip Take your wife away, Brigstock.

Philip's *sudden vehemence causes* **Mrs Brigstock** *to make straight for the edge of her self-control – and over it.*

Mrs Brigstock Yes, and he takes himself away . . . leaves the firm, I should think so, and sorry enough you'll be before we've done. I'll see what the law will say to her . . . and they're not a hundred yards off . . . on the better side of the street too and a plate glass window as big as yours.

Mr Brigstock Do be quiet, Freda!

Mrs Brigstock (*in hysterics now*) Three hundred pounds, and how much did Maple have when he started . . . or

Whiteley . . . and damages, what's more . . . And me putting up with the life I've led. . . !

They wait till the fit subsides – **Philip** *with kindly impatience,* **Brigstock** *in mute apology – and* **Mrs Brigstock** *is a mass of sobs. Then* **Brigstock** *edges her towards the door.*

Philip Wait . . . wait . . . wait. You can't go into the passage making that noise.

Mr Brigstock Oh, Freda, you don't mean it.

Mrs Brigstock (*relieved and contrite*) I'm sure I hope I've said nothing unbecoming a lady . . . I didn't mean to.

Philip Not at all . . . it's natural you should be upset.

Mrs Brigstock And we're very much obliged for your kind intentions to us . . .

Philip Wait till you're quite calm.

Mrs Brigstock Thank you. (*Then with a final touch of injury, resentment, dignity, she shakes off* **Brigstock**'s *timid hold.*) You needn't hold me, William.

William *follows her out to forget and make her forget it all as best he can.* **Philip** *comes back to his chair, still good-humoured, but not altogether pleased with his own part in the business so far.*

Philip I'm afraid you've put yourself in the wrong, Miss Chancellor.

Miss Chancellor One often does, sir, in doing one's duty. (*Then her voice rises to a sort of swan song.*) Thirty years have I been with the firm . . . only thirty years. I will leave tomorrow.

Philip I hope you recognise it will not be my fault if you have to.

Miss Chancellor Miss Yates can obviate it. She has only to speak the truth.

Philip *now makes another effort to be frank and kindly.*

Philip Miss Chancellor, are we quite appreciating the situation from Miss Yates's point of view? Suppose she were married?

Miss Yates I'm not.

Philip But if you told us you were, we should have to believe you.

Miss Chancellor Why, Mr Madras?

Philip (*with a smile*) It would be good manners to believe her. And in matters of this sort we have to take a great deal on trust.

Miss Yates (*who has quite caught on*) Well, I did mean to stick that up on you . . . if any one wants to know. I bought a wedding ring, and I had it on when I saw Dr Willoughby. But when she came in with her long face and her What can I do for you, my poor child? . . . well, I just couldn't . . . I suppose the Devil tempted me and I told her the truth.

Philip Have you that wedding ring with you?

Miss Yates It's not real gold.

Philip Put it on.

Miss Yates, *having fished it out of a petticoat pocket, rather wonderingly does so, and* **Philip** *turns, maliciously humorous, to* **Miss Chancellor**.

Philip Now where are we, Miss Chancellor?

Miss Chancellor I think we're mocking at a very sacred thing, Mr Madras.

Miss Yates Yes . . . and I won't.

With a sudden access of emotion she slams the ring upon the table. **Philip** *meditates for a moment on the fact that there are some things in life still inaccessible to his light-hearted logic.*

Philip There is also, of course, that point of view. But suppose the affair had not got about, Miss Yates?

Miss Yates Well . . . I should have had a nice long illness. It'd all depend on whether you wanted me enough to keep my place open.

Philip You are an employee of some value to the firm.

Miss Yates Yes, I reckoned you would. Miss McIntyre'd be pleased to stay on a bit now she's quarrelled with her fiance-é. Of course if I'd only been behind the counter . . .

Miss Chancellor (*who has drawn the longest of breaths at this calculated immodesty*) And this is how she brazened it out to me, Mr Madras. This is what she told Mr Huxtable . . . and you'll pardon my saying he took a very different view of the matter to what you seem to be taking.

Miss Yates Oh, I've got to go now I'm found out . . . I'm not arguing about it.

Miss Chancellor (*severely*) Mr Madras, what sort of notions are you fostering in this wretched girl's mind?

Philip (*gently enough*) I am trying for the moment to put myself in her place.

Miss Chancellor You will excuse me saying, sir, that you are a man . . .

Philip Not at all!

A poor joke, but **Miss Chancellor** *remains unconscious of it.*

Miss Chancellor Because a woman is independent and earning her living, she's not to think she can go on as she pleases. If she wishes to have children, Providence has provided a way in the institution of marriage. Miss Yates would have found small difficulty in getting married, I gather.

Miss Yates Living in here for twelve years!

Miss Chancellor Have you been a prisoner, Miss Yates? Not to mention that there are two hundred and thirty-five gentlemen employed here.

Miss Yates Supposing I don't like any of em.

Miss Chancellor My dear Miss Yates, if you are merely looking for a husband as such . . . well . . . we're all God's creatures, I suppose! Personally, I don't notice much difference in men, anyway.

Miss Yates Nor did I.

Miss Chancellor Lack of self-control . . .

Miss Yates Oh, yes!

Miss Chancellor . . . And self-respect. That's what the matter is. Are we beasts of the field, I should like to know? I simply do not understand this unladylike attitude towards the facts of life. Is there nothing for a woman to do in the world but to run after men . . . or pretend to run away from them? I am fifty-eight . . . and I have passed, thank God, a busy and a happy and I hope a useful life . . . and I have never thought any more or less of men than I have of any other human beings . . . or any differently. I look upon spinsterhood as an honourable state, as my Bible teaches me to. Men are different. But some women marry happily and well . . . and all women can't . . . and some can't marry at all. These facts have to be faced, I take it.

Philip Miss Yates has, no doubt, been facing them.

Miss Chancellor Yes, sir, but in what spirit? I have always endeavoured to influence the young ladies under my control towards the virtues of modesty and decorum . . . so that they may regard either state with an indifferent mind. If I can no longer do that, I prefer to resign my charge. I will say before this young person that I regret the story should have got about. But when any one has committed a fault, it seems to me immaterial who knows of it.

Philip (*reduced to irony*) Do you really think so?

Miss Chancellor Do you require me any more now?

Philip I am glad to have had your explanation. We'll have a private talk tomorrow.

Miss Chancellor Thank you, sir. I think that will be more in order. Good morning.

Philip Good morning.

Miss Chancellor *has expressed herself to her entire satisfaction and retires in good order.* **Miss Yates,** *conscientiously brazen until the enemy has quite disappeared, collapses pathetically. And* **Philip,** *at his ease at last, begins to scold her in a most brotherly manner.*

Miss Yates I'm sure she's quite right in all she says.

Philip Are you! Then are you the sort of young woman to have got yourself into this scrape?

Miss Yates No . . . I don't want you to think I'm that, sir.

Philip Then what on earth did you go and do it for? You're not a fool.

Miss Yates Of course I didn't set out to.

Philip Why aren't you married?

Miss Yates That's my business. (*Then, to make amends for this sudden snap.*) Oh, I've thought often enough of getting married. But look what it comes to . . . look at the Brigstocks!

Philip No, no . . . why aren't you to be married n o w?

Miss Yates I'd rather not say.

This reticence may be natural enough. But **Philip** *seems to detect something odd in it.*

Philip Very well.

Miss Yates I'd rather not talk about that to you at all, sir, if you don't mind. (*Then she bursts out again.*) I took the risk. I knew what I was up to . . . at least, I thought I knew. And I thought I'd have my fling before I came back here to settle down for ever more, amen . . . to boss the Costumes, which I was to – and set the other girls a good example. And it was fun . . . some of it. That may sound horrid . . . but it was. And it was different. And if I am sorry I did it, I'm not going to say so now.

Philip Well . . . I haven't asked you to, have I? I have unconventional opinions, Miss Yates.

Miss Yates Yes. We're far more frightened of you, sir, than we are of Mr Huxtable.

Philip Why?

Miss Yates We never know what you'll say next.

Philip Still, even I don't do very unconventional things.

Miss Yates Why don't you?

Philip Frankly . . . I prefer a quiet life.

Miss Yates I expect you're right. It is safer.

Philip But if you set out on this adventure believing all the conventional people tell you . . . why, I'm not very happy about your prospects.

Miss Yates Oh, that's all right, sir. When you're up against it you don't bother about believing things or not. I've got my plans. I'll be getting two forty a year living out. (*She grows happily confidential.*) There's a maisonette at Raynes Park and I can get a cheap girl to look after it and take care of . . . I shall call him my nephew, like the Popes of Rome used to . . . or I can be a widow. I can bring him up and do him well on it. Insurance'll be a bit stiff in case anything happens to me. But I've got nearly two hundred saved in the bank to see me through till next summer.

Philip Where are you going when you leave here? What relations have you?

Miss Yates I have an aunt. I hate her.

Philip Where are you going for the winter?

Miss Yates Evercreech.

Philip Where's that?

Miss Yates I don't know. You get to it from Waterloo. I found it in the ABC.

Philip (*in protest*) But, my dear girl. . . !

Miss Yates Well, I want a place where nobody knows me, so I'd better go to one I don't know, hadn't I? I always make friends. I'm not afraid of people. And I've never been in the country in the winter. I want to see what it's like.

Philip surrenders, *on this point beaten; but he takes up another more seriously.*

Philip Well . . . you may not want a husband . . . but a father should help support his child.

Miss Yates *is ready for it; serious, too.*

Miss Yates I know! But I've seen other girls in this sort of mess . . . with people being kind to them . . . and despising them . . . and the fellow who'd done it just hating them . . . while they had to sit around and look ashamed and cry. He can forget about me if he likes . . . which he will. I don't know now if I care whether he hates me or not. But I won't be despised by any jealous old cat. And that's what's wrong with Miss C. Crossed in love she was . . . and we all know it.

Philip Really, I don't think there's any evidence of that.

Miss Yates Then she only wishes she had been. I did cry my eyes out for a start. Then I thought if I couldn't buck up and anyhow pretend to be pleased about it I'd be better in the river. And, d'you know, sir, when I'd been pretending a bit, I found I really was pleased. And I'm really happy about it now . . . if they let me alone . . . I'm not pretending. I've done what I shouldn't. But if any one thinks I'm going to the devil now just because I ought to . . . well, they're wrong. And if I might ask you, sir, not to mention . . .

At this moment a telephone on the table rings violently, and **Miss Yates** *apologises – to it, apparently.*

Miss Yates Oh, I beg pardon.

Philip Excuse me. (*Then answering.*) Yes. Who? No, no, no . . . State. Mr State. Put him through (*He is evidently put through.*) Morning! Who? My father . . . not yet. Yes, from Marienbad.

Miss Yates *gets up, apparently to withdraw tactfully, but looking a little startled, too.*

Miss Yates Shall I . . .

Philip No, no; it's all right.

Belhaven *knocks, comes in and stands waiting by* **Philip**, *who telephones on.*

Philip Yes? Well? . . . Who . . . Mark who? . . . Aurelius. No. I've not been reading him lately . . . Certainly I will . . . Thomas is here doing figures . . . d'you want him . . . I'll put you through . . . No, wait. I'll call him here, if it's not private. (*Then calling out.*) Tommy!

Belhaven Major Thomas is in the counting-house, sir.

Philip Oh. (*Then through the telephone.*) If you'll hold the line I can get him in a minute. Say Mr State's on the telephone for him, Belhaven.

Belhaven Yes, sir . . . and Mrs Madras is below in a taxi, sir, and would like to speak to you. Shall she come up or, if you're too busy to be interrupted, will you come down to her?

Philip My mother?

Belhaven No, not Mrs Madras . . . your Mrs Madras, sir.

Philip Bring her up. And tell Major Thomas.

Belhaven Yes, sir.

Belhaven *achieves a greased departure and* **Philip** *turns back to* **Miss Yates**.

Philip Where were we?

Miss Yates (*inconsequently*) It is hot in here, isn't it?

Philip The window's open.

Miss Yates Shall I shut it?

She turns and goes up to the window; one would say to run away from him. **Philip** *watches her steadily.*

Philip What's the matter, Miss Yates?

She comes back more collectedly.

Miss Yates And I'm sure Miss Chancellor can't expect me to marry one like that now . . . can she?

Philip Marry who?

Miss Yates Not that I say anything against Mr Belhaven . . . he'll grow up a very nice young man. And he did try to propose last Christmas. He was festive . . . and he'd got his first raise of salary. But the fact is it's only the very young men that ever do ask you to marry them here. When they get older they seem to lose heart . . . or they think it'll cost too much . . . or . . . but I'm sure it's not important.

This very out-of-place chatter dies away under **Philip**'*s sternly enquiring gaze.*

Philip There's just one thing more. This trouble isn't in any way due to our sending you to Bond Street, is it?

Miss Yates (*diving into many words again*) Oh, of course it was most kind of you to send me to Bond Street to get a polish on. But I tell you . . . I couldn't have stood it for long. The ladies that come in there . . . it does just break your nerve. What with following them round . . . and trying this for them and that for them . . . and the things they say you've got to hear, and the things they'll say . . .

about you half the time . . . that you've got not to hear
. . . and keep your voice low and sweet, and let your arms
hang down straight. You may work more hours with us,
and I daresay it's not smart, but the customers are
friendly.

Philip . . . Because, you see, Mr Huxtable and I would
feel rather unhappy if it was any one connected with us
who . . .

Miss Yates (*quite desperately*) No, you needn't . . . indeed
you needn't. Though I will say there's something in that
other place that does set your mind going about men.
What he saw in me I never could think . . . honestly, I
couldn't, though I think a good deal of myself, I can
assure you. But it was all my own fault, and so's the rest
of it going to be . . . my very own . . .

Major Thomas's *arrival is to* **Miss Yates** *a very welcome
interruption, as she seems, perhaps by the hypnotism of*
Philip's *steady look, to be getting nearer and nearer to saying
just what she means not to. He comes in at a good speed,
glancing back along the passage, and saying* . . .

Thomas Here's Jessica.

Philip State on the telephone.

Thomas Thank you.

And he makes for it as **Jessica** *comes to the open door.*
Philip's *wife is an epitome of all that aesthetic culture can do
for a woman. More: She is the result – not of thirty-three years
– but of three or four generations of cumulative refinement. She
might be a race horse! Come to think of it, it is a very
wonderful thing to have raised this crop of ladyhood.
Creatures, dainty in mind and body, gentle in thought and
word, charming, delicate, sensitive, graceful, chaste, credulous
of all good, shaming the world's ugliness and strife by the very
ease and delightsomeness of their existence; fastidious –
fastidious – fastidious; also in these latter years with their
attractions more generally salted by the addition of learning*

*and humour. Is not the perfect lady perhaps the most
wonderful achievement of civilisation, and worth the cost of
her breeding, worth the toil and the helotage of – all the
others?*

Jessica Madras *is even something more than a lady, for she
is conscious of her ladyhood. She values her virtue and her
charm: she is proud of her culture and fosters it. It is her
weapon, it justifies her. As she floats now into the ugly room,
exquisite from her eyelashes to her shoes, it is a great relief –
just the sight of her.*

Jessica Am I interrupting?

Philip No, come in, my dear.

Thomas (*into the telephone*) Hullo!

Philip Well, Miss Yates, I'll see, if I can, that you're
treated as considerately . . . as you'll allow me to treat
you.

Thomas Hullo!

Philip You don't know my wife. Jessica, this is Miss
Yates, who is in our costume room. You're not actually
working in your department now, I suppose?

Miss Yates (*as defiant of all scandal*) I am.

Thomas (*still to the unresponsive telephone*) Hullo! Hullo!

Philip (*finding* **Miss Yates** *beyond – possibly above him*)
Very well. That'll do now.

But **Miss Yates**, *by the presence of* **Jessica**, *is now brought
to her best costume department manner. She can assume at
will, it seems, a new face, a new voice; can become, indeed, a
black-silk being of another species.*

Miss Yates Thank you, sir. I hope I've not talked too
much. I always was a chatterbox, madam.

Philip The matter was an important one, Miss Yates.

Miss Yates Not at all, sir. Good morning, madam.

Jessica Good morning.

And there is an end of **Miss Yates**. *Meanwhile the telephone is reducing* **Thomas** *to impotent fury.*

Thomas They've cut him off.

While he raps the receiver's arm fit to break it **Jessica** *produces an opened telegram, which she hands to* **Philip**.

Jessica This . . . just after you left.

Philip My dear, coming all this way with it! Why didn't you telephone?

Thomas (*hearing something at last*) Hullo . . . is that Mr State's office? No! Well . . . Telephone Room, are y o u still through to it?

Jessica *is watching with an amused smile.*

Jessica I hate the telephone, especially the one here. Hark at you, Tommy, poor wretch! They put you through from office to office . . . six different clerks . . . all stupid and all with hideous voices.

Philip *has now read his telegram and is making a face.*

Philip I suppose she must come if she wants to.

Jessica What'll your father say?

Philip My dear girl . . . she has a right to see him if she insists . . . it's very foolish. Here, Tommy! (*He ousts him from the telephone and deals expertly with it.*) I want a telegram sent. Then get double three double 0 Central, and plug through to my room . . . not here . . . my room.

Thomas (*fervently*) Thank yer.

Jessica Got over your temper at the play last night?

Thomas Oh, sort of play you must expect if you go to the theatre on a Sunday. Scuse me.

Having admiringly sized up **Jessica** *and her costume, he bolts.* **Philip** *sits down to compose his telegram in reply.*

Jessica, *discovering that there is nothing attractive to sit on,* *hovers.*

Philip Can you put her up for the night?

Jessica Yes.

Philip Shall I ask her to dinner?

Jessica She'll cry into the soup . . . but never mind that.

Philip Dinner at eight?

Jessica I sound inhospitable.

Philip I've only said we shall be delighted.

Jessica But your mother dislikes me so. It's difficult to see much of her.

Philip We must have patience with her, Jessica.

Jessica So I'm always telling you. I only wish she wouldn't write Mildred silly letters about God.

Philip A grandmother's privilege.

Jessica The child sends me on another one this morning . . . didn't I show it you?

Philip No.

Jessica Miss Gresham writes, too. She puts it quite nicely. But it's an awful thing, she says, for a school to get religion into it.

Belhaven *slides in.*

Belhaven Yessir.

Philip Send this at once, please.

Belhaven Yessir.

Belhaven *slides out. Then* **Philip** *starts attending to the little pile of letters he brought in with him.* **Jessica,** *neglected, hovers more widely.*

Jessica Come out to lunch, Phil?

Philip Lord, is it lunch time!

Jessica I'm lunching with Margaret Inman and Walter Muirhead at the Berkeley.

Philip Then you won't be lonely.

Jessica (*mischievous*) Margaret may be if you don't come.

Philip I can't. I'm not nearly through.

She comes to rest by his table and starts to play with the things on it, finding at last a blotting roller that gives satisfaction.

Jessica Phil, you might come out with me a little more than you do.

Philip (*humorously final*) My dear, not at lunch time.

Jessica Attractive little woman you'd been scolding when I came in.

Philip Is she?

Jessica Didn't you think so?

Philip I'm afraid I don't often notice whether women are attractive or not . . . unless they mean me to. And then I don't find them so.

Jessica What a husband!

Philip D'you disapprove?

Jessica I'm a woman! Last day of Walter's pictures. He has sold all but about five . . . and there's one I wish you'd buy.

Philip Can't afford it.

Jessica I suppose, Phil, you're not altogether sorry you married me.

*Although **Philip** is used enough to her charming and reasoned inconsequence, he really jumps.*

Philip Good heavens! Well, we've survived twelve years of it, haven't we?

Jessica *puts her head on one side and is quite half serious.*

Jessica Are you in the least glad you married me?

Philip My dear . . . I don't think about it. Jessica, in business hours I'm no good at repartee.

She floats away at once, half seriously snubbed and hurt.

Jessica I'm sorry . . . I'm interrupting.

Philip (*remorseful at once, for she is so pretty*) No, never mind. These aren't important.

But he goes on with his letters and **Jessica** *stands looking at him, her face hardening just a little.*

Jessica But there are times when I get tired of waiting for you to finish your letters.

Philip I know . . . I never quite finish my letters nowadays. You've got a fit of the idle-fidgets. Shall we take the car somewhere this weekend?

Thomas *bundles into the tête-à-tête, saying as he comes* . . .

Thomas He'll make an offer for the place here too, Phil.

Philip Good.

Jessica *stands there, looking her prettiest.*

Jessica Tommy, come out and lunch . . . Phil won't.

Thomas I'm afraid I can't.

Jessica I've got to meet Maggie Inman and young Muirhead. He'll flirt with her all the time. If there isn't a fourth I shall be fearfully in the cold.

Philip (*overcome by such tergiversation*) Oh, Jessica!

Thomas *is nervous, apparently; at least he is neither ready nor gallant.*

Thomas Yes, of course you will. But I'm afraid I can't.

Jessica (*in cheerful despair*) Well, I won't drive to Peckham again of a morning. Wednesday, then, will you call for me?

Thomas Wednesday?

Jessica Symphony Concert.

Thomas (*with sudden seriousness*) D'you know I'm afraid I can't on Wednesday either.

Jessica Why not?

Thomas (*though the pretence withers before a certain sharpness in her question*) Well . . . I'm afraid I can't.

It is evident that **Jessica** *has a temper bred to a point of control which makes it the nastier, perhaps. She now becomes very cold, very civil, very swift.*

Jessica We settled it only last night. What's the time?

Philip Five to one.

Jessica I must go. I shall be late.

Thomas (*with great concern*) Have you got the car, or d'you want a cab?

Jessica Yes . . . and no, thank you.

Thomas We might do the next, perhaps.

Jessica All right, Tommy . . . don't be conscience-stricken. But when you change your mind about going out with me, it's pleasanter if you'll find some excuse. Goodbye, you two.

And she is gone; **Philip** *calling after her –*

Philip I shall be in by seven, my dear.

Thomas *looks a little relieved, and then considerably worried; in fact, he frowns portentously.* **Philip** *disposes of his last letter.*

Philip Companionship in marriage isn't so simple a matter as it should be.

Thomas (*without interest*) Oh!

Philip Well, is it? What have we got to settle before this meeting?

Thomas Nothing much. (*Then seeming to make up his mind to something.*) But I want three minutes' talk with you, old man.

Philip Go ahead. (*And he gets up and stretches.*)

Thomas D'you mind if I say something caddish?

Philip Not a bit.

Thomas Put your foot down and don't have me asked to your house quite so often.

Philip *looks at him for half a puzzled minute.*

Philip Why not?

Thomas I'm seeing too much of your wife.

He is so intensely solemn about it that **Philip** *can hardly even pretend to be shocked.*

Philip My dear Tommy!

Thomas I don't mean one word more than I say.

Philip (*good-naturedly*) But what nonsense!

Thomas I don't want you to suppose that I'm the least bit in love with her.

Philip Naturally not . . . you've a wife of your own.

Thomas (*in intense brotherly agreement*) Right. That's good horse sense.

Philip As her husband, I'm naturally obtuse in the matter
. . . but I really don't think that Jessica is in love with
you.

Thomas (*most generously*) Not for a single minute.

Philip Then what's the worry, you silly old ass?

Thomas *starts to explain, a little tortuously.*

Thomas Phil, this is a damned subtle world. I don't
pretend to understand it . . . I don't know that I want to
understand it . . . but in my old age I have got a sort of
rule-of-thumb experience to go by . . . which, mark you,
I've paid for.

Philip Well?

Thomas Phil, I don't really like women and I never did.
But I'm not exaggerating when I say I married to break
the habit of finding myself once every six months in such a
position with one of them that I was supposed to be
making love to her.

Philip *is enjoying himself.*

Philip What do they see in you, Tommy?

Thomas God knows . . . I don't. And the time it took up!
I fell in love with Mary and, thank God, she wasn't
married and she did want to marry me . . . and I wouldn't
be without her and the children now for all I ever saw.
But I don't believe I'd have brought that off if I hadn't
been driven to it, Phil, . . . driven to it. I'm not going to
start the old game again now. (*And he wags his head
wisely.*)

Philip Well, what has Jessica been up to . . . if you must
confide in me?

Thomas *gathers himself up to launch the vindicating
compliment effectively.*

Thomas Nothing . . . nothing whatever! She's a most accomplished and a charming and a sweet-natured woman . . . and an ornament to society.

Philip (*with equal fervour*) You're quite right, Tommy . . . what are we to do with them?

Thomas (*it's his favourite phrase*) What d'you mean?

Philip Well . . . what's your trouble?

Thomas (*tortuously still*) There ain't any yet . . . that's the point. But . . . well . . . I've been dreading for the last three weeks that she'd begin talking to me about you. That's why I'm talking to you about her. (*Then, with a certain enjoyment of his shocking looseness of behaviour.*) I am a cad!

Philip (*still amused – but now rather sub-acidly*) But let her. I don't mind.

Thomas Well, I do. It's one of the ways it begins. Last night in the cab she started about when she a girl . . .

Philip While I walked home. Tactful husband!

Thomas Phil . . . don't you be French.

Philip, *suddenly serious, turns to him.*

Philip But, Tommy, do you suppose she is unhappy with me?

Thomas No . . . not more than any woman would be!

Philip Thank you.

Thomas I mean . . .

Philip You mean t h a t. And thank you is what I mean. You hit the mark.

Thomas Oh, I've always got on with you, Phil. But it is a bit like carrying a razor in one's pocket. And she thinks a bit . . . when she's bored with people and music and her

pictures and her books. And besides, once you begin
putting your feelings into words . . . they grow.

Philip Wholesomer they should, perhaps. I wish she
would talk to you.

Thomas *shakes his head vehemently.*

Thomas Well, I'd rather not.

Philip Heavens above us! You're my friend and you're
hers. And you mayn't be clever, Tommy . . . but you
have a heart!

Thomas That's what I'm telling you . . . and things
always begin this way.

Philip Can't you let a woman talk seriously to you without
making love to her?

Thomas Damn it, that's what they say . . . but it never
made any difference.

Philip Tommy, you're a perfect child!

Thomas I remember when I was twenty-four . . . there
was one woman . . . years older than me . . . had a
grown-up son. She took to scolding me for wasting my
time philandering. Told me she'd done it in her time . . .
and what dust and ashes it was . . . talked like a book to
me. I kept off kissing her for six weeks and I'd have sworn
she never wanted me to kiss her. But I did.

Philip Did she box your ears?

Thomas No . . . said she could hardly take me seriously
. . . I was so young. Well . . . if I'd bolted that would
have been priggish. And if I'd stayed I'd have done it
again.

Philip (*mischievously*) Which did you do?

Thomas Never you mind.

Philip (*with the utmost geniality*) Well, if you think Jessica
wants you to kiss her . . . try it . . . politely!

Thomas Thanks, old man . . . that's very clever and up to date and all the rest of it . . . but I've asked you to chuck me out of the house.

Philip Well, I shan't.

Thomas Then you're no friend of mine.

Philip Let us put it brutally. If Jessica wishes to be unfaithful to me how am I to stop her . . . even if I've a right to stop her? No . . . I've my own self-respect to think of.

Thomas If you can't behave like a decent married man you've no right to be married . . . you're a danger.

Philip I will not play the benevolent Turk. If you can't help making love to my wife . . .

Thomas I'm not making love to your wife. I told you so.

Philip Well, if she's making love to you that's your trouble.

Thomas She isn't making love to me. But if you can't take a hint –

Philip A h i n t! Well . . . I'm dashed!

Thomas All right! I've given you fair warning of the sort of fool I am . . . I'll take no more responsibility in the matter.

Philip (*in comic exasperation*) Why not tell Jessica you're afraid of making a fool of yourself with her?

Thomas (*his eyebrows up*) But that'd be as good as doing it. Good lord, you can't behave to women as if they were men!

Philip Why not?

Thomas You try it!

Philip I always do.

Thomas No wonder she wants to grumble about you.

Philip *takes him seriously again.*

Philip Tommy, I know Jessica pretty well. She doesn't want to be made love to.

Thomas (*positively and finally*) Yes, she does. (*Then with real chivalry.*) I don't mean that unpleasantly . . . but all women do. Some of em want to be kissed and some want you to talk politics . . . but the principle's the same.

Philip (*finely contemptuous*) What a world you live in!

Thomas . . . And the difficulty with me is that if I try to talk politics I find they don't know enough about it . . . or else they know too much about it . . . and it's simpler to kiss em and have done.

Philip Oh, much s i m p l e r !

Thomas (*back to his starting-point – pathetic*) But I'm married now and I want a quiet life . . .

A knock at the door interrupts him.

Philip Come in.

It is **Belhaven**.

Belhaven Will you lunch, sir?

Philip What is there?

Belhaven I'm afraid only the Usual, sir.

Philip Can you manage the Usual, Tommy? What is it, Belhaven?

Belhaven Roast beef and a jam pudding, I think, sir. (*Then as confessing to a vulgarity.*) Roly-poly.

Thomas (*with great approval*) Right. I hope it's strawberry jam.

Philip Sure to be. Put it in Mr Huxtable's room, will you . . . that's airy.

Belhaven Yessir.

Belhaven *vanishes.*

Thomas (*as on reflection*) Not plum, y'know . . . plum's no use.

Philip *gathers up his papers.*

Philip Well . . . we've had some good sensible times together, all three. I'll save the situation if I can.

Thomas Only do be tactful, Phil.

Philip No, I talk to my wife as I talk to myself.

Thomas And that's no sign of sanity either!

Philip Tommy, you're turning into a wit. I shall grow jealous of you.

Thomas Aha! I tell you! You kick me down your front steps while you can.

Philip Come on . . . the roly-poly waits.

They go out. The room is left to its ugliness.

Act Three

Some thirty years back the Madras House was established in its present premises. Decoration in those days was rather trade than art; but **Mr Constantine Madras**, ever daring, proceeded to beautify the home of his professional triumphs according to his own taste and fancy, and being a man of great force of character, produced something which, though extraordinarily wrong, was yet, since it was sincere, effective in its way.

There have been changes since, but one room has remained untouched. This is the rotunda, a large, lofty, skylighted place, done in the Moorish style. The walls are black marble to the height of a man, and from there to the ceiling the darkest red. The ceiling is of a cerulean blue; and in the middle of the skylight a golden sun, with spiked rays proceeding from its pleasant human countenance, takes credit for some of the light it intercepts. An archway with fretted top leads from the rest of the establishment. Another has behind it a platform, a few steps high, hung with black velvet. There is also a small door, little more than head high. On the floor is a Persian carpet of some real beauty. On the walls are gas brackets (now fitted for electric light), the Oriental touch achieved in their crescent shape. Round the walls are divans, many-cushioned; in front of them little coffee stools. It is all about as Moorish as Baker Street station used to be in the days of the old sulphurous Underground, but the general effect is humorous, pleasant, and not undignified. In the grand days of the Madras House the rotunda was the happy preserve of very special customers, those on whom the great man himself would keep an eye. If you had been there you spoke of it casually; and to be free of the rotunda was to be a well-dressed woman; moreover, to be recognised as such. Ichabod! The Madras House is old-

*fashioned now, and county ladies bring their daughters because
it would be such a pity for dear Daphne, or Pamela, or
Cynthia not to have the very latest thing for the County Ball.
Not that its present management doesn't endeavour to keep in
the race. Models from Paris, ladies as chiefs of the various
rooms, who are real ladies, and let you know it, too, by the
glassy graciousness or the off-hand civility with which they
variously greet the too-ready-to-be-intimidated customer. But,
since* **Mr Constantine Madras** *retired, the spirit of the place
has faded, and a board of directors cannot revive it. For the
accommodation of this same board, a large oval 'Moorish'
table had to be imported to the rotunda, and half-a-dozen
'Moorish' chairs provided. They had, in fact, to be designed
and made in the Tottenham Court Road; but they are at least
the appropriate furniture for this scene, as it is to be, of the
passing of the Madras House into alien hands.*

*At three o'clock on the Monday afternoon the deal is to be put
through, and it is now five minutes to.* **Major Thomas** *is
there, sitting at the table; papers spread before him, racking his
brain with a few final figures.* **Philip** *is there, in rather a
schoolboyish mood. He is sitting on the table, swinging his
legs.* **Mr Huxtable** *is there, too, dressed in his best, important
and nervous, and he is talking to* **Mr Eustace Perrin State**.

Mr State *is an American, and if American magazine
literature is anything to go by, no American is altogether unlike
him. He has a rugged, blood and iron sort of face, utterly
belied by his soft, smiling eyes; rightly belied, too, for he has
made his thirty or forty millions (dollars though) in the gentlest
and slickest way. You would not think of him as a money-
maker. And, indeed, he has no love of money and little use for
it, for his tastes are simple. But this is the honourable career in
his own country, and he has the instinct for turning money over
and the knack of doing so on a big scale. His shock of grey
hair makes him look older than he probably is; his voice is
almost childlike in its sweetness. He has some of the dignity
and aptitude for command that power can give.*

From the little canopied door comes in **Mr Windlesham**, *present manager of the establishment. He is a tailor-made man; and the tailor only left off for the wax modeller and wigmaker to begin. For his clothes are too perfect to be worn by anything but a dummy, and his hair and complexion are far from human. Not that he dyes or paints them; no, they were made like that. His voice is a little inhuman, too, and as he prefers the French language, with which he has a more unripe acquaintance, to his own, and so speaks English as much like French as his French is like English, his conversation seems as unreal as the rest of him. Impossible to think of him in any of the ordinary relations of life. He is a functionary. Nature, the great inventor, will evolve, however roughly, what is necessary for her uses. Millinery has evolved the man-milliner. As he comes in – and he has the gait of a water-wagtail –* **Mr Huxtable** *is making conversation.*

Mr Huxtable A perfect barometer, as you might say – when your eye gets trained to it.

Windlesham (*to* **Philip***; and with a wag of his head back to the other room*) They're just ready.

Mr State (*smiling benevolently at* **Mr Huxtable**) Is it really? The Crystal Palace! What a fairy sound that has!

Mr Huxtable (*with modest pride*) And a very ealthy locality!

Philip Come along and meet State. (*He jumps off the table, capturing* **Windlesham***'s arm.*)

Mr State (*enthusiastic*) Denmark Hill. Named so for Queen Alexandra!

Mr Huxtable (*struck by the information*) Was it now?

Mr State Herne Hill . . . Herne the Hunter! That's the charm of London to an American. Association. Every spot speaks.

Philip (*as he joins them*) This is Mr Windlesham . . . our manager. He's going to show us some new models.

Mr State (*impressively extends a hand and repeats the name*) Mr Windlesham.

Windlesham Most happy. I thought you'd like to see the very latest . . . brought them from Paris only yesterday.

Mr State Most opportune! (*Then with a sweeping gesture.*) Mr Philip, I react very keenly to the charm and tradition of this room. Your father designed it?

Philip Yes.

Mr State I thought so.

Philip That used to be his private office.

Mr State (*reverently*) Indeed! Where the duchess went on her knees. An historic spot.

Philip Something of a legend that.

Mr State, *intensely solemn, seems now to ascend the pulpit of some philosophic conventicle.*

Mr State Let us cling to legends, sir . . . they are the spiritual side of facts. They go to form tradition. And it is not given to man to found his institutions in security of mind except upon tradition. That is why our eyes turn eastward to you from America, Mr Huxtable.

Mr Huxtable (*in some awe*) Do they now?

Mr State Has it never struck you that while the progress of man has been in the path of the sun, his thoughts continually go back to the place of its rising? I have found that a very stimulating idea.

Philip (*not indecently commonplace*) Well, have them in now, Windlesham, while we're waiting.

Windlesham You might cast your eyes over these new mannequins, Mr Philip . . . the very best I could find, I do assure you. Faces are hard enough to get, but figures . . . well, there! (*Reaching the little door, he calls through.*) Allons mes'moiselles! Non . . . non . . . par l'autre porte à la gauche. (*Then back again.*) You get the best effect through the big doorway. (*He further explains this by sketching one in the air.*) One, two and four first. (*He rapidly distributes some costume drawings he has been carrying, and then vanishes into the other room, from where his voice vibrates.*) En avant, s'il vous plaît. Numéro un! Eh bien! . . . numéro trois. Non ma'moiselle, ce n'est pas commode . . . regarder ce corsage-là . . .

Mr Huxtable (*making a face*) What I'm always thinking is, why not have a manly chap in charge of the place up here.

Mr State (*with perfect justice*) Mr Windlesham may be said to strike a note . . . and a very distinctive note! . . .

Through the doorway **Windlesham** *ushers in a costume from Paris, which is hung upon a young lady of pleasing appearance, preoccupied with its exhibition, which she achieves by swift and sinuous, never-ceasing movements. She wears a smile also.*

Windlesham One and two are both Larguillière, Mr Philip. He can't get in the Soupçon Anglais, can he? Won't . . . I tell him. Promenez et sortez ma'moiselle.

The young lady, still smiling and sinuous, begins to circle the room. She seems to be unconscious of its inhabitants, and they, in return, rather dreadfully pretend not to notice her, but only the costume.

Windlesham Numéro deux.

Another costume; the young lady contained in it is as swift-moving and sinuous and as vacantly smiling.

Windlesham Pleasant motif that, isn't it? Promenez.

Mr State (*in grave enquiry*) What is the Soupçon Anglais?

Philip A Frenchman will tell you that for England you must first make a design and then spoil it.

Thomas (*whose attention has been riveted*) Don't they speak English?

Windlesham Oh, pas un mot . . . I mean, not a word. Only came over with me yesterday, these three.

Thomas Because this frock's a bit thick, y'know.

Windlesham Numéro trois!

A third costume, calculated to have an innocent effect. The accompanying young lady, with a sense of fitness, wears a pout instead of a smile.

Philip What's this? (*His eye is on the surmounting hat of straw.*)

Windlesham (*with a little crow of delight*) That's the new hat. La belle Hélène again!

Mr State (*interested. Still grave*) La belle Hélène. A Parisian firm?

Windlesham (*turning this to waggish account*) Well . . . dear me . . . you could almost call her that, couldn't you? (*Suddenly he dashes at the costume and brings it to a standstill.*) Oh, la la, le gilet! Quelle tracasserie!

He proceeds to arrange le gilet to his satisfaction, also some other matters which seem to involve a partial evisceration of the underclothing. The young lady, passive, pouts perseveringly. He is quite unconscious of her separate existence. But **Thomas** *is considerably shocked and whispers violently to* **Philip***.*

Thomas I say, he shouldn't pull her about like that.

Windlesham (*skipping back to admire the result*) Là . . . comme ça.

The costume continues its round; the others are still circling, veering and tacking, while **Windlesham** *trips admiringly around and about them. It all looks like some dance of modish dervishes.*

Philip (*heartlessly*) La belle Hélène, Mr State, is a well-known Parisian cocotte . . . who sets many of the fashions which our wives and daughters afterwards assume.

Mr Huxtable (*scandalised*) Don't say that, Phil; it's not nice.

Philip Why?

Mr Huxtable I'm sure no ladies are aware of it.

Philip But what can be more appropriate than for the professional charmer to set the pace for the amateur!

Windlesham (*pausing in the dance*) Quite la haute cocotterie, of course.

Mr State (*solemnly*) Do you infer, Mr Madras, a difference in degree, but not in kind?

Philip (*courteously echoing his tone*) I do.

Mr State That is a very far-reaching observation, sir.

Philip It is.

Thomas Do you know the lady personally, Mr Windlesham?

Windlesham *turns, with some tag of a costume in his hand, thus unconsciously detaining the occupier.*

Windlesham Oh no . . . oh, dear me, no . . . I do assure you. There's nothing gay in Paris for me. Tout à fait au contraire. I was blasé long ago.

Mr State But touching that hat, Mr Windlesham?

Windlesham Oh, to be sure. Attendez, ma'moiselle. (*Tiptoeing, he dexterously tilts the straw hat from the elaborate head it is perched on.*) It's not a bad story. Sortez.

By this two costumes have glided out. The third follows. **State**, *who has found it hard to keep his eyes off them, knits his brows, and turns to* **Mr Huxtable**.

Mr State Does it strike you, now, that there is something not quite natural in their behaviour?

Windlesham, *caressing the hat, takes up an attitude for his story.*

Windlesham Well . . . it appears that a while ago out at the Pré Catalan . . . there was Hélène, taking her afternoon cup of buttermilk. What should she see but Madame Erlancourt . . . one of the old guard, she is! . . . in a hat the very twin of hers . . . the very twin. Well . . . you can imagine! Some one had blundered.

Mr State (*absorbed*) No, I am not with you.

Philip Some spy in the enemy's service had stolen the plans of the hat.

Mr State No . . . Madame What's-her-name might have seen it on her before and copied it.

Philip Mr State, Hélène does not wear a hat twice.

Mr State My mistake!

Windlesham So there was a terrible scene . . .

Thomas With Madame. . . ?

Windlesham (*repudiating any such vulgarity*) Oh no. Hélène just let fly at her chaperone, she being at hand, so to speak.

Mr State (*dazzled*) Her what! (*Then with humorous awe.*) No, go on . . . go on . . . I am with you now, I think.

Windlesham She fetched in out of the Bois the ugliest little gamine she could find . . . put her own hat on its horrid little head . . . sat it at her table and stuffed it with cakes. Then she sent to the kitchens for one of those baskets they bring the fish in . . . (*He twirls the hat.*) . . . see! Then she ripped a bit of ribbon and a couple of these (*These being rosettes.*) off her pantalettes . . .

Mr State (*the Puritan*) In public?

Windlesham (*professionally*) Oh, it can be done. Besides . . . la belle France, you know . . . there is something in the atmosphere! Twisted it round the basket . . . très pratique! And that's what she wore the rest of the afternoon and back to Paris. And it's going to be all the rage.

Having deftly pantomimed this creation of a fashion, he hands the hat with an air to **Mr State**, *who examines it.* **Philip** *is smilingly caustic.*

Philip La belle Hélène has the audacity of genius, Mr State. She is also, I am told, thrifty, inclined to religion, a vegetarian, Vichy water her only beverage; in truth she is a credit to her profession . . . and to ours.

Mr State *hands back the hat with the solemnest humour.*

Mr State Mr Windlesham, I am much obliged to you for this illuminating anecdote.

Windlesham Not at all. Will you see another three? Which shall we have now? (*He dips into his list.*) Here's a Dinner and Dance . . . and a Grande Tenue . . . and a wrap and pyjamas . . . a Nightie-Night.

Mr State By all means.

Windlesham They won't be long in changing . . . but one I must just pin on.

Mr State No hurry . . . sir.

He has acquired a new joy in **Windlesham**, *whom he watches dance away. Then a song is heard from the next room.*

Windlesham Allons . . . numéro cinq . . . numéro sept . . . numéro dix . . . Ma'moiselle Ollivier . . . vous vous mettrez . . .

And the door closes.

Philip (*looks at his watch*) But it's ten past three. We'd better not wait for my father.

They surround the table and sit down.

Mr State Major Thomas, have you my memoranda?

Thomas Here.

He hands them to **State**, *who clears his throat, refrains from spitting, and begins the customary American oration.*

Mr State The scheme, gentlemen, for which I desire to purchase the Madras House and add it to the interest of the Burrows enterprise, which I already control, is . . . to put it shortly . . . this. The Burrows provincial scheme . . . you are aware of its purpose . . . goes well enough as far as the shareholding by the local drapery stores is concerned. And it has interested me to discover which aspects of the Burrows scheme suit which cities . . . and why. An absorbing problem in local psychology. But in a certain number of cases the local people will not come in. Yet in Leicester, let us say, or Norwich or Plymouth or Coventry, the unknown and somewhat uninspiring name of Burrows upon an opposition establishment might cut no ice. But I have a further and I hope not uninteresting reason to put before you gentlemen why it is in these centres that we should look to establish our Madras Houses . . . New Edition. Is that clear so far?

During this **Mr Constantine Madras** *has arrived. He turned aside for a moment to the door that the mannequins came from; now he joins the group. A man of sixty and over, to whom this is still the prime of life. Tall, quite dramatically dignified, suave, a little remote; he is one of those to whom life is an art of which they have determined to be master. It is a handsome face, Eastern in type, the long beard only streaked with grey. He does not dress like the ruck of men, because he is not of them. The velvet coat, brick-red tie, shepherd's-plaid trousers, white spats and patent boots, both suit him and express him subtly and well; the mixture of originality and alien tradition which is the man.* **Philip** *is purposely casual in greeting him; he has sighted him first. But* **Mr State** *gets up, impressed. It is part of his creed to recognise greatness; he insists on recognising it.*

Philip Hullo, Father!

Mr State Mr Madras! Proud to meet you again.

Constantine (*graciously, without emotion*) How do you do, Mr State?

Philip You know every one, Father. Oh . . . Hippisly Thomas.

Constantine (*just as graciously*) How do you do, sir? (*Then, with a mischievous smile, he pats* **Huxtable** *on the shoulder.*) How are you, my dear Harry?

Mr Huxtable *had heard him coming and felt himself turn purple. This was the great meeting after thirty years! He had let it come upon him unawares; purposely let it, for indeed he had not known what to say or do. He had dreaded having the inspiration to say or do anything. Now – alas, and thank goodness! – it is too late. He is at a suitable disadvantage. He need only grunt out sulkily . . .*

Mr Huxtable I'm quite well, thank you.

Constantine, *with one more pat in pardon for the rudeness, goes to his chair.*

Mr State A pleasant trip?

Constantine So, so! Don't let me interrupt business. I shall pick up the thread.

Mr State (*serving up a little re-warmed oration*) I was just proceeding to place on the tablecloth some preliminary details of the scheme that has been elaborating since our meeting last June to consolidate your name and fame in some of the more important cities of England. We had not got far.

He consults his notes. **Constantine** *produces from a case a slender cigarette-holder of amber.*

Constantine You've some new mannequins, Phil.

Philip Yes.

Constantine The tall girl looks well enough. May I smoke?

Mr State Allow me. (*Whipping out his cigar-case.*)

Constantine A cigarette, thank you, of my own.

He proceeds to make and light one. **Mr State** *offers cigars generally and then places one to his own hand.*

Mr State I occasionally seek stimulus in a cold cigar. I do not for the moment enter upon the finance of the matter, because I entertain no doubt that . . . possibly with a little adjustment of the proportion of shares and cash . . . that can be fixed.

Mr Huxtable (*in emulation of all this ease and grace*) I'll ave a cigarette, Phil . . . if you've got one.

Philip *has one. And they all make themselves comfortable, while* **Mr State** *continues enjoyably* . . .

Mr State And I know that you are no more the bond-slave of money than I am, Mr Madras. Any one can make money, if he has capital enough. The little that I have came from lumber and canned peaches. Now there was poetry in lumber. The virgin forest! As a youth I was shy of society . . . but I could sit in silent contemplation of Nature for as much as an hour at a time. Rightly thought of there is poetry in peaches . . . even when they are canned. Do you ask then why I bought that mantle establishment in the city twelve years ago?

Philip (*who is only sorry that some time he must stop*) I do, Mr State.

Mr State Because as the years rolled irresistibly on I came to realise that I had become a lonely man . . . and I felt the need of some communion with what Goethe calls, does he not, the Woman Spirit, which can draw us ever upward and on. Well, the Burrows business was in the market . . . and that seemed an appropriate path to the fulfilment of my desire.

Constantine The fulfilment. . . ?

Mr State Sir?

Constantine The ready-made skirt business has appeased your craving, has it, for the eternal feminine?

Mr State Mr Madras, that sarcasm is deserved. No, sir, it has not. For the Burrows business, I discover, has no soul. Now a business can no more live the good life without a conscious soul than a human being can. I'm sure I have you with me there, Mr Huxtable.

Poor **Mr Huxtable** *quite chokes at the suddenness of this summons, but shines his best.*

Mr Huxtable I should say so, quite.

Mr State *begins to glow.*

Mr State There was fun, mark you . . . there still is some . . . in making these old back-country stores sit up and take notice . . . telling them: Gentlemen, come in, or be froze out. That's for their good . . . and for mine. But Burrows can't answer to the call of the Woman's Movement . . . the great Modern Woman's Movement . . . which is upon us . . . though as yet we may not measure its volume. But it is upon us . . . and our choice is to be in it, to do it glad service . . . or to have it flow over us. Let me assure you so. The old-time business of selling a reel of cotton and tinging on the cash machine . . . there's no salvation left in that. Nothing personal, Mr Huxtable.

Mr Huxtable *is ready, this time.*

Mr Huxtable No, no, I'm listening to you . . . I'm not too old to learn.

Mr State Mind . . . Burrows has not been wholly barren soil. Here and there we have sown a seed and made two ideas to spring where but one sprang before. Now in Nottingham . . .

Mr Huxtable I know Nottingham . . . got a shop there?

Mr State (*with wholesome pride*) In two years the Burrows House in Nottingham has smashed competition. I visited the city last Fall. The notion was our local manager's. Simple. The ladies' department served by gentlemen . . .

and gentlemen's by ladies. Always, of course, within the
bounds of delicacy. You think there is nothing in that, Mr
Huxtable.

Mr Huxtable (*round-eyed and open-mouthed*) Oh . . .
well. . . !

Mr State But are you a Mean Sensual Man?

Mr Huxtable (*whose knowledge of the French language
hardly assists him to this startling translation*) No . . . I hope
not.

Mr State Put yourself in his place. Surrounded by pretty
girls . . . good girls, mind you . . . high class . . . pay
them well . . . let them live out . . . pay for their mothers
and chaperones if necessary. Surrounded, then, by
Gracious Womanhood, does the Sensual Man forget how
much money he is spending or does he not? Does he come
again? Is it a little oasis in the desert of his business day?
Is it a better attraction than Alcohol, or is it not?

Philip (*bitingly*) Is it?

Mr State Then, sir . . . Audi Alteram Partem. See our
Ladies' Fancy Department at its best . . . when Summer
Time brings time for sport.

Philip I must certainly do so.

Mr State Athletes every one of em . . . not a man under
six foot . . . bronzed, noble fellows! And no flirting
allowed . . . no making eyes . . . no pandering to anything
depraved. But the Courtesy of Chivalry and the Chivalry
of Courtesy proffered by clean-limbed and clean-minded
gentlemen to any of the Fair Sex who may step in to buy a
shilling sachet or the like. And pay, sir . . . the women
come in flocks!

Mr Huxtable (*bereft of breath*) Is this how you mean to run
your Madras Houses?

Mr State With a difference, Mr Huxtable. I also live and
learn. I bought and built up the Burrows enterprise when

the Suffrage Question was nearing a solution . . . for I
foresaw that with added freedom womanhood's demands
upon the resources of our civilisation would surely grow.
But even then I saw, too, that political claims were but the
narrowest, drabbest aspect of the matter. What now, *urbi
et orbi*, is the Modern Woman's Movement? It is woman
expressing herself. How? Upon what roads is she
marching? What is her goal? Is it for us to say? No. Nor
as yet for her, it may be. Every morning I have placed
upon my table not only the newspapers that affect her
interests today . . . and they pile high . . . but also those
of the same day and date of five and twenty years ago . . .
no more than that. But the comparison is instructive. And
one thing is certain. Burrows and the ready-made skirt
belong to the dead past.

Windlesham, *pins in his mouth, fashion plates under his arm,
and the fish-basket hat in his hand, shoots out of the other
room.*

Windlesham Will you have the others in now? (*Then back
through the door.*) Allons, mes'moiselles, s'il vous plaît.
Numéro cinq le premier. (*Then he turns the hat upside down
on the table.*) You see they left the handles on. But I don't
know if we'd better. A bit outré . . . what?

There sails in now no end of a creation.

Windlesham (*as he searches for the design*) Numéro cinq
. . . number five.

Thomas *is much struck.*

Thomas I say . . . by Jove!

*But it is not meant for this cold searching light which seems to
separate from the glittering pink affair the poor, pretty smiling
creature exhibiting it, until she looks half-naked.*
Windlesham's *aesthetic sense is outraged.*

Windlesham Mais non, mais non . . . pas en plein jour.
C'est pour un petit souper très particulier, n'est-ce pas?
Mettez-vous par là dans le . . . dans l'alcove . . . à côté du

velours noir. They won't learn English; they simply won't. Lucky the lingo's like second nature to me.

The costume undulates towards the black velvet platform. **Thomas** *is lost in admiration.*

Thomas That gives her a chance. Damn pretty girl.

Philip (*his eyes twinkling*) But she'll understand that, Tommy.

Thomas (*in good faith*) She won't mind.

Mr State (*who has been studying the undulations*) But what eloquence of movement!

Philip Eloquence itself!

Mr Windlesham *turns on the frame of lights which bear upon the velvet platform. The vision of female loveliness is now complete.*

Windlesham There . . . that's the coup d'œil.

The vision turns this way and that to show what curves of loveliness there may be. They watch, all but **Constantine**, *who has sat silent and indifferent, rolling his second cigarette, which he now smokes serenely. At last* **Philip's** *voice breaks in, at its coolest, its most ironic.*

Philip And this also is woman expressing herself? Rather an awful thought!

Thomas (*in protest*) Why?

Philip Does it express your view of her, Tommy?

Thomas It's damned smart.

Mr Huxtable (*who is examining closely*) No use to us, of course. We couldn't imitate this under fifteen guineas.

Thomas (*with discretion*) Would it spoil the effect now if you had the shiny stuff making it a bit clearer where the pink silk ends and she begins, so to speak?

Mr Huxtable (*not to be sordid*) But it's a beautiful thing!

Mr State Yes, Mr Huxtable, and the question is: Do we accept the gospel of beauty, or do we not?

Windlesham But the trouble I'll have to prevent some old hag of seventy buying a thing like that . . . you'd never believe.

He turns off the light. The vision becomes once more an expensive dress, with a rather thin and shivering young person half inside it, who is thus unceremoniously got rid of.

Windlesham Numéro sept.

Another costume.

Mr State Now here again. Green velvet. Is it velvet?

Windlesham Charmeuse. Promenez, s'il vous plaît.

Mr State And ermine . . . Royal Ermine!

Mr Huxtable Good lord . . . more ribbon!

Mr State And this for the adorning of some Queen of the Salons. You are doubtless acquainted with the novels of the Earl of Beaconsfield, Mr Philip?

Philip I have been.

Mr State Now might not that costume step into or out of any one of them? A great man. A man of imagination. He brought your country to a viewpoint of Imperial . . . of Oriental splendour from which it has not receded. Yes . . . some one of your statesmen . . . some soldier of Empire will, we may hope, find repose from his cares and fresh ardour for his ambitions there!

Windlesham Numéro dix.

The last mannequin, attired in dressing-gown and pyjamas, now appears.

Philip Or even here.

Mr State Or even. . . ! No . . . at this point my judgement stands disabled. Still . . . why not be attractive en intimité? Her household motions light and free . . .

Wordsworth, I think. Our human nature's daily food . . .
an unromantic simile. Why now should it n o t be bright as
well as good?

Constantine You are something of a poet yourself, Mr
State.

Mr State I never wrote one in my life, sir.

Constantine How many poets would do well to change
their scribbling for the living of such an epic as your
purchase of the Madras House promises to be!

Mr State (*immensely gratified*) Sir, I shall be proud to be
your successor. But you were for the Old Régime. It is the
middle-class woman of England that I see waiting for me.
Literature and journalism have laid the train. Beneath the
surface of a work-a-day life her own imagination is now
smouldering . . . though too often she still sits at the
parlour window of her provincial villa pensively gazing
through the laurel bushes . . . as I have seen her on my
solitary walks. She too must have her chance to dazzle and
conquer. That is every woman's birthright . . . be she
duchess in Mayfair . . . or doctor's wife or baker's
daughter in the suburbs of Leicester. And remember,
gentlemen, that the middle-class woman of England, as of
America . . . think of her in bulk . . . is potentially the
greatest money-spending machine in the world.

Mr Huxtable (*with a wag of his head; he is more at his ease
now*) Yes . . . her husband's money.

Mr State A sociologist will tell you, sir, that economic
freedom is the inevitable sequel to the political freedom
that women have now gained. And I suggest to you that
any increased demand for spending power which will urge
the middle-class husband to resist the financial
encroachments of your proletariat . . . for something must
be made to . . . may contribute largely to the salvation of
your country.

Mr Huxtable (*overwhelmed, as well he may be*) Oh . . . I
beg pardon.

Mr State (*soaring, ever soaring*) But the seed sown and the soil of their sweet natures tilled . . . what mighty forest, what luxuriant, tropical, scented growth of womanhood may not spring up around? For we live in an ugly world. Look at my vest. Consider your tie, Major Thomas. (*His eye searches for those costumes and finds one.*) But here is living beauty . . . and we want more of it, much, much more! Think of the residential sections of your cities and contradict me if you can. I mean to help that poor provincial lady to burst through the laurel bushes and dash down the road . . . clad like the Rainbow.

For **Mr Windlesham** *had detained this one young lady. She has been standing there, the accustomed smile hardly masking a wonder into what peculiar company of milliners she has fallen. But* **Major Thomas,** *his attention called to her, now jumps up to offer his chair.*

Thomas I say, though . . . allow me.

Windlesham Oh, thanks no end . . . but they never sit.

Mr State Dear me . . . I had not intended to detain mademoiselle. (*Then, to mend his manners, and as if it were an incantation to that end.*) Bon jour.

The young lady departs, a real smile shaming the unreal.

Windlesham D'you notice there hasn't been a mode you could sit in to advantage these fifteen years? But with a couch, y'know, we might get a sort of mermaid effect out of some of them.

Mr State I do clean forget they are there. We gave some time and money to elaborating a mechanical moving figure to take the place of . . . a real automaton, in fact. But sometimes it stuck and sometimes it ran away.

Thomas And the cost!

Philip (*finely*) Flesh and blood is always cheaper.

Mr State But it would have provided every Burrows House with a complete series of the ideal figure from -

youth to age. Do you regret the days of the corset, Mr Windlesham, may I ask?

Windlesham Well, I'm not sure I don't. Line's my problem. And . . . oh woman, woman! . . . she'll fuss over her face by the hour . . . but her figure's up to me. And the embonpoint I have to get away with! All the really nice women seem to eat too much. Sometimes, I tell you, I could cry!

Mr State Did you ever delve into the psychology of the corset? A while ago I had a young historian write Burrows a little monograph on corsets . . . price one shilling. Out of date now . . . for it summed up in their favour. And we made a small museum of them . . . at Southampton, I think . . . but it was not a success. Major Thomas, we must send Mr Windlesham a copy of that monograph. You will find it suggestive.

Windlesham Oh, thanks too awfully . . . I'm sure I shall. Send it me to the farm, will you, Thomas? I do my serious reading there, weekends.

Mr State You have a farm?

Windlesham Just a toy . . . but thank God for it! I'd be a nervous wreck with my mind on this all the time. Nature's my passion. Can I assist you any further?

Philip See me before you go.

Windlesham Then it's only au'voir.

And he flutters away. There is a pause as if they had to recollect where they were. It is broken by **Philip** *saying meditatively . . .*

Philip I sometimes wonder, though, what this fruit of all our labours, the well-dressed woman . . . what the creature really would look like to an uncorrupted eye. Costume . . . let it alone . . . may evolve in utility and beauty. A cowboy, a Swiss guide, an Arab in his burnous! But we deal in fashions . . . in hats too elaborate to stay

on, or so simple that they extinguish sight and hearing
. . . in shoes as useful and as dignified as stilts are . . . and
in skirts that are neither bond nor free. And even fashion
may not find its own salvation. Every season we must give
it some new tweak that will leave last year's dresses
looking dowdy. What can the result be, then . . . in either
utility or beauty?

Mr State Mr Philip . . . that opens up a world of
thought . . .

Mr Huxtable Don't you be too clever, Phil.

Mr State . . . and recalls to me a project I once
entertained for the founding at one of our more
conservative universities of a chair of the Philosophy of
Fashion. Major Thomas, will you remind me to consider
that again?

Mr Huxtable Talk won't bring dividends . . . that's what
I say.

Mr State A fallacy, Mr Huxtable, if I may so far correct
you. Lift your head, broaden your horizon, and you will
see, I think, that all human activities are one. And what
we men of business should remember is that art,
philosophy and religion can and should, in the widest
sense of the term, be made to pay. And it's pay or perish,
in this world.

Mr Huxtable A pretty frock's a pretty frock. What more
is there to it?

Thomas A lot of English women at Ascot, Goodwood, the
Eton and Harrow . . . I'll back it for the finest sight
going.

Philip Have you ever seen an Eastern woman walk
through the crowd at Claridge's?

Thomas No.

Philip (*forcefully*) I did, the other day.

Constantine Ah!

With one long meditative exhalation he sends a little column of smoke into the air. **Mr State** *turns to him deferentially.*

Mr State But we are boring you, Mr Madras, I fear. You were Facile Princeps upon all these questions so long ago.

Constantine *speaks in the smoothest of voices.*

Constantine No, I am not bored, Mr State. Somewhat horrified.

Mr State Why so?

Constantine You see . . . I am a Mahommedan . . . and this attitude towards the other sex has become loathsome to me.

This bombshell, so delicately exploded, affects the company very variously. It will be some time before **Mr Huxtable** *grasps its meaning at all.* **Thomas** *simply opens his mouth.* **Mr State** *has evidently found a new joy in life.* **Philip,** *to whom it seems no news, merely says in light protest . . .*

Philip My dear Father!

Mr State *(as he beams round)* A real Mahommedan?

Constantine I have become a Mahommedan. If you were not, it would be inconvenient to live permanently at Hit . . . a village in Mesopotamia which is my home. Besides, I was converted.

Thomas *(having recovered enough breath)* I didn't know you could become a Mahommedan.

Constantine *(with some severity)* You can become a Christian, sir.

Thomas *(a little shocked)* Ah . . . not quite the same thing.

Mr State *(who feels that he really is rediscovering the old world)* But how very interesting! To a broadminded man . . . how extraordinarily interesting! Was it a sudden conversion?

Constantine No . . . I had been searching for a religion . . . a common need in these times . . . and this is a very fine one, Mr State.

Mr State Is it? I must look it up. The Koran! Yes, I've never read the Koran . . . an oversight.

He makes a mental note. And slowly, slowly the full iniquity of it has sunk into **Mr Huxtable**. *His face has gone from red to white and back again to red. He becomes articulate and vehement. He thumps the table.*

Mr Huxtable And what about Amelia?

Mr State (*with conciliatory calm*) Who is Amelia?

Philip Afterwards, Uncle.

Mr Huxtable (*thumping again*) What about your wife? No, I won't be quiet, Phil! It's illegal.

Constantine (*with a half-cold, half-kindly eye on him*) Harry . . . I shall hate to see you make yourself ridiculous.

Only this was needed.

Mr Huxtable Who cares if I'm ridiculous? I've not spoken to you for thirty years . . . have I? That is . . . I've not taken more notice of you than I could help. And I come here today full of forgiveness . . . and curiosity . . . to see what you're really like now . . . and whether I've changed my mind . . . or whether I never really felt all that about you at all . . . and damned if you don't go and put up a fresh game on me! What about Amelia? Religion this time! Mahommedan, indeed . . . at your age! Can't you ever settle down? I beg your pardon, Mr State. All right, Phil, afterwards! I've not done . . . but you're quite right . . . afterwards.

The gust over, **Mr State**, *who is a little be-blown by it at such close quarters, says, partly with a peace-making intention, partly in curiosity* . . .

Mr State But do you indulge in a harem?

Mr Huxtable *is on his feet, righteously strepitant.*

Mr Huxtable If you insult my sister by answering that question. . . !

With a look and a gesture **Constantine** *can silence him. Then with the coldest dignity he replies . . .*

Constantine My household, sir, is that of the ordinary Eastern gentleman of my position. We do not speak of our women in public.

Mr State I'm sure I beg your pardon.

Constantine Not at all. It is five years since I definitely retired from business and decided to consummate my affection for the East by settling down there. This final visit to Europe . . . though partly to see you, Mr State . . . was to confirm my judgement in the matter.

Mr State Has it?

Constantine It has. I was always out of place amongst you. I have been reproached with scandalous conduct . . . (*A slight stir from* **Mr Huxtable**.) Hush, Harry . . . hush! I do not altogether admit . . . and I never could see my way to amend it. It is therefore some slight satisfaction to me to discover now . . . with a stranger's eye . . . that Europe in its attitude towards women is mad.

Mr State Mad!

Constantine Mad.

Thomas (*who is all ears*) I say!

Constantine You possibly agree with me, Major Thomas.

Thomas (*much taken aback*) No . . . I don't think so.

Constantine Many men do, but . . . poor fellows! . . . they dare not say so. For instance, Mr State, what can be said of a community in which five men of ability and dignity are met together to traffic in . . . what was the number of that aphrodisiac that so particularly attracted Major Thomas?

Thomas *is shocked even to violence.*

Thomas No . . . really . . . I protest. . . !

Mr State (*utterly calm*) Easy, Major Thomas. Let us consider the accusation philosophically. (*Then with the sweetest smile.*) Surely that is a gross construction to put on the instinct of every beautiful woman to adorn herself.

Constantine Please don't mistake me. I delight in pretty women prettily adorned. To come home after a day's work to the welcome of one's women folk . . . to find them unharassed by notions of business or politics . . . ready to refresh one's spirit by attuning it to a sweeter, more emotional side of life . . .

Thomas (*making hearty atonement*) Ah, quite so . . . quite so.

Constantine I thought you would agree with me, Major Thomas. That is the Mahommedan gentleman's domestic ideal.

Thomas (*brought up short*) Is it?

Constantine But the intention of a costume is everything . . . and that one's intention was pretty clear. If a husband found his wife wearing it . . .

Thomas Well . . . that was a going-out dress.

Philip (*greatly enjoying this contest*) Oh . . . Tommy! Tommy!

Thomas (*rounding for a moment upon* **Philip**) What's the matter? I tell you . . . if a woman always kept herself smart and attractive at home a man would have no excuse for gadding about after other women.

Mr Huxtable *joins in the fray, suddenly, snappily.*

Mr Huxtable She sits looking after his children. What more does he want of her?

Constantine Harry, now, is a born husband, Major Thomas.

Mr Huxtable I'm not a born libertine, I hope.

Thomas Oh . . . libertine be dashed!

Mr State (*pacifically*) Gentlemen, gentlemen . . . these are abstract propositions.

Mr Huxtable Gadding after another man's wife, perhaps! Though I don't think you ever did that, Constantine . . . I'll do you justice . . . I don't think you ever did.

Philip (*with intense mischief*) Oh, Tommy, Tommy . . . can you say the same?

Thomas *is really flabbergasted at the indecency.*

Thomas Phil, that ain't nice . . . that ain't kind. And I wasn't thinking of that, and you know I wasn't. And . . . we ain't all so unattractive to women as you are.

Mr State *loses himself in enjoyment of this repartee.*

Mr State Ah . . . sour grapes, Mr Philip. We mustn't be personal . . . but is it sour grapes?

Philip (*very coolly on his defence*) Thank you, Tommy . . . I can do all the attracting I want to do.

That is the end of that little breeze, and **Constantine**'s *voice completes the quieting.*

Constantine My son is a cold-blooded egotist. His way with a woman is to coax her on to the intellectual plane, where he thinks he can better her. My sympathies are with Major Thomas. I also am as susceptible as Nature means a man to be . . . and as all women must wish him to be. And I referred to these going-out dresses because, candidly, I found myself obliged to leave a country where women are let loose with money to spend and time to waste. Where the law and what is called chivalry protect them in their most shameless provocations . . . where they flaunt and flout you in the very streets, proud if they see the busmen wink . . .

Mr Huxtable Not busmen! (*But he is only gently deprecating now.*)

Constantine Let him but veil his leering, my dear Harry, and the lousiest beggar's tribute is but one more coin in the pocket of their shame.

To **Mr State** *this might be a physical flick in the face. But* **Mr Huxtable** *looks round and nods solemnly and thoughtfully.*

Mr Huxtable Now there's no need to put it that way . . . and I'd deny it any other time. But I've been thinking a bit lately . . . and the things you think of once you start to think! And there's something in that. (*But with great chivalry.*) Only they don't know they do it. They don't know they do it. (*Then a doubt occurring.*) D'you think they know they do it, Phil?

Philip Some of them may suspect, Uncle.

Mr Huxtable (*his faith unspoiled*) No, what I say is it's instinct . . . and we've just got to be as nice-minded about it as we can. There was Julia, this summer at Weymouth . . . that's one of my daughters. Bought herself a dress . . . not one of the Numero sort, of course . . . but very pretty . . . orange colour, it was . . . stripes. But you could see it a mile off on the parade . . . and her sisters all with their noses out of joint. I said to myself . . . instinct.

Suddenly **Mr State** *rescues the discussion.*

Mr State Yes, sir . . . the noblest instinct of all . . . the instinct to perpetuate our race. Let us take high ground in this matter, gentlemen.

Constantine (*unstirred*) The very highest, Mr State. If you think that to turn Weymouth for a month a year into a cockpit of haphazard love-making . . . and baulked love-making at that, most of it . . . with the various consequences this entails, is the best way of perpetuating your race . . . well, I disagree with you . . . but it's a point of view. What I ask now is why Major Thomas and myself . . . already perhaps in a creditable state of marital perpetuation . . . should have our busy London lives obsessed by . . . What is this thing?

Philip La belle Hélène's new hat, Father.

Constantine Now, that may be ugly . . . I hope I never made anything quite so ugly myself . . . but it's attractive.

Philip (*with a wry face*) No, Father.

Constantine Isn't it, Major Thomas?

Thomas (*honestly*) Well . . . it makes you look at em when you might not otherwise.

Constantine As I say . . . it's provocative. Its intention is that the world's work shall not be done while it's about. And when it's about I honestly confess again I cannot do my share. A terrible thing to be constantly conscious of women! They have their uses . . . as you so happily phrased it, Mr State . . . their perpetual use . . . and the world's interest is best served by keeping them strictly to it. For are these provocative ladies (*He fingers the hat again.*) so remarkable for perpetuation nowadays?

Once more **Mr State** *bursts in; this time with heartbroken eloquence.*

Mr State I can't bear this, sir . . . I can't bear to have you take such a view of life. It's reactionary . . . you're on the wrong tack . . . oh, believe me! Come back to us, sir. You gave us joy and pleasure . . . can we do without such pleasure and such joy? But find yourself once more among the Loveliness you made more Lovely and you'll change

your mind. How did that story of the Duchess end?
When, on the appointed night, attired in her Madras
Creation she swept into the Ballroom with a frou-frou of
silk skirt . . . wafting perfume as she came . . . while her
younger rivals paled before the splendour of her beauty,
and every man in the room . . . young and old . . .
struggled for a glimpse . . . for one word from her . . .
one look. (*Once again he starts to soar.*) A ballroom sir . . .
one of the sweetest sights in the world! Where bright the
lamps shine o'er Fair Women and Brave Men. Music
arises with its Voluptuous Swell. Soft eyes look Love to
eyes which speak again. And all goes merry as a Marriage
Bell! Byron, gentlemen . . . taught me at my mother's
knee. The poet of Love and Liberty . . . read in every
school in America!

At the end of this recitation, which **Mr Huxtable** *barely
refrains from applauding,* **Constantine** *goes coolly on.*

Constantine Yes, Mr State, that is my case . . . and you
plead it admirably. The whole of our upper-class life,
which every one with a say in the government of the
country must now lead . . . is run as a ballroom is run.
Men swaggering before women . . . the women ogling the
men. Once a lad did have some preliminary training in
manliness. But now from the very start. . . ! And in your
own progressive country . . . mixed education . . . oh, my
dear sir . . . mixed education!

Mr State A softening influence.

Constantine (*unexpectedly*) Of course it is. And what has
all education sunk to nowadays? To book-learning.
Because woman's a dab at that . . . though it's of quite
secondary importance to a man.

Thomas (*feelingly*) That's so.

Constantine And to the exercise of moral influence . . . of
woman's morality . . . the pettiest code ever framed. And
now, with a new divorce law, you've given them, if you

please, a legal title to jealousy. Wait a few years till their purses are fuller . . . and, by God, gentlemen, they'll make you smart for that.

Philip Yes, I think they will.

Constantine And at every university . . . what with women students, married professors and their family luncheons. . . ! Heavens above us . . . no respectable woman under sixty should be let within ten miles of any university. From seventeen to thirty-four . . . these are the years a man should consecrate to the acquiring of political virtue. Wherever he turns is he to be distracted, provoked, tantalised by the barefaced presence of women? How's he to keep a clear brain for the larger issues of life? Why do you soldiers, Major Thomas, volunteer with such alacrity for foreign service?

Thomas (*with a jump*) Good Lord . . . I never thought of that.

Constantine What's the result? We view all our problems today . . . political, economic, religious, through the cloudy spectacles of womanly emotion . . . which has its place . . . but not, heaven help us, in the world of affairs. What wonder, then, that your labouring men, who can keep their womenkind to child-bearing and housework and gossip within doors . . . what wonder if they get the government from you? You, at your luncheon and dinner tables, the news in your newspapers dressed up as fiction, your statesmen and soldiers pursued at their work to fill picture pages, your weekends where women out-gamble you at cards, play up to you at sport, out-do you in the ribaldry of the smoking-room! An effete empire is yours, gentlemen . . . and the barbarian with his pick and shovel and his man's capacities is over its frontiers already. And what has been your defence against him? Soft talk and scoldings . . . coaxings and hysterics . . . and pretty dialectic trickery that your women have applauded. How they'll despise you soon for it! You four unfortunates might own the truth just for once . . . you needn't tell your wives . . .

Mr State I am not married.

Constantine I might have known that.

Mr State (*a little astonished*) But no matter.

Constantine (*with full appreciation of what he says*) Women haven't morals or intellect in our sense of the words. Shut them away from public life and public exhibition. It's degrading to compete with them, or for them. I fear, I greatly fear it is too late . . . but oh, my dear sentimental sir (*He addresses the pained though admiring* **Mr State**.), replant the laurel bushes, and thickly . . . and we might yet recover strength to hold our place in the world.

Except **Philip,** *who sits detached and attentive, they are all rather depressed by this judgement upon them.* **Thomas** *recovers sufficiently to ask . . .*

Thomas Are you advocating polygamy in England?

Constantine That would be a part of the solution.

Thomas A pretty shocking idea, you know. (*Then with some hopeful interest.*) And is it practical?

Constantine I did not foresee even so much reform in my lifetime . . . so I left for the East.

Philip (*finely*) You did quite right, Father. Why don't your many unavowed disciples do the same?

Constantine *is ready for him.*

Constantine Now think, Philip, think! See things as they are and not as you wish them to be. Who, Mr State, in your country, took most kindly to Mormonism, for all its vulgarity? Not men. Think of the women who'd change the West for the East and be off with me tomorrow.

Mr Huxtable *wakes at last from stupefaction to say with tremendous emphasis . . .*

Mr Huxtable Never.

Constantine Wrong, Harry!

Mr Huxtable No, I'm not wrong just because you say so! You ought to listen to me a bit sometimes. I always listened to you.

Constantine Bless your quick temper!

Who could resist **Constantine's** *smile? Not* **Harry Huxtable.**

Mr Huxtable Oh . . . go on . . . tell me why I'm wrong . . . I daresay I am.

Constantine Harry, you have six daughters, neither married, nor now with much hope to be. Even if you like that . . . do they? You'd better have drowned them at birth.

Mr Huxtable You must have your joke, mustn't you?

Constantine How much pleasanter then for you . . . and how much better for them . . . if you could still find a man ready for some small consideration to marry the lot!

Mr Huxtable (*with intense delight*) Now if I was to tell my wife that she wouldn't see the umour of it.

Constantine The woman's emancipator's last ditch, Mr State, is the trust that women . . . their eyes open . . . will side with him. Make no mistake. This is a serious question to them . . . of health and happiness . . . if not of bread and butter. Rule out our customers here, who are kept women nearly every one of them . . .

Mr State (*in some alarm*) You don't say.

Constantine (*gently lifting him from the little trap*) Kept by their husbands. Or somehow kept . . . in return for what they are, not for what they do . . . by Society.

Mr State Culture demands a leisure class, you know.

Constantine But, as I remember, we used to employ, Harry, between us . . . what? . . . two or three hundred free and independent women . . . making clothes for the others, the ladies . . . selling them finery. As free as you like . . . free to go . . . free to starve. Did they rejoice in that freedom to earn their living by ruining their health and stifling their instincts? Answer me, Harry, you monster of good-natured wickedness.

Mr Huxtable What's that?

Constantine You keep an industrial seraglio.

Mr Huxtable A what!

Constantine What is your Roberts & Huxtable but a harem of industry? Yet the sight of it would sicken with horror a good Mahommedan. You buy these girls in the open market . . . you keep them under lock and key . . .

Mr Huxtable I do?

Constantine Yes, Harry, and no harm's done yet. (*Then his voice sinks to the utmost seriousness.*) But you coin your profits out of them by putting on exhibition for ten hours a day their good looks, their good manners . . . hire it out to any stranger to hold as cheap for a few minutes as his good manners may allow. And then . . . then! . . . once you've worn them out you turn them out . . . forget their very names . . . wouldn't know their faces if you met them selling matches at your door. For such treatment of potential motherhood my Prophet condemns a man to Hell.

Mr Huxtable (*breathless with amazement*) Well, I never did in all my born days! They can marry respectably, can't they? We like em to marry.

Philip Yes, Uncle . . . I went into that question with Miss Yates and the Brigstocks this morning.

Constantine (*completing his case*) So I ask you . . . what is to happen to you as a nation? What of your future

generations? Between the well-kept women you flatter and
aestheticise till they won't give you children and the
women you let labour till they can't give you children.

Mr Huxtable (*half humorously sulky*) Miss Yates has
obliged us anyhow.

Philip (*quickly capping him*) And we're going to dismiss
her.

Mr Huxtable *flashes again into protestation.*

Mr Huxtable What else can we do? But I said you weren't
to be hard on the girl. And I won't be upset like this. I
like to take things as I find em . . . that is as I used to find
em . . . before there was any of these ideas going around
. . . and I'm sure we were happier. Stifling their instincts
. . . it's a horrid way to talk. And I don't believe it. I
could send for every girl in the shop and not one of em
would hint at it to me. (*He has triumphed with himself so
far; but his newborn intellectual conscience brings him down.*)
Not that that proves anything, does it? I'm a fool. It's a
beastly world. But I don't make it so, do I?

Philip Who does?

Mr Huxtable Other people. (**Philip**'s *eye is on him.*) Oh, I
see it coming. You're going to say we're all the other
people or something. I'm getting up to you.

Constantine (*very carefully*) What is this about a Miss
Yates?

Philip A little bother down at Peckham. I'll tell you about
it afterwards.

Constantine No . . . no need.

Something in the tone of this last makes **Philip** *look up
quickly. But* **Mr State**, *with a sudden thought, has first dived
for his watch and then at the sight of it gets up from the table.*

Mr State Gentlemen, are you aware of the time? I may
mention that I have a City appointment at four o'clock.

Constantine (*polite but leisurely*) Are we detaining you, Mr State? Not universal or compulsory polygamy, Major Thomas. I should never advocate that. For one thing the distribution of the sexes forbids it. But its recognition in principle is a logical outcome of the aristocratic method of government. And that's the only ultimate method . . . all others are interim plans for sifting out aristocracies. The community of the future will be wise, I think, to specialise its functions, so that women may find, if they so wish, intellectual companions like my son . . . who will then be free to dedicate their emotions to municipal politics. There will still be single-hearted men like Harry, content with old-fashioned domesticity. There will be poets like you, Mr State, to dream about women and to dress them . . . their bodies in silks and their virtues in phrases. But there must also be such men as Major Thomas and myself . . .

Thomas *rises, yet again, to this piece of chaff.*

Thomas No, no, I'm not like that . . . not in the least. Don't drag me in.

Mr State As stimulating a conversation as I remember. A little hard to follow at times . . . but worth the sacrifice of any mere business talk.

Constantine *takes the hint graciously and is apt for business at once.*

Constantine My fault! Shall we agree, Mr State, to accept as much of your offer as you have no intention of altering? We are dealing for both the shops?

Mr State Yes. What are we proposing to knock off their valuation, Major Thomas?

Thomas Eight thousand six hundred.

Constantine Phil, what were we prepared to come down?

Philip Nine thousand.

Constantine A very creditable margin. Your offer is accepted, Mr State.

Mr State *feels he must really play up to such magnificent conducting of business.*

Mr State Sir, I should prefer to knock you down only eight thousand.

Constantine (*keeping the advantage*) Isn't that rather too romantic of you, Mr State?

Thomas But the conditions?

Constantine We accept your conditions. If they won't work you'll be only too anxious to alter them. So the business is done.

Mr Huxtable's *eyes are wide.*

Mr Huxtable But look here.

Philip Uncle Harry has something to say . . .

Mr Huxtable (*assertively*) Yes.

Constantine Something different to say, Harry?

Mr Huxtable (*after thinking it over*) No.

So **Constantine** *returns happily to his subject.*

Constantine What interests me about this Woman Question . . . now that I've settled my personal share in it . . . is to wonder how Europe, hampered by such an unresolved problem, can hope to stand up against the Oriental revival.

Thomas Ah, there've been some newspaper articles about that lately.

Constantine Doubtless. It has been intellectual currency for a good many years. Up from the Persian Gulf, now, to where I live we could grow enough wheat to feed the British Empire. Life there is simple and spacious . . . the air is not breathed out. All we want is a happy, hardy race of men . . . and under a government that can profit by your scientific achievements and not be seduced by your social and political follies we shall soon beget it. But you

Europeans! Is this the symbol under which you are facing the future? (*He has found again and lifts up la belle Hélène's new hat.*) A cap of slavery! You are idolaters of women . . . and they are the slaves of your idolatry.

Mr State (*with glowing admiration*) Mr Madras, I am proud to have met you again. My coat? Thank you, Mr Philip. I must now prepare to consider the intricacies of a new system of country house sanitation I am about to finance. No poetry there, I fear.

Constantine Sanitation? Your great American science . . . by which you foster your conglomerate millions in health . . . with folly enough in their heads to provide for the needful catastrophe when you become overcrowded.

Mr State Admirable! I dispute its truth. But how stimulating! Goodbye, sir. Ah, if you'd only travel West instead of East we'd find you audiences. A lecture tour . . . why not? Good-day, Mr Huxtable. Till tomorrow, Major Thomas. No, Mr Philip, I can find my way. What a mind . . . what an imagination! America could have given it scope . . .

Philip Your car's at the George Street entrance, I expect . . .

Mr State *is off for his next deal.* **Philip** *having civilly taken him past the door comes back.* **Constantine** *is keeping a half friendly eye on* **Huxtable,** *who fidgets under it.* **Thomas** *takes breath and expounds a grievance.*

Thomas That's how he does business . . . and leaves us all the real work. I shall take the papers home. The four-thirty gets me indoors by a quarter to six. Time for a cup of tea! Phil, have you got China tea?

Philip Downstairs.

Mr Huxtable I must be getting back.

Constantine Running away from me, Harry?

Mr Huxtable (*in frank amused confession*) Yes . . . I was. Habit, y'know . . . habit.

Constantine (*with the most friendly condescension*) I'll go with you . . . part of the way. How do you go?

Mr Huxtable On a bus.

Constantine We'll go together . . . on a bus. D'you remember when the new shop opened how we loved to ride past and look at it . . . from the top of the bus?

Mr Huxtable (*desperately cunning*) Well . . . they won't see me. We don't close till seven.

Constantine's *face sours.*

Constantine No, to be sure. Phil, I shan't be with you for dinner, I'm afraid.

Philip Oh, that reminds me . . . Mother's coming. You know the tea-room, Tommy?

Thomas (*all tact*) Oh, quite!

Philip Straight downstairs, first to the left and the second passage. I'll follow.

Thomas *departs.* **Constantine** *says indifferently* . . .

Constantine After dinner, then.

Philip But you don't mind?

Constantine Not at all.

There stands **Mr Huxtable**, *first on one foot and then on the other, still desperately nervous.* **Constantine** *smiling at him.* **Philip** *cannot resist it. He says* . . .

Philip Now's your chance, Uncle. Stand up for Denmark Hill.

And is off. **Constantine** *still smiles. Poor* **Mr Huxtable** *makes a desperate effort to do the proper thing by this*

*reprobate. He forms his face into a frown. It's no use; an
answering smile will come. He surrenders.*

Mr Huxtable All right! Who cares? Never mind Amelia!

Constantine No . . . at least the past is past.

Mr Huxtable Still . . . what else has a chap got to think
of?

Constantine That's why you look so old.

Mr Huxtable Do I?

Constantine What age are you? I forget.

Mr Huxtable Sixty-three.

The two sit down together.

Constantine I'm your senior. You should come and stay
with me for a little at Hit . . . not far from Hillel . . .
Hillel is Babylon, Harry.

Mr Huxtable (*curious*) What's it like there?

Constantine The house is white and there are palm trees
about it . . . and not far off flows the Euphrates.

Mr Huxtable Just like in the Bible. (*His face is wistful.*)
Constantine.

Constantine Yes?

Mr Huxtable You've said odder things this afternoon than
I've ever heard you say before.

Constantine Time was when you wouldn't listen, Harry.

Mr Huxtable (*wondering*) And I haven't really minded em.
It's the first time I've ever seemed to understand you . . .
and p'raps that's as well for me.

Constantine (*encouragingly*) Oh . . . why?

Mr Huxtable Because . . . d'you think it's only not being very clever keeps us . . . straight?

Constantine Has it kept you happy?

Mr Huxtable (*impatient at the petty word*) Anyone can be happy. What worries me is having got to my age and only just beginning to understand anything at all. And you can't learn it out of books, old man. Books don't tell you the truth . . . at least not any I can find. I wonder now, if I'd been a bit of a dog like you. . . ? But there it is . . . you can't do things that aren't in you to do. And what's more, don't you go to think I'd have done them if I could . . . knowing them to be wrong. (*Then comes a discovery.*) But I was always a bit jealous of you, Constantine, that's the truth . . . for you seemed to get the best of everything . . . and I know people couldn't help being fond of you . . . for I was fond of you myself, whatever you did. That was odd to start with. And now here we are, both of us old chaps . . .

Constantine (*as he throws back his head*) I am not old.

Mr Huxtable (*with sudden misgiving*) You don't repent, do you?

Constantine What of?

Mr Huxtable Katherine said this morning that you might have . . . but I wasn't afraid of that. But when I think how, ever since I've known you, you've had us all on the jump . . . and the games you've played . . . why, of course you ought to be ashamed of yourself. Still . . . well . . . it's like the only time I went abroad. I was sick going . . . I was orribly uncomfortable . . . I ated the cooking . . . I was sick coming back. But I wouldn't have missed it. . . !

Constantine (*in affectionate good-fellowship*) Come to Arabia, Harry.

Mr Huxtable (*humorously pathetic about it*) Don't you make game of me. My time's over. What have I done with

it now? Married. Brought up a family. Been master to a
few hundred girls and fellows who never really cared a bit
for me. I've been made a convenience of . . . that's my
life. That's where I envy you. You have had your own way
. . . and, for all the trouble of it, it must have been
exciting . . . and you don't look now as if you'd be
damned for it either.

Constantine (*in gentlemanly defiance*) I shan't be.

Mr Huxtable *shakes a fist, somewhat, though unconsciously,
in the direction of the ceiling.*

Mr Huxtable Well . . . that's not fair, and I don't care
who hears me say so.

Constantine Life isn't fair, dear Harry. And if it were it
wouldn't be life.

As they start, **Mr Huxtable** *returns to his mundane
responsible self.*

Mr Huxtable But you know, old man . . . it's all very well
having theories and being able to talk . . . still, you did
treat Amelia pretty badly . . . and those other ones too
. . . say what you like! Let go my arm!

Constantine Why?

Mr Huxtable (*his scruples less strong than the soft touch of*
Constantine*'s hand*) Well . . . are you really going away
for good this time?

Constantine Tomorrow.

Mr Huxtable (*beaming on him*) Then come on home and
have a talk to mother and the girls.

Major Thomas *comes back, looking about him.*

Thomas Excuse me . . . I left my hat.

Constantine Dare you, Harry, dare you?

Mr Huxtable Well . . . you must mind what you say, of course. But . . . I would like to have us all thinking a bit differently of you when you're gone.

Constantine Ah . . . they'll not dare do that, I fear.

Philip *comes back too.*

Mr Huxtable Phil . . . your father's coming home to see your aunt.

Philip (*after one gasp at the prospect*) Good.

Constantine I'll be with you by nine, Phil.

Mr Huxtable*'s dare-devil heart fails once more.*

Mr Huxtable Don't be too friendly through the shop, though.

Philip And Uncle Harry, by the way, can tell you all about that Miss Yates affair. And your advice may be useful.

Constantine He shall have it.

Off they go.

Thomas (*still searching*) Where the devil did I put . . . I shall miss that four-thirty.

Philip If you do . . . take my father's place at dinner, won't you?

Thomas *stops and looks at him aggrievedly.*

Thomas Phil, stop chaffing me . . .

Philip It's evident I need more light on the great Woman Question. What do my mother and Jessica really think about such men as you and my father? (*He picks up some papers and sits to them at the table.*)

Thomas . . . or you'll aggravate me into behaving rashly. Oh . . . here. (*He has found his hat, and he slams it on.*)

Philip With Jessica?

Thomas (*with ferocious gallantry*) Yes . . . a damned attractive woman.

Philip Well, after all . . . as an abstract proposition, Tommy . . . polyandry is as much Nature's way, in certain of her moods, as the other. We ought to have made that point with the gentle Mahommedan.

Thomas (*after vainly considering this for a moment*) I'd like to see you in love . . . it'd serve you right.

Suddenly **Philip** *drops his mocking tone.*

Philip But what do we get out of it, I ask . . . we slow-breeding, civilised folk . . . out of love-making and romance . . . beauty of women and its setting in art and culture? We pay pretty dear for it. What does it profit us?

Thomas Damned if I know.

Philip Trot along, then, or you will miss your train.

Thomas *trots along.* **Philip** *gets desperately to loathed business.*

Act Four

Philip, *his mother, and* **Jessica** *are sitting after dinner round the drawing-room fire in Dorset Square.* **Jessica**, *rather, is away upon the bench of her long, black piano, sorting bound books of music, and the firelight hardly reaches her. But it flickers over* **Mrs Madras**, *and though it marks more deeply the little bitter lines on her face, it leaves a glow there in recompense. She sits, poor anxious old lady, gazing not into the fire, but at the shining copper fender, her hands on her lap as usual. Every now and then she lifts her head to listen.* **Philip** *is comfortable upon the sofa opposite; he is smoking and is deep besides in some weighty volume.*

It is a restful room. The walls are grey, the paint is a darker grey. The curtains to the two long windows are of the gentlest pink brocade; the lights that hang on plain little brackets from the walls are a soft pink, too; and no other colour strikes you, but the maziness of some Persian rugs on the floor and the mellowed brilliancy of a few minor Edwardian masters of the little picture on the walls. There is no more furniture than there need be; there is no more light than there need be; yet it is not empty or dreary. There is just nothing to jar, nothing to prevent a sensitive soul finding peace there.

The parlour maid comes in; she is dressed in grey, too, capless, some black ribbons about her. (One begins to fear that **Jessica**'s *home inclines a little to the precious!) She brings letters, one for* **Jessica**, *two for* **Philip**, *and departs.*

Philip Last post.

Jessica Half-past nine. I suppose your father does mean to come.

Philip He said so.

Mrs Madras Is your letter interesting, Jessica?

Jessica A receipt.

Mrs Madras Do you run bills?

Jessica Lots.

Mrs Madras Is that wise?

Jessica The tradesmen prefer it.

With that she walks to her writing-table. **Jessica**'s *manner to her mother-in-law is over-courteous, an unkind weapon against which the old lady, but half conscious of it, is quite defenceless.* **Philip** *has opened his second letter and whistles at its contents a bar of a tune that is in his head.*

Jessica What's the matter, Phil? (*To emphasise his feelings he performs a second bar with variations.*) As bad as that? (*For final comment he brings the matter to a full close on one expressive note and puts the letter away.* **Jessica** *flicks at him amusedly.*)

Mrs Madras How absurd! You can't tell what he means.

Jessica No. (*With forced patience she wanders back to her piano.*)

Mrs Madras You might play us something, Jessica . . . just to pass the time.

Unobserved, **Jessica** *casts her eyes up to the ceiling.*

Jessica What will you have?

Mrs Madras I am sure you play all the latest things.

Jessica I'm afraid you don't really like my playing.

Mrs Madras I do think it's a little professional. I prefer something softer.

Jessica *leaves the piano.*

Jessica We are giving you a dull evening.

Mrs Madras (*with that suddenness which seems to characterise the* **Huxtable** *family*) Why do you never call me Mother, Jessica?

Jessica Do I not?

Mrs Madras (*resenting prevarication*) You know you don't.

Jessica I suppose I don't think of you . . . precisely so.

Mrs Madras What has that to do with it?

Jessica (*more coldly courteous than ever*) Nothing . . . Mother.

Mrs Madras That's not a very nice manner of giving way, either, is it?

Jessica (*on the edge of an outburst*) Isn't it sufficiently childish?

Mrs Madras (*parading a double injury*) I don't know what you mean. It's easy to be too clever for me, Jessica. Haven't I a right to respect and affection from you? When an old woman has lost her husband . . . or worse . . . if she's to lose her children, too, what has she left?

The parlour maid announces 'Mr Constantine Madras'. *There stands* **Constantine** *in the bright light of the hall, more dramatically dignified than ever. As he comes in, though, it seems as if there was the slightest strain in his charming manners. He has not changed his clothes for the evening. He goes straight to* **Jessica**, *and it seems that he has a curious soft way of shaking hands with women.*

Constantine How do you do, Jessica? I find you looking beautiful.

Jessica *acknowledges the compliment with a little disdainful bend of the head and leaves him; then, with a glance at* **Philip**, *leaves the room.* **Constantine** *comes towards his wife. She does not look up, but her face wrinkles pathetically. So he speaks at last.*

Constantine Well, Amelia?

For **Mrs Madras** *it must be resentment or tears. Resentment comes first.*

Mrs Madras Is that the way to speak to me after thirty years?

Constantine (*amicably*) Perhaps it isn't. But the English language is poor in greetings.

Philip, *nodding to his father, has edged to the door and now edges out of it.*

Constantine They leave us alone in the firelight. We might be an engaged couple.

She stays silent, distressfully avoiding his eye. He takes a chair and sits by her. He would say (as **Jessica** *no doubt would say of herself) that he speaks kindly to her.*

Constantine Well, Amelia? I beg your pardon. I repeat myself and you dislike the phrase. Don't cry, dear Amelia . . . unless, of course, you want to cry. Cry, then, and, when you've finished crying . . . there's no hurry . . . you shall tell me why you wished to see me . . . and run the risk of upsetting yourself like this.

Mrs Madras (*dabbing her eyes*) I don't often cry. I don't often get a chance.

Constantine I fear that is only one way of saying you miss me.

The handkerchief is put away and she faces him.

Mrs Madras Are you really going back to that country tomorrow?

Constantine Tomorrow morning.

Mrs Madras For good?

Constantine (*with thanksgiving*) For ever.

Mrs Madras (*desperately resolute*) Will you take me with you?

Constantine *needs just a moment to recover.*

Constantine No, Amelia, I will not.

Mrs Madras (*reacting a little hysterically*) I'm sure I don't want to go and I'm sure I never meant to ask you. But you haven't changed a bit, Constantine . . . in spite of your beard. (*Then the voice saddens and almost dies away.*) I have.

Constantine Only externally, I'm sure.

Mrs Madras Why did you ever marry me? You married me for my money.

Constantine (*sighting boredom*) It is so long ago.

Mrs Madras It seems like yesterday. Didn't you marry me for my money?

Constantine Partly, Amelia, partly. Why did you marry me?

Mrs Madras I wanted to. I was a fool.

Constantine We are fools, all of us, I suppose, when we grumble at the consequences of getting what we want. (*Evenly still.*) It would have been kinder of me, no doubt, not to have married you. But I was impetuous in those days and of course less experienced. I neither realised that you never could change your idea of what a good husband must be, nor how necessary it would be that you should.

Mrs Madras How dare you make excuses for the way you treated me?

Constantine There were two excuses. I was the first. I'm afraid you became the second.

Mrs Madras (*with spirit*) I only stood up for my rights.

Constantine You got them. We separated and there was an end of it.

Mrs Madras I've never been happy since.

Constantine That is nothing to be proud of, my dear.

Mrs Madras *feels the strangeness between them wearing off.*

Mrs Madras What happened to that woman and her son . . . that Flora?

Constantine The son is an engineer . . . promises very well, his employers tell me. Flora lives at Hitchin . . . quite comfortably, I have reason to believe.

Mrs Madras She was older than me.

Constantine Very possibly.

Mrs Madras You've given her money?

Constantine (*his eyebrows up*) Certainly . . . they were both provided for.

Mrs Madras Don't you expect me to be jealous?

Constantine (*with a sigh*) Still, Amelia?

Mrs Madras Do you ever see her now?

Constantine I haven't seen her for years.

Mrs Madras It seems to me she has been just as well treated as I have . . . if not better.

Constantine She expected less.

Mrs Madras And what about the others?

Constantine (*his patience giving out*) No, really . . . it's thirty years ago . . . I cannot fight these battles over again. Please tell me what I can do for you . . . besides taking you back with me.

Mrs Madras (*cowering to the least harshness*) I didn't mean that. I don't know what made me say it. But it's dreadful seeing you once more and being alone with you.

Constantine Now, Amelia, are you going to cry again?

Mrs Madras (*setting her teeth*) No.

Constantine That's right.

Mrs Madras *really does pull herself together and becomes intensely reasonable.*

Mrs Madras What I really want you to do, if you please, Constantine, is not to go away. I don't expect us to live together . . . after the way you have behaved it would be wrong of me to consent to such a thing. But somebody must look after you when you are ill . . . and I don't think you ought to go and die out of your own country.

Constantine (*meeting reason with reason*) My dear . . . I have formed other ties.

Mrs Madras And what do you mean by that?

Constantine I am a Mahommedan.

Mrs Madras Nonsense!

Constantine Possibly you are not acquainted with the Mahommedan marriage law.

Mrs Madras D'you mean you're not still married to me?

Constantine No . . . though it was not considered necessary for me to take that into account in conforming to it . . . I did.

Mrs Madras Well . . . I never thought you could behave any worse! Why weren't you satisfied in making me unhappy? If you've gone and committed blasphemy as well . . . I don't know what's to become of you, Constantine.

Constantine Amelia, if I had been a Mahommedan from the beginning you might be living happily with me now.

Mrs Madras How can you say such a horrible thing?

Constantine I came from the East.

Mrs Madras You didn't.

Constantine Let us be accurate. My grandfather was a Smyrna Jew.

Mrs Madras You never knew him. Your mother brought you up a Baptist.

Constantine I was an unworthy Baptist. As a Baptist I owe you apologies for my conduct. What does that excellent creed owe me for the little hells of temptation and shame and remorse that I passed through because of it?

Mrs Madras (*in pathetic wonder*) Did you, Constantine?

Constantine I did.

Mrs Madras You never told me.

Constantine (*with manly pride*) I should think not.

Mrs Madras But I was longing to have you say you were sorry and let me forgive you. Twice and three times I'd have forgiven you . . . and you knew it, Constantine.

Constantine *recovers his cold sense of humour, which he had almost lost.*

Constantine Yes, it wasn't so easy to escape your forgiveness. But for Mahomet, the Prophet of God, Amelia, I should hardly be escaping it now.

Philip *comes delicately in.*

Philip I beg pardon . . . only my book. (*Which he takes from the piano.*)

Constantine Don't go, Phil.

So **Philip** *joins them, and then, as silence supervenes, says with obvious cheerfulness.*

Philip How are you getting on?

Mrs Madras (*her tongue released*) Philip, don't be flippant. It's just as your cousin Ernest said. Your father has gone and pretended to marry a lot of wretched women out in that country you showed me on the map, and I don't know what's to be done. My head's going round.

Constantine Not a lot, Amelia.

Mrs Madras And if anybody had told me when I was a girl at school and learning about such things in History and Geography that I should ever find myself in such a situation as this, I wouldn't have believed them. (*She piles up the agony.*) Constantine, how are you going to face me hereafter? Have you thought of that? Wasn't our marriage made in Heaven? I must know what is going to happen to us . . . I simply must. I have always prayed you might come back to me and that I might close your eyes in death. You know I have, Philip, and I've asked you to tell him so. He has no right to go and do such wicked things. You're mine in the sight of God, Constantine, and you can't deny it.

Without warning, **Constantine** *loses his temper, jumps up and thunders at her.*

Constantine Woman . . . be silent. (*Then, as in shame, he turns his back on her and says in the coldest voice . . .*) Philip, I have things to talk over with you. Suggest to your mother she should leave us alone.

Philip (*protesting against both temper and dignity*) I shall do nothing of the sort. For the few hours left you in England, and while you're in my house, I'm afraid you must treat my mother with what we call politeness.

Mrs Madras (*with meek satisfaction*) I'd rather he didn't . . . it's only laughing at me. I'll go to bed. I'd much rather he lost his temper.

She gets up to go. **Constantine**'s *bitter voice stops her.*

Constantine Phil . . . when you were a child . . . your mother and I once quarrelled in your presence.

Philip (*in bitterness, too*) I remember.

Constantine To this day the thought of it shames me.

Mrs Madras (*quite pleasantly*) Well . . . I'm sure I don't remember. What about?

Constantine Oh . . . this terrible country! Every hour I stay in it seems to rob me of some atom of self-respect.

Mrs Madras *joins battle again at this.*

Mrs Madras Then why did you come back? And why haven't you been to see me before . . . or written to me?

Constantine (*in humorous despair*) Amelia, don't aggravate me any more. Go to bed, if you're going.

Mrs Madras I wish I'd never seen you again.

Philip Good night, Mother.

Philip *gets her to the door and kisses her kindly. Then* **Constantine** *says with all the meaning possible . . .*

Constantine Goodbye, Amelia.

She turns, the bright light from the hall lamps falling on her, looks at him in half-pathetic triumph, one would say; for she has at least won more cause of complaint. But she makes no other reply, and **Philip** *comes back to the fire. All this is bitter to him, too. He eyes his father.*

Constantine I'm sorry. I'm upset. I was upset when I came.

Philip The visit to Denmark Hill?

Constantine No. I didn't go. I hadn't time. You think I've always treated your mother badly.

Philip Was she ever happy with you?

Constantine (*shrugging*) For as long as she'd let herself be. And she could have had me back . . . more than once. I was fond of her . . . she was my wife. I've never found it hard to be kind to women. She could have had more children. Tell a woman in the East she might still bear children at forty . . . she'd ask nothing more of you. Rebellion against nature brings no happiness, Phil.

Philip What else is civilisation?

Constantine And what better condemnation of about half of it?

Philip (*with his ironic smile*) Well . . . I agree that this present stage of our moral progress is hardly suited to your simplicity of temperament, my dear Father. A heart-breaking paradox . . . to find one's manliest virtues turned to mere weakness under temptation!

Constantine You're a queer fellow, Phil. If I'd sat and turned all my vigour into phrases as you do . . . they'd have poisoned me.

Philip That's a home thrust. Thoughts curdling into words . . . and into more thought and more words. Yes . . . it leaves one lifeless.

Exchanging ideas, merely, these two can keep quite friendly, it would seem.

Constantine Well . . . you thrust home too. I couldn't get a cab from Blackheath . . . and, vexed and worried as I was, I found I had travelled a station too far in the tube . . . watching such a pretty little trull sitting opposite. She had that curve of the instep and the trick of swinging her foot which somehow I never could resist. And why should a man resist it? But in this civilisation of yours . . . half-factory and half-hothouse . . . you're right . . . one's wholesomest instincts turn ridiculous and ignominious. An old age for me here . . . of a loose lip and a furtive eye . . . I'd ask you to shoot me first. Thank God . . . I shake free for ever tomorrow.

Philip (*with a watchful little frown*) Was it this upset you?

Constantine No.

Philip What the deuce were you doing at Blackheath?

Constantine I had business there.

Philip (*taking out the letter that came for him by the last post*) Did Uncle Harry tell you about the Miss Yates affair?

Constantine Yes.

Philip I've just had this from Miss Chancellor.

Constantine Who's she?

Philip Surely you remember Miss Chancellor . . . the housekeeper at Peckham? It was she fixed on Brigstock as the other guilty party.

Constantine Is he?

Philip Who's to say but Miss Yates? But now Brigstock's solicitors . . . smart expeditious fellows . . . demand an apology and Heaven knows what else! If the whole silly affair does come into Court! . . .

And without apparent warning, though **Philip***'s smooth implications should have prepared us for it, and though, truly, it is a relief to* **Constantine** *to have it out, his magnificent reserve does utterly break down.*

Constantine Good God, Phil . . . I've been battling with the little baggage these three hours . . . driving in a taxi round and round . . . I made her come and meet me . . . sitting till we were frozen in some asphalted dust-heap of a park at New Cross! . . .

Philip (*apostrophising all the gods at once*) I might have guessed . . . I did guess! Oh, you incorrigible old man!

Constantine How dared she not tell me about it!

Philip The scandal?

Constantine About her baby. She knew . . . before I went to Marienbad.

Philip Well . . . for an appropriate rounding off of your career! I came back in May to find you, didn't I . . . dignified and disdainful . . . in the office at Bond Street? (*Then, as in exasperated bewilderment.*) But why Miss Yates?

Constantine Why not? (*At which riposte even* **Philip***'s jaw must drop.*) You have gathered together in Bond Street, these last three years, let me tell you, Phil, a most inappropriate personnel. These ladies with their social connections ought to be buying clothes there, not selling them. They've the wrong sort of manners too . . . and I should say their morals are doubtful. That's no matter in their own drawing-rooms. But with all the other young women imitating them . . . powder and paint and affectation . . . jazzing by night and smart chatter by day . . . I shouldn't have known the place. However, it's that American booby's business now. Little Yates seemed the only wholesome self-respecting creature in it.

Philip I see.

Constantine (*man of the world, confiding comrade, and model employer once more*) You'll have to help me, and make her take some money.

Philip She was obstinate about that this morning.

Constantine I'd not have believed that any young woman could have vexed me so. I made her every sort of proposal.

Philip (*the ironic smile lighting his face again*) Even to a place in the household beneath the palm trees?

Constantine No.

Philip No, she'd be rather disruptive there.

Constantine But of course she had the last word. The child is hers by law . . . and a scandalous law it is! I've had my troubles with women, heaven knows! But nothing like this has ever happened to me before.

Philip (*the smile grows grim but satisfied*) So . . . it has been left to little Yates to put you in your place!

Constantine (*darkly, resentfully*) It seems funny to you, does it? Well, Phil, I trust no woman may ever make you feel that you've been made a mere convenience of.

Jessica *returns:* **Constantine** *responds at once to the mere feminine presence, is all himself again.*

Jessica Am I intruding?

Constantine No, no, Jessica . . . no, no.

Philip Mother's gone to bed.

Jessica I met her on the stairs. Had she such a very happy talk with you? She actually smiled at me. Why, she hasn't smiled at me since the morning after Mildred was born.

Constantine (*with grandfatherly gallantry*) How is Mildred?

Jessica Growing by inches.

Constantine You must kiss her goodbye for me. Can I have a taxi, Phil? I've an appointment with Voysey at ten.

Philip There'll be one on the stand opposite. (*He still has* **Miss Chancellor's** *letter in his hand.*) What about this? We don't want the thing in court, I think.

Constantine I should dismiss Baxter.

Philip Brigstock.

Constantine Whatever his name is.

Philip What has he done to deserve that?

Constantine He seems a poor sort of fellow. Pay him some compensation.

Philip A hundred pounds to invest in some tame-cat business and lose?

Constantine No doubt he will! Give Miss Chancellor the firm's formal thanks for exposing a scandal . . . that'll smooth her down. And of course Miss Yates must go.

Jessica (*carelessly curious*) The girl in your office this morning?

Philip Yes.

Constantine But after a bit you can find her a place in one of these new Madras Houses of State's.

Philip I'm refusing his directorship.

Constantine Oh! Can you afford to?

Jessica He can't.

Constantine (*not without malice; here is the chance of a pin-prick for* **Philip**) By the way . . . I've to talk to Voysey about my will. You do finally refuse the executorship?

Philip Please.

Constantine And the residue?

Philip We've as much money now as we can spend without giving thought to it.

Constantine You can save.

Philip Mildred's provided for.

Jessica She is not, Phil.

Philip I want to leave her till she's thirty with some little inducement towards earning her living.

Jessica What nonsense!

Philip Jessica and I quarrel once a week about this school she has been sent to. I spent half a day there. Such a pretty place!

Jessica The education's excellent. They learn cooking. Each girl has her garden.

Philip No vegetables allowed in it, I noticed. She'll leave at seventeen, an accomplished young lady . . . able to talk about everything intelligently without knowing anything at all.

Jessica Accomplished women do very well for themselves in this world . . . and capable women don't. You're clever enough to see they don't. I want Mildred to be happy.

Constantine And he has forbidden me to leave her a ten thousand pound dowry. Did he tell you?

Aesthetic, fastidious, detached as our charming **Jessica** *may be, there are some matters upon which she is common sense itself.*

Jessica Philip . . . how dare you do such a thing?

Philip (*really a little guiltily*) Well . . . I did mean to tell you.

Jessica Yes . . . when your father was safely away.

Constantine Don't worry. Even the most ardent social reformers can't prevent people leaving them money. I've told Voysey to make it another five thousand. I very much approve of you, Jessica . . . and I hope dear Mildred will grow to be like you . . . pretty and witty and pleasantly extravagant. And I'm glad to see Phil so delightfully . . . you'll forgive me the phrase . . . so delightfully henpecked. For a man with his views about women should be. And he's luckier than he knows. I really believe, my dear, that your charm and your art and your sense of beauty . . . your civilisation . . . for so it is . . . all yours, all that's worthy to be called so . . . if I'd been broken to it in my young manhood it might even have conquered m e. Good night . . . goodbye.

Jessica Goodbye, Father.

With which gracious peroration **Constantine** *turns to the door and* **Philip** *follows him.*

Constantine And Philip . . . if you could give that Miss Yates her congé with sufficient brutality she might be stung, perhaps, into taking some compensation. If the auditors wouldn't pass it, I'd send you a cheque . . . as a private matter . . . with pleasure.

Philip (*appreciative, ironic*) Yes, that's an idea! Victoria at eleven tomorrow? I shall see you off . . .

They pass out into the hall. After a moment **Philip** *returns, to find* **Jessica** *at her piano making a little casual music, soft-sounding passes over the keys.*

Jessica I do dislike your father.

Philip That's so much to the good.

Jessica But why poor Mildred should be disinherited! I owe you one for that, Phil.

Philip (*his thoughts on the past still*) Did your parents squabble?

Jessica No indeed . . . they so seldom spoke.

Philip (*dismissing them to the past*) Well . . . if only we cultivate our differences in candour and dignity . . . that may be, after all, the best service one generation does the next.

Jessica I'm up to an argument . . . say once a week.

Philip Poor Jessica!

Jessica (*speaking as she plays, playing punctuating speech*) No . . . when you bore me I need only play a little louder. But don't become too much of an intellectual prototype of your dear papa . . . going round . . . seducing all and sundry . . . who've not the brains to resist you . . . to your own peculiar way of thinking. That I should find . . . socially tiresome . . . and rather vulgar of you. Is he, by the way, always so generous with his cheques to young ladies in trouble?

Philip *barks out a contemptuous little laugh.*

Philip Vanity! To think that he couldn't resist dropping you that hint!

Jessica *turns from her piano, one is sorry to say, quite agreeably amused.*

Jessica Has he really been up to mischief again . . . at his age!

Philip If he hadn't been he'd love us to believe it! Vanity! His real spur, I do verily believe, to that fine and flamboyantly amorous career! Nature's energy must be slacking, you'd think, if she can find no other.

Jessica (*with fine impatience*) Let it slack! The way men allow Nature to befool them into swinging the pendulum

. . . they've no other notion . . . between getting babies born and starting wars to destroy the surplus! Let's have some leisure to enjoy our civilisation.

Philip But you don't. (*Then with a sudden explosive vigour.*) Whitechapel High Street's our civilisation.

Jessica *is familiarly alert to the challenge. With a good-natured sigh she leaves her piano and, so to speak, daintily doubles her mental fists.*

Jessica Ah! I've never been there.

Philip Seconds out of the ring! A Manchester cotton mill, then . . . but you've never seen one. The Potteries . . . the Clyde . . . you've never been there. But the life we live! In this room for instance . . . a Persian carpet on the floor . . . Dutch tiles round the grate . . . and one fine piece of Ming on the mantelpiece. My dear, it's a museum! And I notice your taste in music has slipped back a century lately.

Jessica I cannot bear this very modern noise.

Philip Quite so! And Mildred's at that nice old-fashioned school having her mind made a museum lest she should grow into a horrid modern young lady.

Jessica Surely you say God forbid to that.

Philip Oh, I'm a fogey! I'm forty-two next birthday. But the music, art, and manners young people batter us with today . . . what are they but an echo of the world we made . . . and a right revenge upon us for our blindness to it?

Jessica Well . . . are we to move to Manchester?

Philip Don't get desperate! No, as a visionary I'm all for compromise. I'm going in for politics . . . the great art of compromise. Not for high-flying, speech-making politics . . . I'm too apt at speech-making, God forgive me . . .

but for sordid, municipal politics, dull hard work over drains and dentistry in the schools and such like.

Jessica I've never been against public life for you . . . and I'll economise all that need be . . . but this passion to be on the London County Council is really morbid.

Philip I want Whitechapel High Street made a fit place for Mildred to live in.

Jessica Only the people that live in it can make it so. Do they think it ugly?

Philip I fear not.

Jessica Be careful you don't cease to.

Philip I may cease to . . . I must risk that . . . I must save my soul alive. I've been a trafficker in beauty . . . I'm sick of it.

Jessica That is morbid.

Philip It may be.

Jessica Let's go off to Italy for a month.

Philip More art . . . more museums! Oh Jessica, Jessica! When things as they are drive us from sanctuary here . . . run away! I'd have to run very far, now.

Jessica I don't need to run. And I'm not responsible for your ugly world. I've one of my own, thank heaven, to live in. You men have your work . . . whatever you choose. But art has to make life possible for some of us women, Phil.

Philip (*savagely almost*) Give me the art and the artists that'll make most of the life we're content with impossible . . . I've no more use left for the other sort. D'you remember when I was very young and used to salve my social conscience by lecturing on Shelley to select little audiences in the slums?

Jessica When we were engaged. And I nearly threw you over for throwing me over one evening for some wretched lecture.

Philip (*his eyebrows up*) Did you?

Jessica (*pleasantly*) Very nearly.

Philip Fancy that!

Jessica I did think marriage would cure you . . . but now you lecture m e !

Philip Well . . . I remember once travelling in the train with a poor wretch who lived . . . so he told me . . . on what margins of gain he could pick up by standing incompetently somewhere between the cornfield and the baker . . . or the coal mine and the fire . . . or the house and the tenant . . . I forget which. And he was weary and irritable and very unhealthy. And he hated Jones . . . because Jones had just done him out of a half per cent on two hundred and fifty pounds . . . and if the sum had been bigger he'd have sued him, so he would! And the end of Prometheus was running in my head: This like thy glory, Titan, is to be Good, great and joyous, beautiful and free . . . and I thought him a mean fellow. But on he maundered about his dread of bankruptcy. For his uncle, so it seemed, who had been in the insurance business, had come to the workhouse . . . and what a disgrace that was! And I fear he was a little drunk. He'd have found no comfort in Shelley, I felt sure . . . and, with my lecture worrying me, my own well-springs of charity were dry. But when he asked what was taking me to Canning Town . . . somehow I was ashamed to tell him.

Jessica (*not untouched*) Oh yes . . . it's a horrid world . . . an ugly, stupid, wasteful world.

Philip He cured me, I believe, of lecturing on Shelley . . . which was a pity, in a way, for the lectures weren't so bad. But what is more, I've remembered that little swine through all these years with a sort of baulked affection. I would like to know how he is getting on.

Jessica You may meet him County Councilling.

Philip Wangling some shifty contract. By Jove, I'll see he doesn't!

By now they are seated, one each side of the fire.

Jessica Don't turn your new leaf till after tomorrow, by the way. Take me to that concert. Tommy has chucked.

Philip Tommy! That reminds m e. Two words with you about Tommy. Is your sense of humour working? Tommy wants me to play the Turk and turn him out of the house before he finds himself fatally in love with you.

Jessica, *in every sense of the phrase, sits up.*

Jessica What on earth do you mean?

Philip That was the gist of a lunchtime talk today . . . across the roast beef and the roly-poly. Your coming to Peckham precipitated it.

Jessica (*ominously*) Are you serious, Phil?

Philip Tommy was portentously serious.

Jessica How dared you discuss me . . . like that?

Philip (*deliberately at ease*) I didn't . . . he got no change from me. No nice husband discusses his wife. Upon sound Mahommedan principles, he guards her in the harem of his heart. At worst you may catch him saying: Women, my boy, oh, I tell you. . . ! And embedded in the nonsense that follows will be . . .

Jessica Stop trifling, Phil.

Philip Well . . . I listened sympathetically. What else could I do?

Jessica You could have knocked him down.

Philip Don't be histrionic, Jessica. He wants me to play the Turk. You fancy me as the noble savage. I couldn't have knocked him down . . . he'd have knocked me down. Then, if you hadn't despised me and flung yourself into his arms you'd have been no true woman.

Jessica You won't make me laugh.

Philip What do you bet? And would it have solved the difficulty?

Jessica I'll solve that. This is all true, is it? Then I'll not have him inside my doors again nor speak to him again as long as I live. Nor to you . . . till you apologise. Good night.

And off she is going with extreme and icy dignity when his level voice stays her . . . not quite unwillingly.

Philip My dear . . . flourishes apart . . . you are angry?

Jessica Much more than angry.

Philip Hurt?

Jessica I should hope so.

Philip (*gently, reflectively; the soft answer that may turn away half-satisfied wrath*) Tommy's a bit of a fool . . . but I'm fond of him . . . and I hoped you were. I don't want you to part us . . . for your own sake also. I do sympathise with him . . . just a bit.

Jessica (*her exasperation wholesomely set free*) Do you think, may I ask . . . and does he . . . that I've been falling in love with him?

Philip (*judiciously*) No. So I sympathise with him the more.

Jessica (*with tart response for this compliment*) Thank you. That I've led him on?

Philip (*still more judiciously*) We now come to the making of very fine distinctions.

Jessica Oh, I despise men! I grew up despising them. You took me in for a bit. But I come back to despising you all.

Philip (*a grim twist to his voice*) And you take good care to keep us contemptible, don't you?

Jessica How, pray?

Philip I'm the child of a loveless marriage. I grew up disposed to dislike . . . and that's harder to cure than despising: despising will cure itself! . . . most men and all women. Thank heaven I managed to fall in love with you . . . and no questions asked. But I'm a cold-hearted brute. Tommy, now, is a simple sort . . . and what my entertaining friend Mr State calls the Mean Sensual Man . . .

Jessica (*finely contemptuous*) Yes! When we're alone, having an interesting talk, he's all the time thinking I want him to kiss me. Am I that sort of a woman? Answer me.

Philip (*a smile flickering*) Well . . . let me think. No, not quite. What you want is to have him wanting to kiss you but never to kiss you.

Jessica I do not.

Philip I must take your word for it.

Jessica Can I help his wanting to kiss me?

Philip I wonder, now, if you couldn't.

Jessica I'm a flirt, am I?

Philip I believe that's what they are called.

Jessica, *in the small breathing space after this pretty and swift exchange, shifts her ground.*

Jessica I give you my word that I've never flirted with Tommy. He's not the sort of man I could flirt with. And he's always talking of his children . . . and he takes me to help choose a hat for his wife! And I like Mrs Tommy . . . though, of course, she's a goose and she doesn't make him any brighter. Heavens, I'd have to be pretty bored before I'd start flirting with him. But he has been boring me lately . . . and I suppose I've been trying to wake him up a little . . . I should never have called it flirting! If a man can't stand against the simplest sort of temptation, what is he worth? And how caddish to go talking to you about it!

Philip So he said . . . so he said!

Jessica (*in almost pitiful protest*) All my life I've wanted . . . and I've tried . . . to be friends with men . . . just friends. And one after the other they start flirting with me! Why?

Philip (*the smile flickering again*) I've forgotten, of course, what you look like and I never notice what you have on . . . but I suspect it's because you're rather pretty and attractive.

Jessica And am I not to be? Am I to let you choose my hats?

Philip (*whimsically*) As a man-milliner, I might!

Jessica Am I to dress like those six thin girls of your uncle's? . . . though, goodness knows, poor dears, it makes little difference how you dress them!

Philip No . . . I fear they don't profit the world.

Jessica (*with most genuine impatience*) Oh, don't talk about our profiting the world . . . as if we were so many cattle.

The argument ceasing to be so very personal, **Philip** *turns contemplative.*

Philip For this past thirty-six hours . . . now I come to consider . . . I have been perambulating the Woman Question. From the dowdy virginity of Denmark Hill I passed to Peckham and Miss Yates . . .

Jessica Those two wrongs don't make a right!

Philip They must serve to . . . somehow. I wish you could have heard the far-flung nonsense of our business talk in Bond Street today.

Jessica You men parade in words just as fantastically as we do in our fashions.

Philip (*pleased at her happy hit*) That's not untrue. Anything to colour the dull work-a-day! And here I am now at my own fireside . . . and at the heart of the problem, Jessica.

Jessica *turns whimsical now, and oh, so charming.*

Jessica Sorry, I'm sure, if I don't suit! Oh, why don't y o u flirt with me, Phil?

Philip (*won to a quite brotherly good-humour*) I know . . . I know! Such a silly needless choice it seems to have to be making . . . poor you! . . . between me and my father. But that's more or less what it comes to, my dear.

Jessica (*very genuinely indeed*) I detest and despise your father and all he stands for. But I did think that dear old blunt-headed Tommy was safe.

Philip *turns on the charmer, and hits out none the less hard because he hits good-humouredly.*

Philip You unprincipled woman!

Jessica (*genuinely amazed*) I? I've not done a thing . . . that matters.

Philip Quite so.

But **Jessica***'s wits are about her.*

Jessica Now don't let's be subtle and logical . . . that leads to trouble. By nature, perhaps, I'm not so very much nicer than some of you men. Mother tells me to this day that I was a glutton of a baby . . . thank God I grew up fastidious. My art and my culture, then, that you mock at, may have their uses, to start with, for me.

Philip (*giving her, of set purpose, the rough side of his tongue*) My good girl . . . if it's only your culture keeps you from kissing Tommy . . . and Dick and Harry . . . kiss them and have done.

Jessica *is really shocked.*

Jessica Philip . . . how you can say such a brutal and disgusting thing to your own wife, I do not know.

Philip But you do know that the Mean Sensual Man really looks on you all as choice morsels . . . with your charm and your pretty clothes and your pretty talk so much sauce to his appetite. Baulk it and he feels he's made a fool of.

Jessica (*taking swift advantage*) So he is . . . and so he should be.

Philip (*honestly a little puzzled*) You don't feel the whole thing's degrading?

Jessica It's he that's degraded. A woman's either virtuous at heart or she isn't.

Poor **Philip** *relaxes with a sigh.*

Philip One thing seems plain . . . the fireside problem doesn't yield to argument.

Jessica I'd hoped there couldn't be one . . . as long as I loved you, Phil.

Her sweetness and his love for her, he won't try to resist either.

Philip Do you?

Jessica Deeply.

Philip Come here, then . . . and kiss me.

Jessica (*merrily enough*) Nothing on earth should induce me to. You can come over to me.

Philip I won't. I'll meet you half way.

They meet, he takes her hand. Then she finds he is looking at the fire lost in thought.

Jessica And you forget to kiss me!

He kisses her hand, then, and smiles at her, though his eyes look beyond her still.

Philip I have so come to fear the pleasant sounding word.

Jessica Even when it's mine?

Philip Yes. Be a little patient with me, then, my dear, if loving you, which solved the simpler problem, opens a world of others to my restless mind.

Jessica (*but as if she loved this strange thing too*) Restless, ruthless, unsatisfied, mischievous mind! Well . . . after all, Phil, I did make my choice. I like being married to your sort . . . and, at times, when I don't like it, I feel it's very good for me.

Philip (*solidly*) It is! And look here . . . don't be hard on old Tommy. He's a child. Let's ask him to dinner Friday . . . and we'll chaff his head off.

Jessica (*quite her assured self*) No. Your pleasant brutalities I may have to endure . . . but I'll tackle Master Tommy in my own ladylike way . . . and heaven help him! He won't try to flirt with me again.

Philip Then all will be well! But oh . . . but oh, the farmyard world of sex! Have we won nothing nobler from the jungle? Will mankind cease to be if we cease to strut in our finery?

Jessica (*cheerily*) You have ceased to strut in y o u r finery. I shall strut in mine till it ceases to amuse me.

Philip Till you find something better to do. We await your pleasure.

Jessica What do you mean by that?

Philip Here's a whole world that waits to be made both beautiful and fine. We've done our best . . . and our worst. What are you going to do? You've got your freedom. Do you mean to pay the price of it? I love you . . . deeply. And I try to treat you now as I'd treat another man . . . neither better nor worse. What other compliment is there left to pay you? You'd be wise to value it . . . there's no higher code of honour. Our fireside problem is the world's in a sense . . . since male and female created He them, leaving us to do the rest: though men and women have been long enough in the making . . . for we two do sum up most of the differences in life between us. And we don't shirk them . . .

Jessica I do . . . often.

Philip Then don't you dare to.

Jessica (*with a little secret sigh*) I always shall. It's easier for you to face things and not fear if the truth will hurt. You a r e free. You weren't brought up to think you must be either good or bad . . . and wondering whether you'd turn out pretty or plain. Yes . . . you let me forget I'm a female. And I see your vision, too . . . I think I do . . . when we've been frank and friendly with each other . . . when we feel we want to shake hands . . .

Philip Yes, that's the good moment.

Jessica But you can't be wise for us.

Philip I know.

Jessica I suppose we've still to set ourselves free. (*Then, lest life should seem too tremendous, and too dull, she turns to him with her pretty smile.*) So don't talk too much about things you don't understand.

Philip (*humorously meek*) I'll try not.

Jessica Poor Phil!

She pats his cheek, then kisses it. 'Poor Phil' is but pretty irony, of course; such a charming home as he has, such a charming wife! As long as he'll only see his visions in the domestic fire. . . !

His Majesty

1923–28

His Majesty was first performed at the St Bride's Centre, Edinburgh, as part of the Edinburgh International Festival, on 25 August 1992, by the Orange Tree Theatre. The cast was as follows:

King Henry XIII of Carpathia	Sam Dastor
Queen Rosamund	Caroline John
Colonel Guastalla	Brian Hickey
Mr Henry Dwight Osgood	David Timson
Count Zapolya	Barrie Cookson
Countess Czernyak	Auriol Smith
Dominica Czernyak	Janine Wood
Ella	Caroline Gruber
Colonel Hadik	Peter Wyatt
Dr Madrassy	Morris Perry
Count Stephen Czernyak	Geoffrey Church
General Horvath	Richard Owens
Mr Bruckner	Frank Moorey
Captain Roger Dod	Timothy Watson
The Mayor of Zimony	David Timson
Lieutenant Vida	Vincent Brimble
Sergeant-Major Bakay	Richard Owens
Sir Charles Cruwys	Vincent Brimble
Jakab	David Timson

Directed by Sam Walters
Designed by Tom Piper

Author's note
The people of this play are imaginary and the story is fiction; though it had an origin, sufficiently obvious, in fact. Carpathia is nowhere in particular, nor can its towns be identified on any map.

Act One

We are in the petit-salon of a large house near Zurich. Its architecture is a nineteenth-century echo of the eighteenth, and the furniture is the usual Louis Seize sort of thing. Some businesslike-looking letter files and a typewriter on its table have crept in, though; and what must be a rolled-up map hangs between the two long windows which give towards the garden and the lake. The big bronze-featured writing-table in front of this is tidily covered with papers and despatch-boxes. On either side are double doors.

Mr Henry Dwight Osgood, *an American gentleman, aged forty or so, correctly dressed in a recently pressed suit, stands waiting, hat and gloves in hand. To him there enters* **Colonel Guastalla**, *a younger man, in spirit if not in years; ready of speech but discreet, quick, but ever at his ease. He is dressed in a plain uniform which faintly recalls that of the old Austrian Empire.*

Guastalla Yes, Mr Osgood, if you can give us two minutes more his Majesty will be delighted to see you himself. Do sit down. And then y o u can bear witness too that he is still safe here in Switzerland.

Osgood Does not the published assurance of the President of the Federation suffice? By the way, Colonel . . . if I'm to submit you my copy . . .

Guastalla If he talks freely you'd better. I've been discreet, I hope.

Osgood Excessively.

Guastalla But we pay the right sort of compliment, I've been taught, to you gentlemen of the Press when we flavour all we do want published with an occasional something we don't.

Osgood Why, Colonel . . . the press-man is human. Some of us you can trust and some you can't. This is the royal sanctum?

Guastalla It should be! We're cramped. I've only the little cubby-hole you were kept waiting in. There's the large salon, of course. But her Majesty had a whole wing turned into nurseries.

Osgood Is that so?

The cadence of **Mr Osgood***'s response is in itself a cradle song.*

Guastalla I worked in the garden-house all the summer. Things are quiet enough as a rule. People of no importance I can see at my hotel. Were you followed, did you notice, coming here?

Osgood I certainly was. Some brand of policeman . . . by the look of his boots. Are you much troubled that way?

Guastalla Not by the Swiss. The concierge will keep them posted. Quite right! If he didn't I should have to see someone did.

Osgood Spies in a man's very home . . . !

Guastalla Agents . . . they prefer to be called. Oh . . . kings in exile look for these little attentions. When two of the Great Powers withdrew their ambassadors a year ago . . . I was vexed . . . I feared our importance was waning. But we found it was only post-war economy. They were sharing the head-housemaid with Paris. Our own people at home a r e apt to be rather a nuisance. They're anxious . . . and upstart governments always overdo the thing . . . ! His Majesty.

King Henry *comes in; a man in his forties. He wears a simple uniform. He is not a very handsome man, nor probably* *a very clever man; but he is shrewd. His courtesy is innate and he has an ironic, a mischievous sense of humour. He has charm. There are depths in him too; for at times, one may notice, he withdraws into himself, seems to withdraw altogether elsewhere. He gives his hand now to* **Mr Osgood** *with cordial simplicity.*

He has been followed into the room by **Count Zapolya,** *whose appearance proclaims him to be a distinguished diplomat and statesman of the old school. And this – it sometimes happens so – is what he is.*

The King How do you do, Mr Osgood? Always glad to see any citizen of your great Republic.

Osgood Your Majesty.

The King . . . that views the affairs of our old world with such disinterested benevolence . . . and has contributed so generously to its restoration. Seventy-three million dollars and more, I think, sent to my poor starving Carpathia. It would have paid half the war indemnity. What a good thing we didn't get it sooner! Do you know Count Zapolya?

Nothing could be more characteristic of his Majesty than this blend of formality and irony and simplicity. Only very dull men do not find themselves at ease with him.

Osgood I have had the honour.

The King Are you straight from Karlsburg now?

Osgood I left there day before yesterday, Sir.

The King Bringing the newspapers that tell me I left here for Carpathia a week ago travelling under the name of Fischer. Facts inaccurate . . . but the size of the headlines most gratifying! You prefer to get your information first hand. Quite right! Zapolya, won't you join her Majesty? Five o'clock. She'll give you tea in the schoolroom with the children . . . English fashion. I shan't have to keep you long.

Count Zapolya bows acquiescently to the kind command;
then, as he turns to go, asks **Mr Osgood**, very
courteously . . .

Zapolya When did we meet, Sir?

Osgood Paris . . . 1919. And . . . if his Majesty will allow
me . . . I have wanted ever since to tell you, Count, that
we all thought when they presented you with the treaty
you played them off the stage. You had our sympathy.

Zapolya Thank you. It was a melancholy occasion. But
. . . like a true tragedian . . . I ate a good lunch
afterwards.

Bowing once more, he departs. His Majesty seats himself.

The King Now, Mr Osgood. Won't you sit down? Sit
down, Guastalla. Now?

Osgood With your Majesty's permission I will go in off
the deep end. Do you . . . or not . . . expect to be
restored to the Carpathian throne in the near future?

The King You have just come from Karlsburg . . . !

Osgood Not direct, Sir. I have been spending a day at
Eisenthal.

The King (*to* **Guastalla**) You didn't tell me that. I think,
then, I must interview y o u, Mr Osgood.

Osgood Any news I have that is news is at your Majesty's
disposal.

The King No . . . I'd rather not hear it.

The curtness of this brings **Mr Osgood** *deferentially to his
feet.*

Osgood If your Majesty regrets receiving me . . . why, I
have not been received.

The King Never mind! Sit down again. What does it
matter? Now listen to me. Do you want to take notes?

Osgood No, Sir.

The King Do you never take notes?

Osgood I am not that incompetent.

The King You'll carry away all I say in your head?

Osgood Yes, Sir.

The King Dear me! I couldn't do that.

Osgood You'd learn, Sir . . . if you had to.

The King I hope I should. I doubt it. Well! Carpathia was broken in the War . . . and I did not shirk the peace that was offered me . . . that you saw Count Zapolya sign. I made no complaint and no excuses to my people. What thanks had I? You connived at my exile. I was the scapegoat. What followed for Carpathia? Red revolution, bankruptcy and famine . . . with Europe's pawnbrokers and stock-jobbers to the rescue . . . and a Jew's peace now that the Philistines have done. For I know what Karlsburg's like today, Mr Osgood. Police in the streets again . . . trams running . . . shops open. But rotten with intrigue in politics and finance . . . a moral chaos. Yes, I'd be glad to restore some dignity and decency to my country if I could. But I want no more bloodshed. And this young madcap at Eisenthal . . . ! You saw Stephen Czernyak?

Osgood I had an hour's talk with Count Czernyak.

The King He doesn't pretend I've encouraged him?

Osgood He most respectfully complains that you haven't.

The King What sort of men has he got there?

Osgood Youngsters . . . the mass of them . . . that weren't in the War.

The King Quite so. Any guns to count? No . . . don't tell me . . . I'd rather not hear. I'm fond of Stephen Czernyak . . . I've known him from a child. His mother was the first friend her Majesty made in Carpathia. The cutting-up of that Eisenthal province was a scandal. The Neustrians are treating their slice of it abominably . . . and this government in Karlsburg hasn't treated what's left us much better. But I will not win back my kingdom by bloodshed. I inherited one war. One's enough.

Osgood Then you do not propose, Sir . . . may I say? . . . to drop out of the skies to lead these mountaineers down to Karlsburg . . . to kick Madrassy and his government and the Assembly and the British Mission and the French Mission and the Jews and the lawyers all into the Danube with one kick.

The King You may say that I shall not re-enter Carpathia like a thief or as a conqueror . . . however attractive the rest of the programme may be.

This seems to bring the conversation to such a full stop that Mr Osgood gets up again; but this time a more satisfied man.

Osgood Then I will now thank your Majesty for a very challenging talk. With that Colonel Guastalla has told me besides I am confident of making a dignified story of it.

The King rises too, and begins a kindly cross-examination. This habit, bred by countless inspections of regiments, factories, schools, model dwellings and the like, has become second nature with him.

The King Going straight back to Karlsburg?

Osgood No, Sir. Now I know there's nothing doing, I sail on Saturday.

The King Taking a holiday?

Osgood Going home.

The King For good?

Osgood I hope so.

The King I've always wanted to see America.

Osgood Your Majesty may count on a welcome.

The King No Ellis Island? We wretched kings, though
. . . prisoners of custom . . . when we're not exiles!
You're from New York?

Osgood Not to begin with, Sir.

The King Where from, then?

Osgood Iowa City, Iowa.

The King Iowa City, Iowa! You can have found nothing
more romantic in Europe, Mr Osgood, than I find that.
But you've liked my country, I hope.

Osgood A most beautiful country, Sir.

The King D'you speak the language?

Osgood For railroad, hotel and eating-house purposes
only.

The King That's been a drawback. You'd have liked my
people too. Farmers and peasants . . . steady and sensible
. . . if you only leave them alone. Don't judge by
Karlsburg and its mob. Comic operas and stock-exchange
scandals are the chief crops there. Interested in farming?

Osgood Mrs Osgood and I, Sir, operate a small farm in
New Jersey. S h e does, I should say.

The King Jersey? Cows!

Osgood Chickens with us, mostly.

The King But I breed poultry!

Osgood I have that in mind, Sir.

The King What's your fancy, now?

Osgood Mrs Osgood's for Rhode Island Reds. I've stood
by Wyandottes. We consider utility.

The King But prize birds pay. The soil's wrong here. I've
not done badly, though. (*He takes from his writing-table a
triple photograph frame.*) My Bourbourgs. Mark me now
. . . they've a future as a dominant. Louis Quatorze . . .

Louis Quinze . . . Louis Seize! A family joke . . . not for publication.

They really do call to mind the state portraits of these gentlemen, though the birds are the more majestic. **Mr Osgood** *conscientiously plays the connoisseur; and the* **King** *finds this a far more cheerful subject than Carpathian politics.*

Osgood Magnificent lobes!

The King Aren't they? Try cod-liver oil. Do my people want me back, d'you think?

He replaces the frame. With the question his voice has shifted to a minor key. **Mr Osgood** *looks a trifle uncomfortable.*

Osgood Is it for me to say, Sir?

The King Come . . . to a mere exile . . . not yet so used to the truth that I don't sometimes prefer it!

The frank charm of this would be hard to resist indeed. And, button after button undone, **Mr Osgood**'s *studied reserve at last slips off him.*

Osgood Your Majesty . . . what an opening! And how I'd have jumped for it once on a time! Ten years ago my considered opinion upon the whole European problem should have been placed at your disposal. My God, Sir . . . you couldn't have found a more rusé young fellow than me . . . shipped eastward, nineteen eighteen.

The King In your army?

Osgood Attached Political Intelligence. I have flat feet . . . which disqualified me from tramping to the trenches with the rest and being shot like a man. Not that I felt quarrelsome! I came full of pity for you all . . .

The King That is apt to turn to dislike.

Osgood Sir . . . my first sight here was a hospital and my second a battlefield two days old . . . and my first clear

thought that there were men here . . . statesmen, so-called
. . . who'd had such things in mind all along.

The King They hadn't, I assure you.

Osgood Well . . . I could better forgive them that than
some of their jobbery since. I know lots less than I did.
But I've sat in my machine by roadsides and had the
common countryfolk stand round me with distrustful eyes.
If their talk's been strange their meaning's been plain . . .
and your Majesty put it pat. For the dear Lord's sake
leave us in peace. I don't know now which rile me more
. . . the men that fool their fellow-men and call it
government or the fellows behind that they let fool t h e m
. . . that stir the mud and fish their dirty profit from it.
But if for five short minutes I could be God Almighty I'd
make a handful of the lot and drop them in the cold
Atlantic . . . and we'd hear the joy-bells ring. Me, Sir . . .
in my intellectual shirtsleeves . . . with my New York
culture shed! What's wrong with an axe and a spade and a
bit of land to clear, said my grandad when he went West
. . . and I'll pity the government that had tried monkeying
with him. And what's wrong with exile from a world like
this? That's the question . . . man to man . . . I'd like to
have been asking you. Colonel, I fear you should never
have presented me.

With which apology **Mr Osgood** *buttons on his perfect
manners again. But the* **King** *is undisturbed, is much
refreshed, indeed, by this Western breeze.*

The King Not at all, Mr Osgood, not at all! What you say
is most interesting . . .

At this moment the **Queen** *appears; and they all three turn, as
people do turn, and even instinctively stand to attention at the
sight of her. She is a woman old enough to have a son of
sixteen, robust enough to have borne six children besides and to
feel the better for it. Whether she is beautiful or not one would
never stop to ask: there is a natural magnificence about her
that puts aside all such questioning. She is utterly*

*unselfconscious. Her manner is usually gracious, for graciousness has been bred into her as one of the attributes of a queen. When she does not wish to be gracious – how should she ever suppose she is being rude? She is showing people what she thinks of them; and the sooner they know it the better. She is never – in any sense – slow to move; and she now comes into the room quickly, as if she thought to find her husband alone. She certainly shows no pleasure at finding **Mr Osgood** there; and the temperature of Switzerland seems to fall a degree or two. But the **King**, with his charming smile, sets things right again.*

The King My dear . . . this is Mr Osgood of the United Press and of Oyua City, Oyua, North America. He has been ten years in Europe finding out all about it . . . but he doesn't like it and he's going home.

*If there should be any irony in this **Mr Osgood** does not perceive it; he is fully occupied in bowing to the **Queen**, who inclines her head, eyeing him steadily.*

Osgood Your Majesty.

*Once more the **King** proffers a cordial hand.*

The King Goodbye then. You did choose a bad time for a first visit. After a war things are always in a bit of a tangle. But think kindly of us. There's a lot in what you say. Even in the old days one wished now and then one wasn't a king. But being a king . . . one had to do one's best to be a king, you know.

Osgood Your Majesties.

Mr Osgood *has evidently studied the old Carpathian Court etiquette; for he bows once where he stands, three paces back bows again, and yet again at the open door where he finds* **Guastalla** *waiting for him. The* **Queen**, *her eyebrows lifting slightly, is not unpleased by this.*

Guastalla I'll come down with you.

The King Bon voyage! Oh . . . Guastalla!

Mr Osgood *has departed.*

The King D'you know his hotel? We might send him . . . send his wife . . . a couple of cockerels and a pullet or so, if he'd care to take them. From the number five pen, will you say? Friendly fellow!

Guastalla *follows* **Mr Osgood**. *The* **King** *and* **Queen** *are alone.*

The Queen Why do you waste time with such people?

The King My dear Rosamund! The Press! Besides . . . one must be extra civil to America.

The Queen Why?

His blandness takes on a whimsical tinge.

The King That is a searching question. We always are. I don't know why. Where's Zapolya?

The Queen He never takes tea.

The King No . . . but I do. And I thought he'd like to see the children.

The Queen He's looking old.

The King He's growing old. Time passes.

The Queen It does indeed! You've not finished your talk with him. Do you want me here?

The King Yes . . . I'd only have to tell you all about it after. We'd not got beyond his asthma when this American man arrived. I always begin with his asthma. He's just come from Eisenthal.

The Queen The American?

The King Yes.

The Queen Did you tell him you'd never countenance Stephen Czernyak?

The King What else could I tell him?

The Queen Henry . . . if you'd listened to me . . . if Cyril and Margaret hadn't had chickenpox and I'd not been nursing them . . . you'd have been in Karlsburg weeks ago. What came of all the bargaining with Madrassy? Nothing . . . and I said nothing would. This talking to journalists . . . it's so undignified! And now Zapolya's to tell us what Paris thinks! Who cares? I wish you'd not sent for him . . . he's a pessimist. And who is Madrassy that he should presume to bargain with you?

The King He's the head of the present Carpathian government, my dear.

The Queen Nonsense! Carpathia is yours, Henry. Go and take it. Go to Eisenthal. Ride into Karlsburg at the head of your army . . .

The King Dear Rosamund . . . you're romantic. The problem's not so simple.

The Queen When you know what you want all problems are simple.

The King Well . . . I want my tea at the moment. And I hope you've not eaten all the muffins between you.

He has been locking away a paper or two taken from his pocket. He slips his arm in hers and walks her off to the nursery.

*   *   *

The falling of the dusk tells us that an hour or more has passed. The talk with **Count Zapolya** *has reached that stage when its pendulum is slowing but will not stop, when a half-hearted shove at intervals does not suffice to set it at full swing again; a recognisable moment in all such talks. The* **Queen** *sits enthroned;* **Count Zapolya** *is in a small chair, in respectful discomfort; the* **King** *paces the room, at times drifts to the windows, then comes back to his table looking idly for nothing in particular.*

The King No . . . Madrassy won't fight if he can help it. Fighting's not his line.

Zapolya With Czernyak one step nearer Karlsburg he may have to give place, then, to those that will.

The King I don't see this Opposition taking office. There's nothing they agree upon.

Zapolya. They'll manage to agree upon taking office if they get the chance. They could govern for a little if the Activists would join.

The King Who's the best man in that gang?

Zapolya New men . . . all of them.

The King I get their paper . . . a readable rag! Up and be doing's their motto . . . no matter much what apparently! Does the wily Madrassy count on my stopping Czernyak, then?

Zapolya He must think you set him on to start with.

The King Takes me for a fool as well as a liar!

Zapolya And he spun out his parley with you to make you hold him back.

The Queen Of course he did!

Zapolya For Czernyak has a fighting chance, Sir.

*The **King**'s attention is fixed.*

The King With five thousand men . . . armed anyhow? The Treaty leaves us ten thousand.

*The **Queen** sits up very straight.*

The Queen Us!

The King Carpathia. Madrassy.

The Queen Carpathia's not Madrassy . . . not yet!

The King (*smoothly*) . . . leaves the government in Karlsburg ten thousand troops.

Zapolya Mostly boys . . . going stale in barracks.

The King The militia besides.

Zapolya Villagers mainly. Will they march against you?

The Queen No.

Zapolya . . . or at all, if they can help it!

The King . . . and ten batteries. Nothing heavy, of course.

Zapolya He has a fighting chance.

The King I want no bloodshed.

Zapolya That is another matter, Sir.

What is it that is really vexing his Majesty?

The King Why didn't Madrassy move troops up there three months ago?

Zapolya When he was raising his American loan! New York bankers have all your Majesty's objections to bloodshed.

The King . . . before Stephen had men enough to make any sort of fight for it?

Zapolya I see Stephen Czernyak with two men and a boy making some sort of fight for it.

The King Why didn't he make a fuss at Geneva about these Neustrian guns?

Zapolya He did, Sir.

The King No, no . . . a r e a l fuss!

Zapolya The mischief was done. Neustria apologised. The culprit is being tried. Everything's correct. Besides . . . while Madrassy was wondering whether he wouldn't want you back, your flag hoisted in the mountains was an asset to him . . . with his own Opposition.

The King He was always too subtle, was Madrassy.

The Queen A time-server!

Zapolya If a politician can serve his moment of time to any purpose, Ma'am . . . that may not be a reproach. Why didn't your Majesties go back when he gave you the half-chance?

The Queen He made conditions. He had no right to.

Zapolya I should have gone.

The Queen To put ourselves in his power?

Zapolya He was evidently afraid you wouldn't be.

The Queen He never meant us to accept them.

Zapolya What better reason could you want, Ma'am, for doing so?

The King He was my tutor in classics, you know, when I was a small boy. He has got on . . . since. I made him Minister of Education. I've never quite outgrown the feeling that if I don't please him he'll give me fifty lines of Virgil to learn.

The Queen He took an oath of allegiance to you, Henry. He has broken it and he'll be damned everlastingly. I hope he remembers that, sometimes.

The King He has enough else to worry him now. The country's in a devil of a mess.

The Queen And deserves to be!

His Majesty's mind returns to its vexations.

The King Why were these Neustrian banks allowed to find Czernyak money? Why wasn't that stopped at once?

Zapolya Geneva can't touch t h e m, Sir.

The King Their own government could.

Zapolya Yes . . . but Neustria has a first-class political scandal of her own blowing up . . . and civil war in Carpathia will leave her looking comparatively virtuous.

The King A nice neighbour! But now they've stopped supplies!

Zapolya Yes.

The King Finally?

Zapolya I think they want to see if your Majesty will make a move . . . and the effect of it. I think the rumour you'd gone back may have been of their spreading.

The King The effect of t h a t was that Carpathian securities went down with a bump.

The Queen Madrassy would see they did!

The King But if I'll make a move now this new Paris group will find the money for it.

Zapolya Yes.

The King Unconditionally?

Zapolya They've made no conditions.

The King Would you risk your money like that?

Zapolya I am not an expert, Sir, in this post-war warfare. And like the old crossbowman I can't help chuckling when sometimes the guns do more hurt to the gunners than the enemy. But I grasp its principles . . . so called. You look for trouble . . . or discreetly foster it. Securities go down and you buy. When the trouble's over they go up and you sell. And there's a profit.

The King They may not go up. Then you're ruined.

Zapolya Not if you've been reckless enough . . . for then your rivals step in to save you. High finance has its altruism. It desires not the bankruptcy of a sinner . . . of a sufficiently spectacular sinner. Bankruptcy is catching. I think the Crédit Ponthyon . . . to do it justice . . . wants a settled Carpathia. That is why they want your Majesty back there. Monsieur Ferdinand . . . a-straddle on the hearthrug, his morning cigar in his mouth . . . took a high moral tone with me. Oh . . . the international Jew with his gospel may sell the poor world salvation yet, at a price . . . make us members one of another . . . since the Christian Church cannot. Mere prejudice, no doubt, to balk at the price . . . as I do.

The **Queen** *rises impatiently.*

The Queen Nothing's being settled! Things are at a crisis. We must be practical. How does this map let down?

The King Pull the red string. No, my dear . . . that's blue! The r e d string.

For her Majesty is not so practical as all that; few of us are. **Count Zapolya** *goes to her rescue . . .*

Zapolya Allow me, Ma'am.

. . . and the map is lowered. It shows us Carpathia, all belittled as she now is, powerful neighbours elbowing round her. Karlsburg stands out as a knot of roads and railways in the centre; Eisenthal and its mountains are over to the north, near the Neustrian border. The **Queen** *turns businesslike.*

The Queen Where's Eisenthal? And railhead? It's not a hundred miles from Karlsburg.

Zapolya A hundred and twenty, Ma'am.

The King Surely the railway's cut. Their War Office can't be all that incompetent.

The Queen It's a week's marching.

Zapolya Nine days, Ma'am.

The Queen Go to Eisenthal, Henry . . . and the whole country will rise. Ride into Karlsburg at the head of your army . . .

*The **King**'s voice strikes calmly, coldly through her enthusiasm.*

The King London may be for recognising me, you think, if the recall's constitutional?

Zapolya Constitutional is music in London's ears. But popular clamour . . . enough of it . . . might do.

The King Paris?

Zapolya . . . is against you.

The King Then why is the Crédit Ponthyon ready to back me?

Zapolya Once the Crédit Ponthyon is backing you Paris may change its mind.

The King If I borrow their money first . . . they'll see I can pay it back!

Zapolya That puts it crudely, Sir.

*At this moment **Colonel Guastalla** comes in, and rather hurriedly. He is now in civilian clothes.*

Guastalla You've not needed me, I hope, Sir. I was called away to my hotel.

*The **Queen** disapproves, first, of **Guastalla**'s bouncing into the room like this; secondly, of his bouncing in without his uniform; thirdly, of his speaking before he is spoken to. It is, therefore, in her iciest tones that she points out even a fourth offence . . .*

The Queen And you have now left the door open, Colonel Guastalla.

He has not only done this, but he crosses to open the other door as he says . . .

Guastalla Yes, Ma'am . . . I have something private to say . . . if his Majesty will allow me. (*And he looks carefully into the room beyond.*)

The King Frederika Bozen's there, isn't she?

The Queen Yes.

Guastalla No, Sir.

They are all now in a thorough draught.

The King The colds we catch talking secrets in this house!

The Queen Tiresome woman! I told her to sit there.

The King And the money spent spying on us! Piles of reports . . . can't you see them? If I hatch out a dozen chickens every Foreign Office in Europe rings with it. Well?

Guastalla Captain Dod, Sir, sent to say that if the weather does break flying mayn't be too safe for some weeks . . . and the authorities have dropped him a strong hint that the repairs to his engine are taking too long.

The King I thought he'd been sent about his business.

Guastalla You gave no positive orders, Sir.

There is something a little disingenuous in the tone; a very sharp eye might detect that **Guastalla** *avoids looking at the* **Queen***. The* **King***'s eye is sharp enough; nevertheless his voice is quite casual as he explains to* **Zapolya** . . .

The King Dod is the Englishman that . . . is he English or American, Guastalla?

Guastalla English, Sir.

The King . . . that was to have flown us . . . home. Very well. We can have the doors shut now.

The Queen And you would like to resume your uniform, Colonel Guastalla.

She sounds slightly mollified. **Guastalla** *shuts one set of doors; and, departing, the other, with a cheerfully deferential . . .*

Guastalla Certainly, Ma'am.

The King Poor Guastalla! In and out twenty times a day . . . and has to change each time.

The Queen To pander to a Swiss Government and its dignity! They'd make us dress like grocers within doors if they could.

Poor **Guastalla** *gone, the* **King** *quietly re-links the broken chain of their talk.*

The King But if I make no move . . . and these Neustrian banks have stopped supplies . . . what is Czernyak to do? He can't live on the country. He'll have to disband.

The Queen Henry!

The King It's hard on him, I know. If I write him a letter . . . will that help? . . . telling him to disband . . .

Before **Count Zapolya** *she really should not! But the* **Queen** *can endure this no longer.*

The Queen Henry . . . you'll break my heart! You bargain with that scoundrel Madrassy for weeks . . . though it's plain as daylight that he's tricking you. You talk to journalists and give them chickens. But when ten thousand men want to lay down their lives for you . . . all you'll do is to tell them not to.

The King Six thousand at most.

The Queen What's the difference?

The King If it comes to fighting there's some difference. Can you see that a letter gets to him?

Zapolya I'll try, Sir.

The King I've no right to countenance such folly.

Zapolya But, sooner than disband, he may choose to fight . . . while he still can.

The King D'you think he will?

Zapolya Don't you?

*The **King** – as he can when needs must – looks facts in the face.*

The King Yes, I do. Do these Neustrian gentlemen think so too?

Zapolya They're tired of waiting. I fancy their game is to force him to.

The King Knowing he can't win?

Zapolya What do they care for that, Sir? They want three months' anarchy in Carpathia . . . and they'll get it. Whatever happens they won't lose.

At which conclusion his Majesty looks pretty grim; and for all comment . . .

The King I hope there's a Hell.

*He walks up to the map and stands studying it. The **Queen**, a little wide-eyed at this new prospect, turns to **Count Zapolya** in almost childish appeal . . .*

The Queen Can't he win?

Zapolya Not by all the rules, Ma'am. Miracles happen.

The Queen I think he might.

*The **King** is intent on the map still.*

The King Eisenthal! Ever there?

Zapolya I was born twenty miles away . . . across the present frontier, Sir.

The King Of course! Stupid of me!

The Queen Why do you use that map, Henry?

The symbolic sight of poor despoiled Carpathia is more than she can bear.

The King It's the latest. I keep it rolled up.

The Queen Did they know, Count Zapolya, when they handed you that infamous treaty, that they were asking you to sign away the very house you were born in?

Zapolya So long ago, Ma'am, that no doubt they thought I'd forgotten.

The King has begun to pace the room.

The King How could Stephen let himself be tricked like this?

Zapolya Has he been tricked, Sir? He always meant to fight. He has had their money. They leave him in the lurch. He's free of them . . . and so would you be.

The King He can't think he'll win.

The Queen I think he'll win.

The King If he did . . . I can't go back on such terms. I've said I won't.

Zapolya How could you refuse to . . . if he really won?

The King I'll have no bloodshed.

The Queen Dear Henry . . . don't keep saying what you won't have. What will you?

Lashed by her vehemence, Henry comes to a standstill, facing the facts again.

The King The plain truth is, I suppose, that I don't much want to go back . . . upon any terms. With things as they are! Would you? Would you take office again?

He appeals to Zapolya, who responds smilingly, sadly; for indeed he is both looking old and growing old.

Zapolya I, Sir? Oh, yes! The old horse dies happier in the shafts.

The Queen I trust we s h a l l see you in office again, Count Zapolya.

*But this is for the **King**'s benefit and encouragement rather than his, and he knows it.*

Zapolya Thank you, Ma'am . . . but I could not advise his Majesty to recall me. True . . . I am one of the few elder statesmen that did not make the War. But worse . . . I made the Peace. This new democracy has no faith in God . . . but it still needs a Devil to believe in . . . to cast the burden of its follies and sins upon. Leave me in exile to play that harmless part. Find some respectable demagogue . . . when the time comes . . . to make a fresh start with . . . who'll give the mob its stomachful of flattery and sensation. Fed fat, the beast will be less trouble to you.

Her Majesty dislikes irony.

The Queen You are not serious, I think, Count Zapolya.

*The **King** is pacing the room again, half attentive, half wrapt in his thoughts.*

The King Back to that puppet-show! Poultry farming's a man's job beside it! But I used to have some quite good ideas about being a king.

Zapolya Government is a strange art, Sir. An expert calling at which the expert fails . . . and the wise man when he is too wise!

The King You'll stay and dine?

Zapolya Your Majesty is most kind.

The King I shall write to Stephen to disband.

Zapolya Yes . . . I should, Sir.

The King But you think he'll disobey me.

The Queen I hope he'll disobey you.

The King I know you do, Rosamund . . . but you really mustn't say so.

Zapolya I venture to hope he'll disobey you, Sir. But write the letter. Five thousand men facing such odds for you . . . shows you are still to be counted with. The letter will free you from blame for the folly of it. And if by chance he should win . . . success never needs much explaining away.

The King gives him a sidelong look.

The King There's even the chance that he might obey me. Not that anyone ever has yet!

Zapolya The letter will take some days to reach him.

The King True! Dinner's at half-past eight.

His reputation for subtlety thus sustained, **Count Zapolya,** *bowing, departs. The* **Queen** *bends her head in punctilious acknowledgment, but then gives an exasperated little sigh.*

The Queen Why can't he bow properly? Even he!

The King He did bow.

The Queen Once! Who told that American what to do?

The King They know all these things.

The Queen Our own people think they can treat us as they please now. Guastalla bounces into this room . . . as if it were any room. While we're living like this, be more strict about such things . . . not less! And you leave all the scolding to me.

The King I do wish, by the way, you wouldn't seduce Guastalla from his duty.

The Queen Henry . . . what a thing to say.

The King He knew perfectly well that I meant Dod and his machine to be sent about their business. But you're his goddess . . . you've only to lift your finger! You and he think, I suppose, that you've only to say Go Back or Go to Eisenthal often enough for it to end in my going!

The Queen Not at all.

The King Well . . . that is how most people are persuaded to do things. Czernyak has been a fool. No man is safe from his supporters . . . that's the first lesson every leader has to learn.

The Queen Don't be paradoxical.

The **King**, *having coasted the room again, looked out of the window, glanced again at the map, now comes to a standstill, flings himself into a chair and lets his thoughts drift away.*

The King If you could begin again, Rosamund, would you choose to be a queen?

The Queen Yes, of course.

The King (*with his whimsical smile*) Even mine?

The Queen But I a m a queen.

The King This place is cramped, I know. And it's very Swiss . . . naturally! But it's not uncomfortable. You'd never come to think of it as home?

The Queen How can you ask?

The King What made my grandfather build that great stucco barrack of a palace? Dreary and draughty! Put less than twenty at table and the private dining-room's a desert. And one winter when I was a boy . . . and the city electricians had struck and it was foggy . . . I lay in bed there by candlelight and I could not see the ceiling! That's a fact. You've never stayed at the Castle. Charming! But its drains are wrong.

The Queen Your grandfather thought of what was due to the greatness of his country.

The King He did! And look at it! But he was a nice old man when you knew him. Do you carry in your mind, I wonder, any constant picture of me? What is it?

The Queen Whenever I'm angry with you . . . then I try to think of you standing that day before the altar . . . crowned, with your sword stretched out, taking your oath to save Carpathia in her need.

The King Or die.

The Queen Or die. And riding back with the crowd cheering you!

The King It didn't.

The Queen Henry . . . I heard it!

The King It yelled at me. I might have been a circus. But they weren't very cheerful yells. The war was going badly. Was there much to choose between that noise and the shouting in the square the night they bombed Grandpapa's statue . . . the night we ran away?

The Queen And I wish we'd died rather!

The King It seemed the sensible thing to do . . . to give the Democrats their chance.

The Queen Much they made of it!

The King But it may have been my chance . . . to be a king and not a puppet for five minutes . . . and to die. It so seldom occurs to the well-meaning man that sometimes the best service he can do the world may be to get out of it.

The Queen Cyril would have revenged us when he grew up.

The King The silly sort of thing he'd have found expected of him! (*She is sitting by him now, and he puts a friendly hand on hers.*) But as we did very sensibly make a bolt of it, I wish it amused you more now to think of us togged up as chauffeur and lady's maid . . . though anything less

like one than y o u looked! The man at the barrier was a
fool not to spot you.

The Queen (*miserably*) I believe he did. Why else did he
grin?

The King I never thought of it! Yes . . . they were all
glad to be rid of us.

The Queen I try not to let little things humiliate me.

The King I drove the two hundred and thirty-five miles in
nine hours and forty minutes . . . and we stopped once for
petrol. There's nothing humiliating in t h a t.

In sudden surrender to Fate she breaks out . . .

The Queen Henry . . . why don't you abdicate? Send to
Madrassy and tell him you'll abdicate. I'll never say
another word about it to vex you. You can run the farm
and enjoy yourself. And we're still fit to bring up the
children, I suppose.

The King No . . . while they're all supposed to be
squabbling about m e I can't abdicate. No . . . if that
flying man can be ready I shall go back tomorrow.

The **Queen's** *spirits leap from misery to hope; to ecstasy
almost.*

The Queen To Eisenthal?

The King No, Rosamund! My dear . . . I've said No to
that so many times. Please don't suggest it again.

The Queen But you can't go to Karlsburg . . . as things
are.

The King Not very well.

The Queen Where will you go, then?

The King I'm considering. (*He rings the little telephone on
his table.*)

The Queen But w h y?

The King Zapolya's an old fox! I won't have civil war started. Stephen must come to heel. And I must have a good talk with Madrassy.

The Queen He'll have you murdered . . . if he gets the chance.

The King I don't think so.

The Queen Of course he'll have you murdered.

The King No . . . No . . . it wouldn't do.

The Queen He could hang the man that did it.

The King Rosamund . . . don't be so tortuous.

The Queen He's a traitor! He's a Republican! He's a trickster and a Socialist! Why shouldn't he have you murdered?

The King . . . or so passionate! You set me defending people I disapprove of . . . and it warps my judgment.

The **Queen** *accepts the situation – whatever it puzzlingly is.*

The Queen Very well! I think you ought to fight . . . and I think it's wicked to stop men fighting in a good cause. But we'll go.

The **King***'s eyebrows lift.*

The King You can't go.

The Queen I shall certainly go.

The King I'll take Guastalla. It'll be a risky journey . . . whatever happens when I get there.

The Queen Do you expect me to sit here and wait? I'm your wife, Henry . . . even if I might be a better one.

The King My dear . . . if we both came to grief the children would be left pretty helpless.

The Queen I'm sorry . . . I'm not that sort of a mother.

The King Well, perhaps they're not that sort of children . . . as they're yours.

They are now standing affectionately together. Her eyes, he sees, are filling with tears.

The Queen You think if I come I'll upset everything. I know I'm unpleasant to people. I wasn't always. It's this life here. I know I worry you! I try not to! You're so patient! I wish you weren't. You think me a fool!

The King Far from it. I think you t a l k nonsense now and then. But we all do that. And you're often right by instinct when my judgment's wrong. I only wish you didn't want me to be something I'm not.

*The **Queen** dries her eyes and breaks out in humorous desperation.*

The Queen You're so g o o d, Henry!

The King (*whimsically*) That's against me, I admit.

The Queen And I want you to be great . . . and I mean you to be. But I never forget, I hope, that I'm only your wife and the mother of your children.

The King You're a bit of a child yourself, you know.

The Queen So are you!

*And **Guastalla** comes in, answering the bell, to find them laughing happily at each other. He has put on his uniform, and his manner is now, surely, all that could be desired.*

Guastalla Your Majesty rang?

*The **King** is dismayedly apologetic as he says . . .*

The King Oh . . . have you changed! You'll have to run down to your hotel again to get in touch with Dod. I'm so sorry. And I must send a couple of messages through our friend in Karlsburg. We'll do that first. Bring your cipher. We shall want some money. That means a letter to Paris.

Guastalla They're opened now, Sir, whichever way I send them.

The King It won't matter much.

No bustle so pleasant as that which ends indecision, wisely or no. **Guastalla** *vanishes. The* **King** *is at his table, businesslike. The* **Queen** *surveys him with such puzzled affection.*

The Queen Oh . . . I wish I understood you! You're not a coward . . . and you won't fight. You argue like a lawyer . . . and let anyone get the better of you. You ask everyone's advice and agree with all they say . . . and now you do this foolhardy thing.

The King It's the right thing to do. You can come if you like.

She might be a child promised a treat; sedate, though, in her pleasure.

The Queen Thank you, Henry. I must go and kiss Teresa good night.

The King Don't tuck her up for five minutes. I'll be there when I've sent these telegrams.

He has a note-block and pencil in hand; and he turns now to consult the map again. She comes up and gives him a shy little kiss on the cheek before she leaves him.

Act Two

A salon in an eighteenth-century Carpathian chateau, built under French influence, of course. It is a beautiful room; but it is now incongruously furnished with a kitchen table, five or six old wooden chairs and a grand piano, and there are no curtains to the long windows that give upon the terrace. One can tell that pictures have been taken from the walls; and the glass chandelier has been badly smashed. The place has in fact been looted; only the grand piano was too cumbrous to be carried off. At right angles to the windows, a double door opens into one of the other salons; at right angles to this a small doorway in the panelling leads along the corridor.

It is late afternoon.

At the kitchen table, where they have evidently been having some sort of a rough meal, sit **Countess Czernyak** *and her daughter* **Dominica**. **Countess Czernyak** *is fifty or over; and, by her face, one may tell her for a woman who has come, through whatever storms, into an autumn calm that is very beautiful, who is content now to be a sensitive, tolerant, humorous observer of the world.* **Dominica** *is young and has spirit, the livelier for its being under control. Both she and her mother are dressed for a journey.*

Dominica . . . so if you don't want that grey silk, Mamma, I could dye the stuff and it would do for a dinner dress.

Countess Czernyak There might be other things in those old trunks.

Ella, **Countess Czernyak**'s *maid, comes in; a buxom young woman in her twenties. She also is dressed for a journey. This* *can hardly account, though, for her present excitement, which good manners hardly suppress.*

Dominica Well, next time we come . . . ! Ready to start, Ella?

Ella If you please, my lady, there are three strange people in the garden. Yes, just ready! And the Colonel has got his gun . . . so I thought I'd better warn you. I hope the coffee wasn't very nasty. He says he gives them while he counts ten to say who they are and then he shoots. It's the only way now he is alone here, he says.

Dominica What are they like?

Ella One's dressed as a woman. Oh . . . !

Countess Czernyak God be good to us . . . it's the Queen.

It is indeed the **Queen***, who, weary and dusty as from tramping the roads, has appeared at one of the windows.*

The Queen Oh, my dear Ja-ja . . . at last!

Ja-ja*, we find, is* **Countess Czernyak** *(it is a nursery name the children gave her; she was their 'official governess' in the old Court days); and the* **Queen** *is ready to fall on her neck in relief.*

Countess Czernyak We'd given you up, Ma'am. We've been here since the day before yesterday.

The Queen The King and Guastalla have gone round the back way . . .

With a gasp, and as if moved by the same spring, **Dominica** *and the buxom* **Ella** *vanish down the corridor.*

The Queen What's the matter?

Countess Czernyak Nothing, I hope.

But for her fatigue, the **Queen***'s nerves might be still more on edge.* **Countess Czernyak** *is calm, but her lips are pressed tight – and tighter as, in the near distance, a shot is heard.*

The Queen What's that? What has happened?

Countess Czernyak We'd better wait here now . . . till we know.

But the **Queen** *realises what it might mean.*

The Queen Oh, Ja-ja . . . that couldn't happen! Yes . . . it could!

Countess Czernyak Here's somebody.

We hear steps down the echoing corridor and, to the **Countess's** *unspeakable relief, the* **King** *comes in. The* **Queen** *shuts her eyes, crosses herself, and, to our knowledge, says nothing. The* **King's** *uniform is as dusty and travel-stained, even more; but he is in high spirits. He has been followed into the room by* **Dominica**, *who now grasps a kitchen poker.*

The King It's all right. No one's hurt. How are you, Countess? He had me covered. Guastalla let fly at him from the back of the dustbin . . . missed him by an inch! And were you coming for us with the poker?

Dominica I broke the window, Sir. I saw he couldn't hear me . . . !

The Queen Who was it? Who did it?

The King I don't know. He apologised. Nice old man! There's no harm done. Took us for brigands! Well, we look it.

Countess Czernyak I'm so sorry, Sir.

And, as far as his Majesty is concerned, that ends that.

The King Sit down, my dear . . . you're dead tired. But here we are . . . safe and sound . . . at last!

Countess Czernyak We'd given up hope of you . . . we were just leaving.

The Queen How long since we left?

The King It's twenty past five now by Swiss time. We got up from the aerodrome at a quarter to six yesterday morning. Thirty-six . . . thirty-five hours and a half. Not so bad . . . considering!

The Queen We had to come down in a fog . . . and sleep by a haystack . . . and wait all this morning while Guastalla and the Englishman went trying to find oil. And now we've walked ten miles.

Countess Czernyak You've had no dinner! There's nothing in the house, Ma'am, but scraps. But the car can go to the village.

The Queen Give me some coffee.

The King I'm not hungry. We've been eating sausage and cheese and raw onion all day. Most sustaining!

Colonel Guastalla *now arrives, laden with three rucksacks; the contents of two of them he empties on the table.* **Countess Czernyak** *is managing to wash out a coffee-cup for the* **Queen**. *She and* **Guastalla** *greet each other with friendly formality.*

Countess Czernyak Sugar, Ma'am?

The Queen Please.

Guastalla Countess!

Countess Czernyak Colonel!

The King Well, Countess . . . where's Madrassy?

Countess Czernyak He was here by midday yesterday. He has been gone two hours.

The King Can't be helped! He came, anyhow . . . and came quick. And where's your belligerent son?

Countess Czernyak Was Stephen to come here too, Sir?

The King If he got my message.

Dominica *hands the* **Queen** *her coffee.*

The Queen Thank you, Dominica. You're looking very pretty. When did I last see you?

Dominica Two years ago, your Majesty.

The Queen Long years, my dear!

Countess Czernyak Did Dr Madrassy know?

The King Yes.

Countess Czernyak He said nothing. There's been no word from Stephen. I've had not a word from him since he went to Eisenthal four months ago.

The Queen How's that, Ja-ja?

Countess Czernyak Letters would be stopped, Ma'am, in any case. There's a price on his head. It's placarded all over Karlsburg. They pasted one up in front of my window.

The Queen Time we were back, indeed!

The King He could get here safely enough. Madrassy came alone?

Countess Czernyak With a secretary . . . and another car full of detectives.

The Queen (*scornfully*) Detectives!

Countess Czernyak Nobody seems to know hereabouts . . . or to care much . . . w h o's governing the country.

The King It all looked so peaceful from the air. I know now just what it feels like to be Providence . . . and preside calmly over everyone's troubles. A pity we had that breakdown . . . but we could not keep our bearings.

The Queen Captain Dod did wonders, I'm sure . . . but I do think he found it all much too amusing.

The King I've enjoyed the jaunt thoroughly so far. And you were splendid. Now the dull part begins. What's this, Guastalla? (*He is at the table surveying the packages.*)

Guastalla The Paris code, Sir. I couldn't manage much but money and papers. But I could drive back for the bigger things now. Dod must stand by his machine.

For the first time the **Queen** *becomes aware of the strangeness of her surroundings.*

The Queen What h a s happened to this room, Ja-ja?

The King Are you on the telephone?

Countess Czernyak *manages to answer both questioners at a time.*

Countess Czernyak It hasn't been put back, Sir. Well, we saved the big Velasquez, Ma'am . . . it's rolled up and hidden in the laundry . . . and some of the Sèvres. But of course there was a lot of looting. They took the telephone wire and the posts to make fences.

Guastalla There'll be one in the village, Sir. It's probably working.

Dominica The detectives were using it yesterday. Mamma . . . why not take the Velasquez back with us?

Countess Czernyak My dear . . . what should we do with it?

Dominica Sell it to the Jews. We could now.

Dominica *should not, first, talk to her mother, except very indirectly, in the* **Queen's** *presence; secondly, she should not be so flippant. The discipline that follows, though kindly, is cold.*

The Queen Dominica.

Dominica Yes, Ma'am.

The Queen Put my cup down. You've grown a little wild.

The **King** *is now bending over a map.*

The King If he only left two hours ago he can't be back in Karlsburg yet.

Countess Czernyak He was to stop and dine at Gratz, I think, with the Cardinal Archbishop.

This is altogether too much for her Majesty.

The Queen With the Archbishop!

The King Good! He can wait for me there. No! His car will be faster than yours, Countess.

The Countess Much.

The King He'd better come back here to me, then . . . detectives and all! Be off, Guastalla! If you miss him at Gratz . . . well, we'll see.

Countess Czernyak Let Dominica drive you down, Colonel. The car knows her!

Guastalla Thank you.

Dominica, *curtseying to the* **Queen,** *departs.* **Guastalla** *follows her.*

The King Her Majesty will sleep here, in any case, Countess.

Countess Czernyak It'll be a harder bed than the haystack, I fear, Ma'am.

The King A troublesome house party for you. Sorry! I didn't know you'd be so put to it to entertain us.

Her Majesty's indignation now boils over.

The Queen Madrassy! You made him a minister and he betrayed you. He betrayed his fellow-traitors. He has been leagued with murderers . . . and he left them to their fate. And he's dining with the Archbishop!

The **King** *is busy over his map; and philosophical.*

The King Yes . . . the world's like that. I must get hold of Stephen somehow . . . and quickly. I must have a light on this map.

Countess Czernyak We've a big table in there, Sir.

The King Any notepaper?

Countess Czernyak They were writing all day
yesterday . . .

The King Don't trouble.

*He carries his map into the other room. With a certain
formality – which does not in the least traverse her gentle
affection for the* **Queen** *–* **Countess Czernyak** *asks . . .*

Countess Czernyak What can I do for your Majesty?

The Queen Nothing, dear Ja-ja. But it's like old times to
hear you ask that. Sit down. Shut the door first . . . we
mustn't disturb the King. Now tell me all your news.
Letters and newspapers only tantalise one. The children
are nearly well again. I thought for three days Sophia
would catch chickenpox too. So hard to isolate them in
that wretched villa. A sensible little doctor . . . did
everything I told him. But, oh, what a country! Crevices
between rocks! What a climate . . . and what people! I got
bronchitis in June. But I'm quite strong now.

If **Countess Czernyak** *smiles at this sequel to 'Tell me all
your news' it is inwardly.*

Countess Czernyak I've heard every now and then from
Frederika Bozen . . .

The Queen A good creature. Clever with her needle. A
little selfish! Do you think I ought to have let Margaret
cut her hair?

Countess Czernyak She sent begging me to beg you to let
her.

The Queen They all think Ja-ja has still only to say the
word! She'd set her heart on it. But it looks so . . . up-to-
date.

*Dusk is falling; and in the dimmer light the room looks yet
more stark and bare. The* **King** *returns.*

The King Better not leave this money lying about!

The Queen How much did you bring?

The King A million marks . . . a hundred thousand francs' worth. And a hundred thousand francs . . . which may be two million marks more by tomorrow morning.

The Queen I don't understand that.

The King If the mark slumped six weeks ago at the rumour that Madrassy was parleying with me . . . what will it do when it hears I'm back? May I have that candle?

It stands on the piano, stuck in a wine bottle. **Countess Czernyak** *lights it for him.*

The Queen It ought to go up!

The King Yes . . . that's what a loyal mark would do! You've not seen this morning's paper?

Countess Czernyak No, Sir.

The King Our leaving must have leaked out by now. Thank you.

Countess Czernyak Forgive the candlestick.

The King They'll censor the news here, I suppose.

He goes out, his hand protecting the faint candle-flame. **Countess Czernyak** *sits by the* **Queen** *again.*

The Queen I'm sorry you had to receive Madrassy here. But the King thought it best.

Countess Czernyak I had some interesting talks with him, Ma'am.

The Queen Really! You couldn't have found much to agree upon.

Countess Czernyak That made them the more interesting.

The **Queen** *gives her a sidelong glance – and changes the subject.*

The Queen You must be very proud of Stephen.

Countess Czernyak Yes. When he was a naughty boy . . . and very naughty . . . one was proud of him somehow, still.

*The **Queen** is not too pleased with her friend's tone. She puts a plump question.*

The Queen And you're glad to see us back?

Countess Czernyak It's like old times, Ma'am.

The Queen Then why don't you seem glad? Ja-ja . . . things m u s t have changed if you've changed!

Countess Czernyak No, Ma'am . . . I'm too old to change. You can count on me.

The Queen I'd no idea your home had been so wrecked. Why did you never tell me? The Russians are savages . . . and always were . . . though one can't say that now.

Countess Czernyak They were only here a day. Our troops began it.

The Queen Are you sure? Who says so?

Countess Czernyak They were retreating . . . they'd been beaten. And when you're beaten . . . if you've any strength left . . . it's a relief to smash something. I daresay they thought that if they didn't do it the Russians would.

The Queen I begged the King to punish all that propaganda in the army.

Countess Czernyak I came back as soon as I heard . . . and by then our own people from the farms were looting. When they knew I was packing what was left here they came in a crowd. And I stood in this room, Ma'am, and saw it wrecked round me by men and women I'd known, some of them, as children . . . and I'd tried, I did think, to be kind to them. One or two wanted to stop it . . . and one of them snatched back a silver Madonna they'd taken . . . I suppose he thought I valued it. They killed him . . . there by that window. His own brother helped to kill him.

(*There is a moment's empty silence.*) I walked through the village yesterday . . . I'd not been here since. They smiled at me . . . they were kindly. I believe they've forgotten. Better so.

The **Queen** *is really fond of her.*

The Queen Poor Ja-ja! We'll build it all up again.

Countess Czernyak No, Ma'am . . . I mean to leave it like this while I live. I shan't be coming back often . . . Dominica's so busy in Karlsburg . . . and we've a comfortable, ugly, little flat there. But I find myself here among the wreckage. For my life's like this, Ma'am.

The **Queen** *almost shakes a finger.*

The Queen That's morbid.

Countess Czernyak One mustn't complain. We lucky ones have been borrowing prosperity for these few hundred years. But the older the debt the less one likes paying.

The Queen And that's Dr Madrassy talking, I think.

Countess Czernyak Oh no, Ma'am! . . . it's not at all the sort of thing I say to him. We were arguing about French poetry most of the time. He'll have none of these new young Catholics . . . but I think there's a lot in them.

The **Queen** *hardly hears this; she too is finding something of herself in the wrecked room.*

The Queen I dreamt last night . . . I woke with such a jump and the moon was shining on me . . . about that last Birthday ball . . . d'you remember it? . . . before the War. I think of it so often . . . the men in their uniforms and all those pretty girls kissing my hand. Oh . . . surely that wasn't just show! It meant something, didn't it? What has happened to them that they've done nothing to set the world right again? Not a thing . . . till Stephen shames them! What h a s happened to them all, Ja-ja?

Countess Czernyak Some are living on what they've got left . . . and some are in Paris. Some are earning their living.

The Queen Well . . . as things are . . . we mustn't blame them for that.

Countess Czernyak Here and there they haven't done badly. Andrew Palffy's a partner in the Bibiena Bank. He says he blackmailed the Levinskys into making him one . . . though what worse he could tell about them than everyone knows, I can't imagine. He gives his friends work. My sister Kate does typing there.

The Queen (*kindly*) She was always so practical.

Countess Czernyak Little Countess Sarkotie runs a teashop. You remember, Ma'am . . . she used to fancy herself in a cap and apron handing cups round at bazaars. Oh, sometimes it has made no real difference. Hilda Lenygon's professionally disreputable now . . . all but! . . . and I begin to respect her.

Her Majesty is not amused.

The Queen And you still cut your jokes . . . which I always appreciate. Will you have my rooms made ready now, please? I may be able to lie down for an hour.

Countess Czernyak Very good, Ma'am.

It does indeed seem like old times. **Countess Czernyak** *rises, curtsies and goes. Left alone, the* **Queen** *lights a cigarette. The* **King** *comes from the inner room. He has a written sheet of notepaper in his hand and is waving it about to dry it.*

The King You didn't bring your fountain pen?

The Queen No.

The King This ink's atrocious. Cigarette to spare? I've smoked all mine. And there's no blotting paper.

She gives him – and he achieves the lighting of – a cigarette, the letter still in his hand.

The Queen Time we were back indeed! I wish we were going on to Gratz. I'd like to tell the Cardinal Archbishop what I think of him.

The King Cardinals, alas, care less than most people what one thinks of them . . . unless, of course, one's the Pope!

The Queen This money you've brought . . . it's not the kind without your head on it, I hope.

The King My dear . . . there's no other kind now.

The Queen Your money is the real money, surely.

The King There's a Karlsburg restaurant has its walls papered with hundred mark notes with my head on them.

The Queen You've told me that before. I don't think it amusing.

The King Do you want to hear my letter to Stephen?

The Queen Now that you're back every other sort of banknote should be burned.

The King The banks would be much obliged to us.

The Queen Why?

The King Aha! You should have read that little book on currency I sent up to you when you were ill. A banknote is a note of the bank's debt to its holder. Therefore if you burn it . . .

No; after thirty-six hours of aeroplane, haystack and cross-country tramp, she really cannot!

The Queen Never mind! I'm sure there's trickery somewhere.

The King Well . . . there often is! (*He has waved the letter dry, and now starts to read it . . .*) My dear Stephen . . .

The Queen Don't you write a letter of this sort in the third person?

But he too is weary enough to be shorter of patience than usual.

The King No, I don't! I've known him from a baby . . . and after three sentences my grammar goes all to pieces. Do let us be sensible.

The Queen Henry . . . here we are . . . dropped out of the air . . . helpless . . . ridiculous! Look at you . . . and I've not had my hair done since yesterday. But you're God's anointed and I'll die with you if need be. We should think of that, and not try to be . . . sensible.

He puts a gentle hand on her rumpled hair.

The King Dear heart . . . you're worn out.

The Queen I'm not . . . I'm not! I'll sit with my eyes shut for ten minutes. At least we've a roof to cover us.

On his way back the **King** *notices, among the others on the table, a little packet tied up with pink ribbon.*

The King What on earth's this?

The Queen Two Grand Crosses of St Anne and five Second Class St Andrews. They were in the cupboard in your bedroom. I thought they might be useful.

This most happily restores him his sense of humour.

The King I daresay they will be.

He goes to finish his letter. It is almost dark now, and the flickering candlelight casts, through the half-open doors, queer shadows about the bare room. The **Queen** *sits motionless; her eyes closed. After a moment* **Colonel Hadik** *appears at the little door. He is old, and more than old; the life of the body has lost its meaning for him. He is dressed in rough country clothes. But, whatever his birth and breeding, he is an aristocrat, and would look it whatever he wore. Silently though he comes, the* **Queen** *senses his presence and opens her eyes.*

The Queen What is it?

Hadik I beg your Majesty's pardon . . . I thought
Countess Czernyak was here.

The Queen No.

He bows and is going, when . . .

The Queen Are you the caretaker?

Hadik Yes, Ma'am.

The Queen Was it you that fired at his Majesty?

Hadik No . . . I recognised him in time, Ma'am.

The **Queen** *has now become fully aware of him.*

The Queen Were you always a caretaker?

Hadik No, Ma'am. My name is Hadik. I was Colonel and
chief instructor in Ballistics at the Military Academy. The
Peace Treaty closed it.

The Queen I know. Are you related to Countess
Czernyak?

Hadik Her cousin, Ma'am.

The Queen What are Ballistics?

Hadik The mathematics of gunnery, Ma'am.

The Queen But have you no pension?

Hadik There are . . . so I'm told . . . to be old-age
pensions for all when the Budget is balanced. But I am not
counting on that. May I look for Countess Czernyak now,
Ma'am?

The Queen She is giving orders about my rooms. Who
else is here in the house?

Hadik No one, Ma'am . . . except, for the moment, her
maid. They will be moving your Majesty's bed into the
State Apartments . . . and I had better help. It is only my
camp-bed, I fear. But it is not uncomfortable.

The Queen Thank you, Colonel. I disapprove of your being in this menial position. I shall tell Countess Czernyak so. And those responsible for your neglect will be punished.

Hadik I am content, Ma'am. I want no one punished.

The Queen But how can you manage? What do you do?

Hadik I study mathematics still. In the higher mathematics lies knowledge that has hardly yet been cursed by man's use of it. I can still work in the garden. I need only bread besides . . . and a little wine. I'll kill a man in self-defence if I must. I do not justify that. But such is the nakedness of our nature . . . of which I am no longer ashamed. May I go now and help move that bed, Ma'am?

As she does not answer – for indeed she is at a loss for further comment and she is not accustomed to reiterating her wishes – he bows and goes. After a moment the **Queen** *calls . . .*

The Queen Henry!

. . . and the **King** *appears in the doorway.*

The King Yes, my dear.

The Queen The man that shot at you is Ja-ja's cousin and a Colonel of Ballistics at the Military Academy . . . and he's the caretaker here . . . and he's quite mad. What has come to this country?

The King But he didn't. Guastalla shot at him.

The Queen Dear Henry . . . don't be so literal!

The **Queen** *leans back again and closes her eyes; the* **King** *disappears.*

★ ★ ★

The room is now sufficiently lit by a new and very brassy oil lamp, bought in the village evidently. In the **Queen's** *chair – the only fairly comfortable one – sits* **Countess Czernyak** *asleep, and settled to sleep, if we may judge by the rug she spread over her knees that has now slipped down. There is light in the other room too, as we see when* **Colonel Guastalla**, *coming out, quietly opens the half-door. And from it – between this opening and a closing as quiet – comes the sound of voices, high in argument. Two we know; the third is a strange one. It is* **Dr Madrassy**'s. *So he is back from Gratz and his dinner with the Cardinal Archbishop, and some hours must have passed.*

The King's voice But my good Madrassy . . . here we are . . . two men with wills of our own . . .

Madrassy's voice Helpless, Sir, I assure you!

The King's voice Nonsense!

The Queen's voice And very wicked nonsense!

Guastalla *is crossing the room to the little door in the panelling; but he sees that the rug has fallen to the floor, and he comes back to pick it up. As he puts it over the Countess' knees she opens her eyes.*

Guastalla It grows chilly about now.

Countess Czernyak What is the time?

Guastalla Twenty-five past four.

Countess Czernyak Will they never have done?

Guastalla Nothing harder, is there, than to agree to disagree!

Countess Czernyak We might all have been in our beds . . . if we had any . . . hours ago.

Guastalla Who's for the top of the piano?

Countess Czernyak You can toss for it with Dr Madrassy.

Guastalla *gives – one cannot think why – a grim little smile.*

Guastalla He shall have it if he'll stay.

Countess Czernyak Why do you keep fidgeting in and out like this?

Guastalla Come now . . . I didn't wake you the last time. We want an evening paper. The enemy's chauffeur may have one.

Once more the half-door opens and again **Madrassy***'s voice is heard, more emphatically this time; the interview is evidently coming to a full close.* **Guastalla** *slips quietly away.*

Madrassy's voice. Very well, Sir . . . we've said all the sensible things we can say. We'll part . . . and do the least foolish possible.

With which rather calculated farewell, he takes leave of their Majesties and joins **Countess Czernyak.** **Dr Madrassy** *is a man of sixty, the scholar turned politician. His exact, fastidious mind makes the brutalities of politics seem more brutal by its clear recognition of them, and offers itself as a sacrifice to their brutality. Not a happy man, therefore! Only a sense of the need for going on sustains him; only the salt of a bitter humour lets him palate life for the time at all. He closes the door and stands looking at* **Countess Czernyak** *as in mute appeal for understanding, though not sympathy. All her response is . . .*

Countess Czernyak What made you suppose they'd go back without more ado . . . looking ridiculous . . . feeling ridiculous?

Madrassy I didn't! But I had to give them the chance to. I haven't spared them. I always liked him. Broken loyalties lie heavy on a man.

From the inner room come the **King** *and* **Queen.** *The dispute is taken up as if it had never been interrupted.*

The King You won't force me to fight you, Madrassy, and don't think it.

Madrassy It won't be my policy to begin, Sir.

The King I am not a puppet in Czernyak's hands . . . and you've no right to doubt my word.

Madrassy You can sensibly do one of two things, Sir. Be off back again. Or head this rabble from Eisenthal . . . blaze your way to Karlsburg . . . and try me as a traitor when you get there . . . if you catch me.

The Queen You are a traitor, Dr Madrassy . . . and if his Majesty had you taken out and shot here and now you'd have no right to complain.

The King Nonsense! If we're to come to that Madrassy could better have me shot. He has a dozen men here.

Madrassy I shan't, Sir. I've my reputation as a moderate man to keep up. But after this most compromising talk to you I'll be getting back to Karlsburg, if you please, to reconstruct my Cabinet . . . while I still can.

The Queen By bringing men into it who've boasted they'd have us killed like vermin if we dared set foot in our own country again!

Madrassy Yes! The only way left me, Ma'am . . . now you've done so . . . to stop them doing it.

Colonel Guastalla *has returned, a newspaper in his hand.*

Guastalla A three o'clock edition, Sir. Racing tips mainly. But the mark has started sliding.

Madrassy And now I'll be told that I held back the news while I speculated. Czernyak's advance leaking out has done it, I suppose.

The **King** *wheels round.*

The King Has he advanced? When?

Madrassy Early this morning. He'll be in Zimony by tomorrow.

There are times when his Majesty can lose his temper; and, for a moment, this looks like being one of them.

The King We've been talking for two hours . . . and you never tell me that.

Madrassy *smiles his wryest smile.*

Madrassy I thought you knew, Sir . . . and didn't know, perhaps, that I did.

The King Then he has never had my message. I sent him strict orders not to move a man.

Madrassy He got it. A little late . . . but in time to obey you. We tapped it . . . but I had it sent on.

The King Zimony! How far from here, Guastalla?

Guastalla Sixty miles.

The King And where's Czernyak himself at the moment? Perhaps you can tell me that.

Madrassy On his way here with a dozen cars and fifty men to try and capture me. And if I wait much longer he will.

The King He will not. I am responsible for your safety.

Madrassy Thank you, Sir . . . I won't risk it.

The King D'you think I knew such a trick was being played on you?

Madrassy No need you should. But Colonel Guastalla was in and out a good deal while we were talking, I noticed.

The King Did you know of this, Guastalla?

Guastalla *owns up – and with confident rectitude.*

Guastalla Count Czernyak passed Pfalz with eight motor cars an hour ago, Sir.

His Majesty is speechless; **Madrassy** *is very cool.*

Madrassy Pfalz? The road's trenched and wired ten miles on.

Guastalla Yes . . . I'm waiting to hear if he's through.

He faces Dr Madrassy squarely. Hostilities are evidently commencing, while the King looks on. But now they are all conscious that Colonel Hadik is on the threshold, pausing there as if he had not expected such a roomful.

Hadik I beg your Majesty's pardon.

The King No . . . come in.

He says this amicably enough; how has poor Colonel Hadik offended? – who now does his errand, speaking more to Countess Czernyak than to anyone, yet, somehow, not exclusively to her.

Hadik Dominica would like to know whether she shall bring in some hot malted milk and biscuits. The kitchen stove is lit.

Madrassy Which means perhaps that he is!

The King Does it, Guastalla?

Guastalla Yes, Sir.

The King How perfectly childish!

Madrassy But I congratulate your Majesty upon so efficient an Intelligence Service! How have you worked it, Colonel? Are my fellows asleep? They ought to have warned me.

Guastalla They're at the telephone in the village. Czernyak's headquarters has wireless. We've been picking up Morse with our aeroplane set. The air's buzzing with news. It doesn't need much de-coding.

Madrassy He's two hours away still.

Guastalla About that.

The King Then have some malted milk before you go . . . as the stove is lit.

Colonel Hadik *gravely departs; and after this flash of sarcasm the* **King** *himself turns grave.*

You have done your duty, Guastalla, no doubt . . . but in future let me know what you're doing, please. I came back to stop this sort of folly . . . not to profit by it. When I've stopped it I'll be off again . . . I give you my word . . . if there's no more use I can be. Run your Republic . . . who cares? . . . if you've turned republican . . . why not? But if I were the fool or the trickster you seem to take me for, I'd surrender my sword to the first soldier you could send against me with honour enough to . . . ! By the bye, Guastalla, I must have a sword. Why was mine left behind? (*He speaks of it as John Citizen speaks of his umbrella.*)

Guastalla In the hurry, Sir. I'm sorry.

The King Well . . . find me one somehow. Rosamund, do sit down . . . then we all can. I'm dead tired.

The **Queen** *does not know whether she is standing or sitting; her body is weary, but her spirit is afire. She sits down, however; and the rest dispose themselves,* **Guastalla** *near the* **King**, **Countess Czernyak** *discreetly apart.*

The Queen Dr Madrassy . . . was there ever a moment when you meant to give us back our own?

The King Better have been frank with me!

Madrassy Old habit clings, Sir. We never were very frank with you. If Czernyak hadn't played the fool . . . or if you'd been content to let him . . . ! If you'd been patient till these new people with money to spend had begun crying out for a king and a court again . . . ! They're a vulgar lot, though . . . you wouldn't have liked them. But remember . . . it's little more than a year yet since the red flag was flying over Karlsburg.

The Queen And you were saluting it.

Madrassy As it happens, Ma'am, I never did . . . I never had to. While the Red Terror raged I was down with rheumatic fever . . . and through the White Terror that followed I had shingles.

The Queen How lucky for you!

Madrassy Yes . . . I used to lie awake at night with the shingles and think so.

The Queen Were you in the Revolutionary Government or not?

Madrassy To this day, Ma'am, I don't know. I was Minister of Education . . . and nobody bothered about such amenities . . . or about me. They were shooting and hanging people and in far too much terror themselves to think of anything else.

The Queen You could have resigned . . . on principle.

Madrassy. No. On principle . . . it's the only one I've clung to . . . I never resign. Perhaps I was dismissed. Perhaps someone reappointed me when the tumult was over. I had a bed in my office and telephones by the bed. And if anyone came to talk politics my secretary said that whatever I'd got was undoubtedly catching. My staff stuck to me . . . a sound lot . . . and the work went on somehow. And through Red Terror and White Terror not a school in the country was closed.

The **King** *smiles gravely.*

The King You're proud of that?

Madrassy Yes. I'm proud of that. I don't suppose the children were taught much. But we fed them a little and kept them off the streets . . . street sights weren't pretty just then. When I did get out of bed I found my dear countrymen weary of Red Terrors and White Terrors too. Reconstruction was the cry . . . which meant that we all sat round trying to guess what would happen next.

Dominica Czernyak *has now brought in the malted milk in cups on a tray and is handing one to the* **Queen**. **Colonel Hadik** *follows with a tin of biscuits.*

The Queen Thank you, my dear. Aren't you very sleepy?

Dominica Oh no, Ma'am . . . it's all much too exciting.

Madrassy And I guessed right.

The **King** *gets his cupful.*

Dominica The one with the spoon is your Majesty's. It has sugar in.

The King Thank you.

Madrassy So I found myself my country's saviour. And really . . . considering . . . I've not done so badly.

The Queen You're an opportunist, Dr Madrassy.

Madrassy That is the word, Ma'am.

The Queen You were a defeatist in the war, I think.

Madrassy History had taught me the use men make of victory.

The Queen Are we much better off for being beaten?

Madrassy We've saved our souls alive. Little else, I know. But when your conquerors overreach themselves . . . as conquerors will . . . urge them to the extreme of their folly. You get your revenge . . . if that's what you want . . . the sooner. No biscuits, thank you.

Hadik Your car is waiting.

Madrassy Thank you. High time too! My fellows will be furious you've been too clever for them. Furious with me! They wanted to come half a regiment strong . . . with machine guns and searchlights and heaven knows what else.

He is gulping down his malted milk as he stands ready to go.
The **King** *rises too.*

The King So you must put me in the wrong.

Madrassy If I can, Sir.

The King You're not jealous of my coming back to make
peace? I apologise for asking.

Madrassy A little jealous. I'm human.

The King Not afraid for your job?

Madrassy I've a wife and children to keep.

The King Is there nothing reasonable we can agree to do?

Madrassy Much, Sir. But by tomorrow you'll have
borrowed a sword . . . and if I've a good word for you I'll
be out of office the day after.

The King Who are these gentlemen that want to hang me
that you want for colleagues?

Madrassy Brisgau, Bruckner . . . and probably Medrano.

The King Activists all?

Madrassy I must hook them if I can. I must keep them
quiet somehow.

The King Is this the Bruckner that shot the President of
the Assembly?

Madrassy No . . . that was Bruckner the Christian
Democrat. He has given up politics.

The King He was acquitted.

Madrassy Yes . . . but he can't get on with his party. Too
thorough-going! This one's a silent fellow. May I wish
your Majesties good night?

The King If you make me fight you I give you leave to
hang me.

Madrassy My work'll be cut out to stop my hotheads making me attack y o u, Sir. I shall isolate you at Zimony and cut off supplies. With six thousand men to feed you'll be looting the town in a day or so.

The King I shall pay for every loaf.

Madrassy A starving town won't sell food. So you'll have to surrender . . . or attack. I'm told, though, those Neustrian guns are no good. They need calibrating.

The King They'll not fire a shot . . . unless you fire the first.

Madrassy I'm the slippery politician, Sir . . . I don't fight. I hope you won't. But it may be your task to fight . . . if not to fight and win to fight and fail. To fight . . . knowing you'll fail . . . hating to fight and with no faith in fighting.

The King Pretty damnable doctrine!

Madrassy Is it? We must not be egoists . . . even in virtue. And if a few months' more ignorant war are needed in this war-rotted country to prove that such well-meaning people as you and I, Sir, are none of us any use here . . . the price must be paid. What has our credit with our fellows or ourselves or with history to do with it? Good night, Countess.

A little quiet mischief is in **Countess Czernyak**'s *response, mischievous friendliness almost.*

Countess Czernyak I hope Stephen won't catch you.

Madrassy I hope . . . after your kindness . . . that I shan't catch him. May I have back . . . if you've done with it . . . that little pamphlet on rickets which you thought might keep you awake? I must thank the author for sending it to me.

She finds it for him.

The King Rickets?

Madrassy Rachitis, Sir . . . a very common child's disease
. . . due to under-feeding. It came as I was leaving . . . I
read it on the journey . . . with a letter from its eminent
author thanking me for the chance I gave him to examine
our Karlsburg school children while the Peace Treaty was
in the making . . . when they were dying like flies. Well
. . . we know all about rickets now . . . so he tells me. I
only hope it's true. That much reality made sure of! We
do wring a little knowledge from the God above our
warring gods. A bitter fruit . . . but sound. Good night,
Sir.

Dr Madrassy *departs,* **Guastalla** *accompanying him but
almost immediately returning. The* **Queen** *rises, relieved of the
burden of such a presence.*

The Queen A perverse mind! You've given him his
chance. He's a beaten man . . . and knows it!

The **King** *is at his map again; it still lies on the table.*

The King Plucky of him to come back though, and risk
being caught! Pfalz . . . sixty miles. Stephen should be
here by seven. Zimony . . . fifty . . . fifty-five. Guastalla
. . . take notes, please.

The Queen Colonel Hadik . . . what is calibrating?

Hadik The adjustment of the bore of a gun, Ma'am.

The Queen Is it hard to do?

Hadik Given the machinery . . . no, Ma'am.

The Queen We must make the machinery.

The King We shall want more money. Can we keep in
touch with Paris? Yes . . . we've our backs to the frontier.

Guastalla Paris will keep in touch with us, Sir . . . as long
as they want to provide it.

The **Queen** *has seated herself at the piano, and she begins to
strike resoundingly magnificent chords, which after a little
resolve themselves into the last dance of Borodin's* Prince

Igor *ballet*. *The* **King**, *concentrating his tired mind, is moved – even he! – to protest.*

The King Oh, my dear Rosamund . . . at this time of night!

The Queen I feel alive again.

The King Is Zimony friendly, I wonder. We must have a proclamation out before Czernyak's troops arrive.

Guastalla I could start now . . . if you'll draft it . . . and knock up a printer early.

The King You must have some sleep.

Guastalla I shall manage. You'll send Dod there with his aeroplane? He's keen as mustard.

The King He knows there'll be no fighting?

Guastalla He can drop propaganda . . . and there'll be reconnaissance . . . and he'll look dangerous up aloft. It'll all help.

The King Very well. Now then! To my people . . .

The **Queen** *has relapsed to the slow movement.*

The Queen D'you remember this, Henry . . . at the Opera in Zurich . . . on my birthday? And I cried . . . we felt so lonely . . . with that crowd of Swiss staring at us.

The King I remember. To my people . . .

The Queen Dominica . . . the piano's out of tune.

Dominica Yes . . . it must be, Ma'am.

The Queen Very bad for it. Have it seen to.

Dominica Yes, Ma'am.

Guastalla *has brought the lamp to the table to concentrate its light on the map and his notes. We hear her Majesty at the* *piano plainly enough. The rest of the assemblage are discreetly in the shade.*

The King To my people . . .

The Queen And did you know, Henry, that your state charger is in the farm stables here?

This really does interest the **King**.

The King Snowjacket!

The Queen Ja-ja bought him from the dealer they sold him to. Colonel Hadik gives him exercise.

The King How does he go, Colonel? He was always doped when I got on him.

The Queen Henry!

The King My dear . . . if you'd ever been drifted sideways down the street . . . saluting and saluting . . . with brass bands blaring at you! Thank you, Ja-ja . . . it was like you.

Hadik He needs corn, Sir.

Guastalla is intent on the map now, and the soldier in him speaks.

Guastalla Suppose Madrassy does attack us, Colonel?

Hadik Occupy the station and the bridge.

The King Surely they could shell us out of that.

Hadik They've no big guns, Sir. Their seventy-five's a pretty thing . . . six batteries of them! And it carries my range-finder . . . which your Majesty was once good enough to praise. I have the letter you wrote me.

The King Did I? Have you? That's right! You must come along too . . . and give us good advice.

The Queen And will you please see, Colonel Guastalla, that Snowjacket goes to Brantomy?

Guastalla I'll do my best, Ma'am.

The King My dear Rosamund!

The Queen Do trust my judgment . . . in some things.

*The **King** makes another try at the proclamation. The **Queen** plays on.*

The King To my people. Relying only upon the justice of my cause . . . (*His inspiration flags.*)

Countess Czernyak Won't you go to bed, Ma'am? It's nearly five.

The Queen In a minute. I'm not tired.

*Having said so, however, she discovers that she is – and indeed has some right to be – simply extenuate with fatigue. It is creeping on them all. And now the **King** looks up to find **Colonel Hadik** at his side, trembling a little, anxious to speak.*

Hadik Would your Majesty perhaps give me some less responsible appointment? I was proud of my guns once . . . but I am not very wise now. I could still fight . . . but you never know who guns kill . . . and I think now it may not be right to . . .

*The old man trembles more and more. **Countess Czernyak** comes to give him a reassuring touch on the arm.*

Countess Czernyak Basil . . .

Hadik If I might wait upon your Majesties . . . as a servant . . .

The King You shall do whatever you like best to do, my dear Colonel.

*The kind voice steadies him. The **Queen** has stopped playing now.*

The Queen How still!

The King Well, these will be the main points. Peace at home and abroad . . . due observance of Treaties with hope of readjustment . . .

Guastalla I have your draft of a year ago, Sir, if that'll help.

The Queen Your poor beautiful home, Ja-ja! But we'll build it up.

The King I'd like to say something different if I could. Adherence to League of Nations . . . good government under Constitution . . . union of all classes and parties . . .

He goes on trying to find something different to say, while the **Queen** *strikes a few last, desolate, single notes before she betakes herself to the camp-bed in the state apartments upstairs.*

Act Three

The King did establish his headquarters at Zimony railway station. Though all the engines were got away when orders came from Karlsburg to cut the line, one or two coaches were left; and these, drawn up to the platform, serve their Majesties to live in. Cramped accommodation certainly; but by putting up two rough wooden hoardings between the coaches and the platform wall, a spacious, though rather draughty, ante-room is made. One of the waiting-rooms has contributed a large table and some chairs; so it serves its purpose well enough.

Sitting round the table, at the moment, we find the **King,** **Colonel Guastalla** *and* **Dr Madrassy.** *Besides these there are* **General Horvath** *and his aide-de-camp;* **Count Stephen Czernyak** *and* **Mr Bruckner.** *The table is ranged with papers and pens and ink; a conference is evidently in progress, over which the* **King** *is presiding.*

General Horvath *is an old soldier, upon whose more military virtues good living and an easy good nature have told, by the look of him, pretty severely. A gentleman withal. His aide-de-camp is remarkable for nothing but the extreme correctness of his uniform.* **Stephen Czernyak** *is a man in the early thirties; handsome, not merely nor necessarily in feature, but in virtue of a certain nobility of spirit that informs him; there is something of the panther about him, his strength seems a coiled-up spring; he is a born leader of men, though where he will lead them is another matter.* **Mr Bruckner,** *who (with* **Dr Madrassy**) *is the only man not in uniform, might be passed over by a casual observer, and might for a while defeat the curious, so closely can he wrap himself in dull taciturnity. He can sit at such a meeting as this immobile and apparently indifferent, till his presence is forgotten. He prefers to have a paper or a book to rest his eyes upon, for when he looks at you* *there is a brooding strength in them that you do not forget. He is plebeian, but not vulgar; the temptations of the flesh pass him by. We are at a pause in the proceedings.* **Guastalla** *is busy writing and the others sit silent. But there is an unrelaxed tension to be felt, a sign that all is not over. After a moment the* **King** *speaks, a touch of suppressed impatience in his tone.*

The King Finished, Guastalla?

Guastalla Just about, Sir! '. . . and except for the matters here set down, either party . . .' Receives?

Madrassy Reserves. I write a shocking hand, I fear.

Guastalla (*as he copies on*) '. . . reserves full liberty of action.' Finished, Sir. Shall I read it over?

The King Yes.

Guastalla 'Protocol of armistice concluded at Zimony railway station November 11, 1923. Present: His Majesty King Henry, Count . . .'

Czernyak His Majesty the King of Carpathia.

Guastalla *pauses. No one takes up the challenge. After a moment the* **King**, *catching* **Guastalla**'s *eye, says quietly* . . .

The King Go on.

Guastalla '. . . Count Stephen Czernyak, commanding his Majesty's forces; Guastalla, aide. On behalf of the Government established at Karlsburg, General Horvath, Dr Madrassy, Mr Bruckner . . .' (*To the aide-de-camp.*) I fear I haven't your name.

The aide-de-camp confides it to him voicelessly.

The Aide-de-camp Papp.

Guastalla (*noting his badges*) Captain.

The Aide-de-camp Yes.

The King I think we can take it as read. I'll sign.
Guastalla and Captain . . .

Guastalla Papp.

The King . . . can certify copies while you and the
General mark your maps, Czernyak, and make your
dispositions. Here?

The document is before him.

Guastalla Yes, Sir.

The King Give me a pen that will write.

Dr Madrassy *hands his own fountain pen to* **Guastalla**, *who
gives it to the* **King**, *who signs.*

The King Now, General.

The document passes in turn to **General Horvath**, *to*
Stephen Czernyak, **Dr Madrassy**, **Mr Bruckner**; *and they
sign it. Meanwhile the* **King** *has himself handed the pen back
with a courteous* . . .

Thank you, Dr Madrassy.

And the signing over, he rises abruptly with a . . .

Good afternoon, gentlemen.

*As he passes towards the railway carriage they also rise,
respectfully and silently;* **Mr Bruckner** *is a bit behindhand in
this tribute. As the* **King** *mounts the steps, however,* **General
Horvath** *breaks forth in a voice that has echoed over many a
barrack-yard, mellowed now by time and five courses for
dinner.*

Horvath Your Majesty!

The King Yes?

Horvath Will your Majesty now permit me to express the
most profound regret that circumstances should have
brought me into apparent conflict with your Majesty? I
have endeavoured to combine duty to my country with all

possible respect for your Majesty personally. And I pray that from this moment the spectres of discord and anarchy . . .

The King I make no complaint, General . . . nor need you feel self-conscious. I hope your wife is quite well, by the way.

Horvath I thank your Majesty . . . she is pretty well.

The King My compliments to her, please.

He goes into the carriage. His tone has been – and for the first time since we knew him – slightly acid. But **General Horvath** *was too deeply moved by his own oratory to notice that. He turns to find* **Stephen Czernyak** *looking at him with the politest contempt. But he does not notice this either.*

Czernyak Will you come to my office, General? Our maps agree, I expect. I can show you the doubtful place from the top of the signal-box if your glasses are good enough. I've broken mine.

Horvath At your service! What I said to his Majesty surprised you, Count Czernyak . . . vexed you, Madrassy.

Madrassy Not at all!

Horvath It came from my heart. This is an honourable armistice for all concerned. (*To* **Czernyak** *again.*) You'd have liked a little fighting first. I understand that. You're young. But what is the object of war? The making of peace. You tell me we've been Europe's laughing-stock, sitting facing each other these three weeks . . . and not a shot fired. No, Czernyak! Between fellow-countrymen . . . a bloodless campaign, brought to a creditable conclusion . . . rightly thought of, what can be more glorious? Where is your office?

Czernyak Fourth door down the platform. The Ladies' Waiting-Room!

Briskly and impressively the **General** *departs. His intellectual diet, one fears, has also been rather debilitating. He must have* *fed full upon stories of iron-handed soldiers with the hearts of children, upon praise of the soldier as the true enemy of war and the like. The ghastly fiasco of the Great War being over, he now prefers to see himself in this light; a very fine light too!* **Guastalla** *finds that* **Captain Papp** *is waiting with perfect politeness, in the most correct of attitudes. He responds with . . .*

Guastalla I'll follow you, Captain Papp.

So **Captain Papp** *follows his chief. He out of hearing,* **Czernyak** *allows himself the slight relief of . . .*

Czernyak I thought you and your colleague had come to do the necessary twaddling, Dr Madrassy.

And he follows. **Guastalla** *meanwhile has opened the door in the opposite hoarding: he now calls through . . .*

Guastalla Dod!

Dod's voice Hullo!

Guastalla Conference over! (*Then, returning, to* **Madrassy**.) Captain Papp is a fair specimen, is he, of your new army officer?

Madrassy Very.

Guastalla What relation . . . forgive me! . . . to the General's tailor?

Madrassy A good guess. He's his son.

Guastalla Old Horvath never did pay his bills!

Captain Roger Dod *appears: an Englishman in his thirties. Good health, good temper, unselfconsciousness and tolerance, and a cheerful ability to turn his hand to anything and do it well enough – and to enjoy doing it – are his passport all over the world.*

This is Mr Roger Dod . . . who flew us from Zurich . . . commands our air force . . . edits our official gazette . . .

distributes our propaganda. Dr Madrassy is anxious to meet you.

Dr Madrassy's *manner is cool in the extreme; but if he thinks* **Dod** *cares a rap for that he is much mistaken.*

Madrassy We are flattered, Mr Dod . . . just to say to you personally what I said to the British Minister about you some days ago . . . by the interest you take in our country's affairs.

Dod Don't mention it, Sir. I'm enjoying myself.

Madrassy I don't doubt that. You've been dropping on us nothing deadlier than pamphlets and newspapers so far.

Dod They've done a bit of damage, I hope.

Madrassy Are you author-in-chief as well?

Dod Bless you, no! I only run the team. All the bright young spirits we could comb out who've a turn for literature. Quite a few! And it keeps them out of mischief.

A young officer comes in and salutes.

Guastalla What is it?

Young Officer Lieutenant Vida, Sir . . . asking for Count Czernyak.

Guastalla In his office.

Young Officer And would his Majesty see Mr Nagy?

Guastalla The Mayor?

Young Officer Yes, Sir. He has been waiting about since twelve o'clock. And the old farmer wants to know if his Majesty means to take his evening walk round the farm.

Guastalla He can wait.

Young Officer He won't wait, Sir. It's milking time.

Guastalla Ask Colonel Hadik then. He's inside.

The **Young Officer** *passes on into the railway carriage.*
Guastalla *turns to go.*

Madrassy I must telephone the text, please, to Karlsburg
as soon as it's verified.

Guastalla I've nowhere less draughty to ask you to wait, I
fear.

Madrassy You can't be very comfortably installed.

Guastalla There were houses in the town for the asking.
But her Majesty won't leave headquarters.

Madrassy A train without an engine. Symbolic! Is the
famous Snowjacket still in his horse-box?

Guastalla He was kicking it to bits. Too much corn. He's
out at grass.

Madrassy Symbolic indeed!

The **Young Officer** *comes from the railway carriage and
speaks to* **Guastalla**.

Young Officer Will y o u please see the Mayor, Sir?

Guastalla Curse the Mayor! I'm busy.

*So whether he will or won't is not quite clear. He departs,
however, and the* **Young Officer** *follows him.* **Dod** *takes up
the thread of his own discourse, as if it has not been
interrupted.*

Dod No . . . politics aren't my pigeon. I don't really know
what all this row's about. Nor is journalism.

Madrassy You have a gift for it. You have added
appreciably to the confusion of the public mind.

Why waste these delicacies of sarcasm?

Dod But your king's a good fellow . . . and I'm for him.
And the country's for him, my belief is . . . if you'd give
it the chance to say so. We've fought clean at least.

Couldn't you have censored that caricature of the two of
them . . . riding bareback into Karlsburg?

Madrassy It w a s vulgar.

Dod It was vile. If at any time you care to introduce me to
the fellow that did it I'll have pleasure in horsewhipping
him.

Madrassy The world looks like that to him . . . and I find
the groups of people round the kiosks grinning at his
grossness begin to look like that to me. Your view of life is
a prettier one, I'm sure. But is it any truer?

Dod I don't see what that has to do with it. Good
afternoon.

With which most British remark **Dod** *leaves them. Not one
sign of interest has* **Mr Bruckner** *shown so far in the
proceedings; and there is a shade of irony in* **Madrassy's** *tone
as he turns to him now – for, really, such silence seems almost
a pose.*

Madrassy Well, Bruckner?

Bruckner *looks up to ask in his turn with matter-of-fact
readiness.*

Bruckner Back to Karlsburg tonight?

Madrassy Or finish the business while we're at it?

Bruckner You and his Majesty seem to get along
famously.

Madrassy What do you make of him?

Bruckner We'd better have forced him to fight.

Madrassy Suppose he had beaten us?

Bruckner How sorry would you be?

Madrassy When I do go over to the enemy . . . I shall
hope to take you with me.

Bruckner That's a bargain.

This little duel of edged humour is brought to an end by the **King**'s *return, cap on head, stick in hand, on his way for a walk evidently.* **Dr Madrassy** *rises to ask . . .*

Madrassy What time will it suit you, Sir, to renew our discussion?

The **King** *turns, most amiably.*

The King Now, if you like. I was only going for my walk. I want some tobacco . . . and I've a few serious words to say to my bootmaker. Why don't you come too . . . both of you? Or would it compromise you to be seen with me? What have we to discuss?

Madrassy The week's none too long to turn round in. There are various questions. We shall demobilise when your Majesty has disbanded . . . not before. You'll need transport.

The King Come . . . you can find us transport. Back to railhead, at any rate! The men must be got home comfortably.

Madrassy Then there are your personal plans.

The King True.

Madrassy What are they?

The **King** *is frankness and simplicity incarnate; and surely, they think, there must be something behind this. Is there?*

The King Well . . . I gave you my word I'd be off again once this trouble was ended . . . if I found I wasn't wanted. Thanks for your help . . . and yours, Mr Bruckner . . . in ending it so harmlessly.

Madrassy You're content to be off?

The King No . . . I'm not. I've had a happy time here . . . playing at soldiers . . . and at being a king again. And I don't want to boast . . . but we've been quite popular. You're not . . . so I gather . . . in Karlsburg, for the moment. Money market hectic . . . trade upset . . . strikes to be settled! And you're to blame . . . because you're there to be blamed. A soulless city! But here it has been all quite simple and human . . . and I've felt at home. For, indeed, I am! However . . . if you're sure I'm not wanted . . . I gave you my word.

Bruckner Who wants you, Sir . . . and what for? That's the question. Can you answer it? We'd have to . . . if we weren't to get rid of you once and for all now while we can.

His Majesty seems to become simpler and franker still.

The King I suppose we've all lain awake a night or two at some time hoping the morning might bring us an answer to that. Well . . . the power and the glory are yours nowadays, Mr Bruckner . . . and I hope you'll enjoy them! I get on with my fellow-man. I'm afraid that's my only gift. But I really like the creature . . . Homo sapiens, you know . . . even when he isn't . . . and he usually isn't . . . I like him! (*From his place at the head of the table he picks up the blotting pad; and on it . . .*) Here we have him complete . . . head, body, two arms, two legs! Sitting in Council and listening by the hour . . . I used to find myself drawing him again and again . . . like this . . . and wondering what he'd say to it all. For you gentlemen that govern him . . . and there are so many of you nowadays . . . despise him, don't you? He knows that. You flatter him . . . because you're afraid of him . . . and you come at last to hate him. He knows! He can't do without you for the moment. But it's a sort of comfort to him . . . tussling with life . . . to feel that there's one fellow-creature, at least, free enough from the tussle to want nothing from him . . . not even his vote . . . who'll wish him well now and then with a word or two, if that's all there's the chance to do . . . and no questions asked. A most unpretentious job! But . . . strip it of its flummery . . . it might be a real job still. However . . . I gave you my word.

Being answered, **Mr Bruckner** *makes no further remark. But he keeps his eyes on the* **King** *for a little.*

Madrassy Switzerland won't receive you again, Sir.

The King That complicates matters.

Madrassy And we've our conditions to make now for letting you go.

The **King** *looks from one to the other before he asks, with a smile . . .*

The King Abdication?

Bruckner Yes.

The King Is this wise of you? It wasn't in the bargain. You won't let me go unless I formally abidcate. But if I don't want to go . . . suppose I say No?

Madrassy How can you? In a week's time . . . with your men dispersed . . . you'll be helpless.

The King While I've breath in my body I can still say No.

Madrassy The answer to that, Sir, is one I don't want to make . . . even in words. Nor does Mr Bruckner, I feel sure.

But the **King** *will have none of 'It hurts me more than it does you.'*

The King But why not? You could retire again . . . with whooping-cough, perhaps, this time . . . to your Ministry of Education, while they tried me and shot me. Your views upon regicide, Mr Bruckner, are very practical, I understand. There's no surer way, of course, to bring back my son in my place able to make a clean sweep of the lot of you. But you'll have thought of that.

Madrassy Does it follow, Sir, because nothing could be sillier than to make a martyr of you . . . that we shan't do it . . . shan't have to do it whether we like it or not?

The King Madrassy, you won't frighten me . . . and I'm sorry you think you can. But you'd depress anyone . . .

friend or foe! Are you really so helpless? Is this what
democracy has come to? Are you sure I'm not wanted here
. . . are you quite sure?

*Through the door in the hoarding there approaches somewhat
diffidently* **Mr George Peter Nagy,** *the* **Mayor of Zimony.**
*A plump little robin redbreast of a man, all that a mayor
should be.*

The Mayor Most humbly begging your Majesty's pardon.

The King Not at all! Come along, Mr Mayor. Sorry
you've been kept about. Seen Colonel Guastalla?

The Mayor The Colonel was too busy.

The King He is busy for the moment. Quite right to come
to me, then. What can I do for you? Do you three know
each other? Dr Madrassy . . . Mr Bruckner . . . Mr
George Peter Nagy, Mayor of Zimony.

The Mayor Perhaps your Majesty will be good enough to
tell me . . . since no one else takes the trouble to . . . if
everything has been settled . . . what is settled about u s?

The King Why . . .

Before he can get further **Stephen Czernyak** *returns, enough
of angry import about him for the* **King** *to ask quickly* . . .

What's wrong, Stephen?

Czernyak's *eyes fall on the* **Mayor;** *a pleasing civilian object
for any soldier in a rage.*

Czernyak Oh . . . you've sneaked in, have you? Just as
well! Horvath insists he may occupy the town, Sir. I
object. You support me, may I take it?

The King After four hours' talk . . . aren't we clear about
that?

Czernyak I think so. He's not to advance his troops.

Madrassy The town's on our flank, does he say?

Czernyak A trick, was it?

Madrassy We settled in Council before we left that whatever happens we were to occupy. I told Horvath to be precise. He said he hated to hurt your Majesty's feelings.

If the **King** *did not scent trouble ahead he might laugh outright at this.* **Czernyak**, *meanwhile, rounds furiously on the* **Mayor**.

Czernyak And you told General Horvath this morning, did you, that you'd welcome his troops?

The Mayor I did.

Czernyak (*to the* **King**) The thanks you get, Sir, for not billeting and requisitioning. The town has been in bounds, Dr Madrassy, for five hundred men a day . . . and only side arms carried . . . so that this fellow's tradesmen could rob them at leisure . . . while we've been lying out in barns and pigsties.

Madrassy And you've been running my blockade, Mr Mayor.

The Mayor We have. I couldn't let the town starve . . . and hungry soldiers wouldn't have sat quiet here very long. They'd have been at our throats first and at yours next. But it has been a pretty poor blockade. I've not been so certain you didn't mean us to run it.

Madrassy You must not accuse me of duplicity, if you please.

The Mayor Everything has cost more in consequence, of course!

The **King** *cannot let this pass unappreciated.*

The King I take off my hat to you, Madrassy. But why did you say you would welcome the troops, Mr Mayor?

The Mayor Because he told me he meant to march in on me whether I liked it or not. So what better c o u l d I say?

Czernyak Can you and your kind never think of anyone's interests but your own?

The Mayor It's not for me to indulge in fine feelings at this town's expense. I'm not made Mayor for that. Give me my own choice . . . I'm for his Majesty.

The King Thank you, Mr Mayor.

The Mayor It stands to reason! I look up to your Majesty . . . and that makes it easier for others to look up to me. And your Majesty . . . and her Majesty, I must say . . . have been most affable. A good deal affabler than ever the Mayoress and I can afford to be. And here's real history going on. I could wave a flag with the best. But then again . . . what's all this to-ing and fro-ing f o r? To do us plain folk good . . . if what we're told is true. We thank you. Zimony was fought over in the War . . . you won't expect us to forget that, will you? We've built it up again . . . not so different to what it was. Leave us the good we've got . . . that's all we ask. This country's a bit sick of these squabblings and manœuvrings . . . if I may say so . . . and we did hope your Majesty's coming back meant that you'd just say the word . . .

The King What word, Mr Mayor?

The Mayor Ah . . . well . . . there! People come quarrelling to me . . . I listen . . . I've got to. I let them talk till they're tired . . . there's not much else I can do . . . and as often as not they don't seem to know what they're quarrelling about. And I say to myself: Now, there ought to be some word . . . ! But if your Majesty doesn't know it . . . I'm sure there's nobody does. Well . . . if it's still not settled what's to happen to us, I must wait till it is. Honoured and obliged by this interview, your Majesty, General and gentlemen, I'm sure. (*The* **Mayor** *departs, carrying off, we must agree, the honours of the discussion.*)

The King He has done his best for everybody, has the Mayor. You must see he doesn't suffer, Madrassy.

Czernyak Meanwhile, Sir . . . is Horvath to put his troops in the town? With his guns over the river . . . when the armistice ends he could tell us to surrender or shoot us to bits.

Madrassy Shall we have Horvath back and discuss the point, Sir?

The King Certainly not. We settled and signed. Tell General Horvath from me that as a soldier and a gentleman I expect him to behave like one.

Madrassy We shall have to override him, then.

The King You may. You won't override me.

Madrassy If we'd brought up the point, Sir, you'd have yielded it.

The King How do you know?

Madrassy Now that you're beaten . . .

Czernyak We're not beaten.

Madrassy . . . your troops may get out of hand.

The King Nonsense! I give you my word to keep order in the town.

Madrassy If we'd chosen to fight . . .

Czernyak Well . . . you didn't.

Madrassy But if you mean to disband when the week's over, Sir . . . what difference does it make? Be reasonable!

The King Here are men ready to give their lives for me. And you ask me to put them to shame before you? They shall go home as honourably as they came.

Madrassy I can't give way now. And I don't go back to Karlsburg, Sir, without your word that you'll abdicate.

The King Or your loyal colleagues will be saying that I've bribed or cajoled you. Mr Bruckner's a witness I don't try to. Isn't that what he's here for? Or will he be suspect now? I condole with you both. I'd sooner sweep a crossing than make one with such a crew.

Madrassy Do you mean to make us fight you . . . after all?

The King Give me choice of weapons . . . yes, I'll fight you and beat you! And you'd thank me.

Madrassy Well, Bruckner?

Mr Bruckner *takes a second or so to consider.*

Bruckner We'd better go and talk to Horvath.

Madrassy Can we load the blame on him? I'll try if you will. There's his professional pride to reckon with. Ours . . . as you say, Sir . . . is to save our skins.

These scholastic ironies do not interest **Mr Bruckner**, *and he has gone.* **Dr Madrassy** *follows. He can hardly be out of hearing before* **Czernyak** *lets loose with . . .*

Czernyak Sir . . . Sir . . . break off with them! They've given us the chance. Send them packing. Give me my head now and I'll have you in Karlsburg in a week. I can do it! Horvath's been blabbing. His command's at sixes and sevens . . . rotted with politics. It may be a bloody business with the regiment on our flank here. But mop that up . . . the rest won't fight. They might come over . . . be thankful to have gentlemen to officer them again. Bruckner thinks so . . . you can see. He's had a quiet look round and he's for backing down. And what the devil do you want?

This last is to **Lieutenant Vida**, *who has appeared, saluting.*

Vida Sorry, Sir. Didn't know you were with his Majesty.

The King Never mind!

Vida Bakay's here, Sir.

Czernyak I can't bother with him now.

Vida Very well, Sir. His sentence was read to his battalion. They didn't take it well.

Czernyak What do I care? Keep him locked up till tomorrow.

Vida Very good, Sir. Have you ordered the goods-siding guns to be shifted?

Czernyak No.

Vida I thought perhaps you didn't want these gentlemen from Karlsburg to get too close a look at them.

Czernyak Massimo has done it on his own account. Quite right.

The King Who's Bakay? What's he sentenced for?

Czernyak Our crack sergeant-major. Six months' cells, isn't it?

Vida Yes, sir . . . for spreading disaffection.

Czernyak I'll have to let him off. We've no place left to put him. How many in the sheds now, Vida?

Vida Thirty-four I think.

Czernyak Keep the fellow about. I may find time for him.

Lieutenant Vida *salutes – smartness itself; discipline seems good under* **Stephen Czernyak** *– and goes.* **Czernyak** *turns to the* **King** *again, as if there'd been no interruption.*

Czernyak For God's sake, Sir! Before they give in and send back to tell me! It's our last chance. Take it . . . for God's sake!

The **King** *is looking at him affectionately; but he shakes his head.*

The King We must wage a war for you some day . . . against the heathen.

Czernyak Very well. Since you came I've obeyed orders . . . I can do that. But I don't understand you, Sir. Every chance we've given you . . . you've thrown away. It's

wicked! I'll say it . . . if it's no use to say it. You don't
want to win.

The King I want to do more than that now.

Czernyak But disband us . . . you've nothing left even to
bargain with.

The King I can't bargain. You think I'll never get to
Karlsburg unless I fight my way there. You're a soldier
. . . you must think so. But men, remember, are held
prisoners of their success . . . they walk ever after in the
way of it. These two . . . Bruckner . . . Madrassy!
They're in power . . . and helpless . . . prisoners of the
men that keep them there. Helpless, we may find soon,
not to bring their guns up and start blowing us to bits . . .
though they don't want to . . . they know what comes of
that in the end. If I let you start blowing them to bits,
dear Stephen . . . I may ride Snowjacket into Karlsburg in
triumph . . . but I should be a prisoner of that power.

Czernyak It seems to me, Sir . . . once you win . . . no
matter how you win . . . you can have your own way
after.

The King Do you believe that? I recommend you not to
believe it. When I'm rid of you all, I'm not sure I shan't
walk to Karlsburg. It's only sixty miles . . . and a straight
road. Who could stop me? The people would be friendly.
And when next I open Parliament I shall walk down the
hill from the Castle . . . frock coat, top hat, with an
umbrella if it's raining. That's half a mile, no more. The
police could keep the street clear. Will it be very
unkingly?

Czernyak Not if you do it, Sir.

The King Worth trying . . . d'you think?

Czernyak I don't believe in miracles, I fear.

The King Nor I. And I don't know the Mayor's magic
word. It would be the natural thing to do. You don't

believe in my divine right, Stephen. But the fact is . . . if
I haven't that, I've no other. Nor has any man. This time
I must put it to the proof. I'll be off for my walk round
the farm now. If they don't knuckle under . . . those three
. . . you can send for me. But I fancy they will.

And the **King** *departs, leaving* **Czernyak** *to set his teeth to the
worst. He rouses himself as one does to carry on routine, and
calls . . .*

Czernyak Orderly!

*The door in the hoarding through which all the main traffic
has been passing (the one opposite that of the* **King**'s
departure) opens. Almost before the orderly can appear . . .

Have that prisoner sent in.

The door closes. **Czernyak** *drops into a chair and sits
brooding. Meanwhile his mother has appeared at the railway-
carriage door.*

Countess Czernyak She wants news, Stephen.

Czernyak We've signed . . . but there's a hitch.

Countess Czernyak She won't stir out till they've gone.

Czernyak I'm to offer her Horvath's profoundest homage.

Countess Czernyak For heaven's sake, don't! She's up, at
any rate! Cousin Basil's playing chess with her. But I've a
mind to pack Ella home and sprain my ankle and take to
my own bed. Then she'd have her clothes to brush, at
least. This is a bitter business for you, my dear.

*A few years ago – for he is still young enough – the last words
would have broken him down; a few years hence he might
soften to them. Now he only sets his teeth the harder.*

Czernyak I'd not have asked him to thank me, even! I
wish she were the man.

Countess Czernyak She's not very wise.

Czernyak What does that matter?

Lieutenant Vida *now returns with his prisoner under guard, and* **Countess Czernyak** *discreetly stands aloof.* **Sergeant-Major Bakay,** *the prisoner, is a hard-bitten soldier with all the marks of long service on him. He fought through the Great War, evidently. He is disciplined to the last inch of self-control and can conduct himself with dignity even under these circumstances, though one can tell that he takes them very badly indeed.* **Vida** *hands* **Czernyak** *the paper with the man's sentence on it, and everyone stands to attention.* **Czernyak** *glances through the paper and then scowls at its victim.*

Czernyak Three days' field-punishment . . . ! Pleasant for his regiment . . . won't it be . . . to see their senior sergeant-major chained to a gun-carriage! And six months' cells . . . as and when possible.

Bakay I'd rather be shot, General.

Czernyak Who asked you what you'd rather be? Am I to waste good bullets on you?

Bakay We've not spent many of 'em so far.

Czernyak Hold your impertinent tongue when I'm talking to you! Why isn't the fellow's face washed before he's brought to me? Can't you be shut in a coal-shed for a few hours without messing yourself up like this? What sort of a soldier are you?

At this juncture **Roger Dod** *strolls back; but, finding a row on, he also discreetly stands aloof.*

Bakay Try me and see! Put me to fight, I say . . . which I came for. Bring a bull out of those fields and I'll fight it.

Czernyak You'll fight or not as you're ordered. And you won't ask why. You're fed . . . you get your pay.

Bakay And let's earn it honest . . . was all I ever meant . . . for that swine of a corporal to go peaching on me. He's for it . . . front or back . . . the first scrap that sees me alongside him. This whole countryside's making game of us. Push through then, I say . . . and show 'em. Let us loose a day or two in Karlsburg . . . and we'll show 'em. And let the cowards go home again . . . whoever they are!

The last three words show us well enough what **Sergeant-Major Bakay**'s *real offences of the tongue were.* **Czernyak** *now 'plays the game' with a vengeance – a vengeance on himself and the prisoner and all the world for having to play it.*

Czernyak Listen you to me. His Majesty is graciously pleased on the happy occasion of this armistice to remit your sentence. And I reduce you to the ranks. Cut off his stripes. Cut them off with that penknife here and now. Give him double fatigues. Set him digging latrines for a week. And I trust you're grateful.

As an experienced sergeant-major, **Bakay** *can at least admire the artistry of abuse.*

Bakay His Majesty's a kind gentleman, I don't doubt. And I'd follow you to hell, General . . . which I set out to . . . and you know it!

Czernyak Much obliged! See I'm told, Vida, when they want me in the office. Take him away. Wash his face!

Bakay *is removed. In the succeeding calm* **Dod** *strolls forward, and* **Countess Czernyak** *leaves the lobby of the carriage too.*

Dod Feel better? Nothing like a bout of slanging for expelling poisons from the system. Discipline's been amazing good though . . . considering. I give you full marks. A little sport might have helped. Or even theatricals! When bad blood's brewing set fellows to making fools of themselves!

Czernyak We've managed to give you a sporting enough time, I hope.

Dod Thank you.

Czernyak The whole business ordained by Providence, no doubt, to that end.

Dod Providence can beat you . . . and the rest of us . . . when it comes to irony, General.

Czernyak *surrenders to this impervious Englishman at discretion; he has a liking for him and some respect, too.*

Czernyak Have you settled on your next adventure?

Dod Yes. Air surveying in South Siam. Come along and learn to click the camera. You'll need a change. I must see this through, though.

Countess Czernyak How will it end, Captain Dod? As you don't care . . . perhaps you know.

Guastalla *arrives, in a bit of a hurry.*

Guastalla You're wanted.

Czernyak *gives him a glance; then, without a word gets up and goes. A glum silence falls.*

Dod Has the enemy given in?

Guastalla Oh, yes!

Dod Poor Czernyak! Cheer up . . . lots of queer things may happen yet.

Countess Czernyak They should never have come back. It was hopeless. That world has vanished. Why did you let them come, Colonel?

Guastalla How could I stop them? They had to try. I didn't think it was hopeless.

Countess Czernyak Then you didn't think.

*The worries of the affair – and they all fall on him, the bigger ones at second hand, the smaller quite his own – are beginning to try **Guastalla**'s perfect temper.*

Guastalla I'm not asked to think. I'm a shorthand typist with good table manners, warranted to look well in uniform.

Countess Czernyak He must abdicate now.

Guastalla She'd sooner die.

Colonel Hadik *has appeared in the doorway of the railway carriage, and he stands there as if listening — not to the now desultory conversation below him, however.*

Dod Of course I may be wrong in thinking I could settle the whole business in ten minutes if everyone concerned would only show a little common sense. But in my dear country we do learn to settle things. We're always scrapping . . . no harm in that! But no good in it unless you make friends after . . .

Hadik Did you hear gunfire?

They all turn at the sudden question — and stare; but **Colonel Hadik** *is an odd old gentleman.*

Guastalla No.

Dod No.

Guastalla The armistice is signed, Colonel.

Hadik So I'm told.

Countess Czernyak How goes the game, Cousin Basil?

Hadik I now give her Majesty a rook and a knight only. With patience she might make a player.

He does not move from where he stands, but listens still. The rest take up the train of their thoughts again; and **Dod's** *talk flows sententiously on.*

Dod Frontiers are your trouble. Frontiers make for xenophobia . . .

Guastalla For what?

Dod A pet of a word, ain't it? . . . and I know what it means! There's a lot to be said for landing in a country from the sea . . . especially if you've been sick on it . . . makes you feel friendlier to the foreign devil.

Countess Czernyak I see anarchy ahead here.

Guastalla The Powers might interfere then. I wish they would.

Dod That's when they won't. There's prestige in a little peaceful Occupation. But when bombs go off . . . and soldiers get nerves . . . and someone says Shoot . . . and you hit the wrong people . . . and the pacifists at home make a fuss . . . ! I say, Colonel . . . your ears are good. (*For now they have all heard it.*)

Hadik Our twenty-pounder with the faulty primer, that time, I should say.

Guastalla But nobody can be firing now!

Dod Whose car can I steal?

Hadik It's a mile away and more . . . coming into the wind.

Dod It's towards the town.

Dod *is already off and away.* **Guastalla** *calls after him.*

Guastalla Send word!

Dod Right!

Into the doorway of the other carriage comes the **Queen**. *She is pale and excited. She looks a tragic figure as she stands there, a long wrap thrown round her.*

The Queen There's fighting!

Guastalla Something's wrong, Ma'am.

The Queen They've attacked us?

Guastalla Our guns are firing.

The Queen Thank God!

Guastalla But we signed the armistice . . . not half an hour ago.

She does not hear this . . . or heed.

The Queen Ja-ja . . . we're fighting . . . we're not disgraced.

Guastalla Where's his Majesty?

Countess Czernyak He went for his walk.

The Queen There's another!

Guastalla Ours?

Hadik I couldn't tell.

Guastalla Will he hear them? Please don't stir from this spot, Ma'am. (**Guastalla** *goes after the* **King**.)

The Queen That last was closer, wasn't it?

Hadik The wind.

Colonel Hadik *has come down from the carriage doorway and in it there appears* **Ella, Countess Czernyak's** *maid, looking a little startled.*

The Queen They've tried to trick us . . . I prayed God they might . . . and we're paying them out. I thought first: Henry kept it as a surprise for me. Dear Colonel . . . did you think you'd never hear your guns again? And I'd taken your bishop . . . the one on the left. I was wondering where you'd gone.

Hadik You should not have taken that bishop, Ma'am.

More firing, evidently; and the **Queen's** *spirits rise higher still.*

The Queen Two together!

Countess Czernyak Get her Majesty's fur cloak, Ella. You mustn't catch cold.

The Queen I want my field-glasses . . . quick. We'll climb the signal-box . . . we can see lots from there. And another!

Hadik That makes the full battery.

Ella *having gone for the cloak,* **Countess Czernyak** *must needs go herself for the glasses. The* **Queen** *turns to* **Colonel Hadik** *again in childish joy.*

The Queen This waiting here . . . I don't know how I've borne it! We won't stop so long at the next station . . . will we?

Hadik Very undisciplined practice! I hope they won't fire Number Four again too soon . . . or they'll hurt themselves.

The Queen What's that queer buzzing?

Hadik Machine guns, Ma'am.

The Queen Let's get as close as we can.

She can wait no more, but is off just as **Ella** *appears with the cloak, which* **Colonel Hadik** *takes from her with . . .*

Hadik Give it to me, Ella. Stay you here.

And he follows the **Queen** *with it as* **Countess Czernyak** *comes out with the field-glasses and speeds after her too.* **Ella** *is left with eyes staring wide.*

* * *

Some little time must have passed, for though the dusk was gathering as the firing started, it would be quite dark now if the platform were not lit by the steel glare of the high-swinging arc lamps. The **Queen,** *glad enough (if she thought about it) of her fur cloak, is waiting, still and tense.* **Countess Czernyak** *is watching at one of the hoarding doors.* **Ella** *comes to the door of the railway carriage.*

Ella There's another motor car come back, please.

Countess Czernyak Whose?

Colonel Guastalla *arrives in all haste, and her Majesty pounces on him.*

Guastalla Here's the King, Ma'am.

The Queen You're to tell him they're not to blame. You're to praise them . . . you're to praise them!

Guastalla Ma'am . . . it's a terrible business . . . and a very difficult business. I beg you to be careful what you say.

The **King** *comes quickly in; and there is a look on his face that we have not seen before.*

The Queen Henry . . .

The King Fetch me my sword, somebody! Don't talk to me now, please. Where's General Horvath? Guastalla . . . Find Czernyak. He's to come here to me.

Guastalla General Horvath has just driven up, Sir!

The King Will somebody fetch me that sword?

They are all staring at the **King**; *and, no one else moving, with a half-articulate 'Yes, y' Majesty'* **Ella** *vanishes into the carriage.*

Guastalla I've not seen Count Czernyak, Sir. I'll send to find him.

Guastalla *departs. That word 'sword' has been music to the* **Queen**.

The Queen Henry . . . you're going to lead them! Oh, at last! You'll draw your sword and lead them!

The **King** *stares at her in blank angry amazement.*

The King Do you know what has happened?

She meets him with defiance.

The Queen Yes, I do.

The King Blackguards and brigands!

The Queen But not if you lead them! God's giving you another chance . . . to draw your sword and lead them. On your horse too . . . your white horse!

He rasps out a very harsh . . .

The King Nonsense!

The Queen I could!

And harshness turning cold . . .

The King Please try not to make a fool of yourself.

The **Queen** *cries out in despair.*

The Queen What does t h a t matter!

Stephen Czernyak *is here now; wrought to a desperate pitch, and controlled. He salutes and stands to attention as might any subaltern.*

Czernyak Sir?

The King What section began it?

Czernyak Battery A took their guns across the bridge about two o'clock.

The King Without orders!

Czernyak The men themselves.

The King No officers?

Czernyak Two went later, Sir. They didn't know the armistice was signed. It's fair to say that. Nor was it.

The King It was when the Kathy battalion went in.

Czernyak Yes, Sir.

The King Officers too.

Czernyak Seven, Sir.

The King They knew by then?

Czernyak I can't say, Sir.

The King You're their chief. You've no excuse?

Czernyak I don't make any.

Suddenly the **King's** *wrath blazes.*

The King Mother of God! Couldn't they at least find armed men to shoot at? None of Horvath's troops in the town?

Czernyak No, Sir.

The King Did you know t h a t, Rosamund?

He is met again with an obstinately defiant . . .

The Queen Yes.

Czernyak They went for the Town Hall. They didn't shoot at first. They warned all the women to stand clear. These tradesmen have been cheating them for weeks. They'd thought when we d i d advance . . .

The King There'd be looting.

Czernyak They're human. They want their own back. So did you, Sir.

The King Finish your report.

Czernyak They're barricaded now in the big square . . . where the White Hart Inn is . . . fifteeen hundred of them. I kept Horvath with me . . . and the telephone's cut, so his staff has had no orders yet . . . unless those politicians have chipped in . . .

The King And we gave him our word to protect the town if he'd keep his troops out of it?

Czernyak Yes. I sent for my own Eisenthalers to come and round the fools up . . . (*He stops. This is, to him, the worst of all.*)

The King Well?

Czernyak *can only make a helpless gesture.*

They won't stir!

Czernyak They're paraded. I've been talking to them.

The King Where?

Does his Majesty mean to see what he can do? **Czernyak**
checks him with the bitter chivalry of . . .

Czernyak No . . . don't, Sir. They've been talking to me
. . . some of them! I'd no answer. Give me my orders,
please.

The King I've no orders.

For the first time **Stephen Czernyak** *loses self-control.*

Czernyak I wish to God I were with them, then . . .
waiting to be shot! You've broken me, Sir . . . you've
broken me!

By this **Ella** *has returned with the sword. She has indeed been
standing with it at the* **King***'s side for several moments before
he perceives her.*

The King What is it?

Ella Please, your Majesty . . . the sword.

The King Thank you, Ella.

*Though he thanks her with his customary courtesy and takes
the trouble to remember her name,* **Ella** *is glad enough to be
off. A silence falls. The* **King** *stands there, sword in hand,
motionless. At last the* **Queen** *asks (though by the tone of her
voice we may guess she knows the answer) . . .*

The Queen What are we waiting for, Henry?

The King For General Horvath. Won't you go in?

The Queen No.

The King Very well.

Silence again. Then comes **Guastalla**, *ushering in* **General
Horvath**, *who is followed, shadow-like, by the correct*
Captain Papp. **Horvath** *is in a state of empurpled
distraction.*

Guastalla General Horvath, Sir.

The King General . . . my troops have mutinied and
disgraced me. I surrender my sword to you.

While **Horvath** *is recovering from the shock of this, we can just hear the* **Queen's** *low, bitter . . .*

The Queen God forgive us!

Horvath, *when he does recover, all but bursts into tears. Anything – anything sooner than take this sword that the* **King** *is holding out to him!*

Horvath Oh . . . please don't! No . . . I do beg your Majesty not to! Anyone else, of course, that's mixed up in it . . . if they'd like to surrender I'd be only too pleased . . . and to see they come to no harm. But not your Majesty. No . . . I really couldn't!

The King I am offering you my sword, Sir.

Horvath But I only took command . . . I told them . . . because I was devoted to your Majesty's true interests . . . and feeling in a sense I was still in your Majesty's service . . . for your Majesty's dear grandfather gave me my commission with his own hands . . . forty-six years ago in April. And how can I . . .

The **King's** *black rage has abated; but he is now very rapidly losing his temper.*

The King How much longer am I to hold this sword?

Horvath And everything can be settled quite simply. There are four inns in that square . . . and the silly fellows will all be drunk by tonight. And I've talked to the Mayor and he's most amenable. And if Count Czernyak will be good enough to help me I can arrest the lot without any trouble. And Madrassy will keep the worst out of the papers . . .

The **King** *can stand no more of it; he throws the sword on the ground with a great clatter and vanishes into the railway carriage. While this parley has been on,* **Dod** *and, a little later,* **Bruckner** *have arrived on the scene. Needless to say they do not obtrude themselves.* **Dod,** *one notices, has been in the wars. The* **King** *departed, that emblematic sword draws all looks to it, till the looker can break the spell. Then the*

Queen's *voice again ends the silence – though she is speaking half to herself.*

The Queen Common men do the brave thing. Why isn't it the right thing? I'm sorry they fired on the town. Why should they surrender? What happens if they won't? I hope they won't.

By this she has turned to **Horvath** *with something of her old defiant fire. He puffs protestingly.*

Horvath But they must! It's most irregular! We must have order. My own men may go next. The whole country's in such a state! But you're not to distress yourself, Ma'am. Count Czernyak and I will settle it all in the friendliest way.

He turns, and is most surprised to find the correct **Captain Papp** *at his heels.*

Where's Doctor Madrassy? Didn't you find him? Don't follow me about. Don't stand there like a tailor's dummy. Tongue-tied fool!

Poor **Captain Papp**, *at this cruelly appropriate placarding, turns and flees.* **Horvath** *feels a little better for his outburst.*

Your Majesty will excuse me . . . if I leave you.

As if they were back in the Palace and the old days had come again, he makes the ceremonial triple bow of leave-taking before he goes. No one else moves. They have their eyes on the **Queen**. *She must speak, she feels.*

The Queen Is there nothing left to do?

Then, suddenly, she begins to shake all over. **Countess Czernyak**, *who has not been far from her, comes up and touches her arm.*

Countess Czernyak My dear . . . how cold you are! Come in.

The Queen No . . . I'm not cold. (*With a great effort she steadies herself.*) Has much damage been done? Some to you, Captain Dod, I fear. How was that?

Dod It's nothing, Ma'am. I was helping put out a fire. An enraged old lady threw a chopper at me. The men had a gaudy hour of it. Not so many casualties . . . no one dead yet, I think.

The Queen Countess Czernyak will bandage you properly if you'll go in with her. We had everything ready . . . in case.

This, in all its courtesy, is a command; and without a word **Countess Czernyak** *and he go into the carriage. Once more she must speak.*

The Queen Are we prisoners?

Czernyak If Mr Bruckner will be good enough to pick up that sword.

No one so far has noticed **Mr Bruckner**, *commonplace and obscure in the background. The* **Queen** *looks at him now as she might at the incarnation of some dangerous disease that had just declared itself. He shakes his head, with what passes, on his countenance, for a smile, as who should say 'It's none of my business'.* **Guastalla** *interposes with . . .*

Guastalla May I present Mr Bruckner, Ma'am?

Mr Bruckner, *being presented, and becoming the centre of attention, proceeds deliberately and very forcibly and rather more elaborately to present himself.*

Bruckner Haven't we had enough of this foolery? If we've anything to fight about we ought to be fighting. If you still want to win you've a chance left. A long chance! But if it's your last . . . better than none!

The Queen What chance?

Bruckner As you h a v e started in . . . why not keep Horvath chatting a while and dash for the best of our guns? If you get them you might beat us. Not a pretty trick! But if you win you'll be whitewashed. And if you're not . . . you'll have won.

Guastalla His Majesty has surrendered.

Bruckner What does that matter? Lock him in . . . before we lock you in. Haven't you been itching to? Why didn't you . . . weeks ago? You might have been in Karlsburg by this. Now it won't be so easy. You can let him loose and stick a crown on him once you've landed him there.

All this leaves them dumbfounded a moment – well it may! Then, for all comment, comes Czernyak's cold . . .

Czernyak You had better find somebody, Sir, to pick up that sword.

Bruckner Very well.

He turns on his heel. But suddenly the Queen's voice stops him.

The Queen Mr Bruckner.

Bruckner Madam.

The Queen Are you laughing at us? Is this a trap?

Bruckner No.

The Queen I'm stupid, then. If it's good advice . . . why do you give it us? Suppose we take it?

Guastalla *gasps with horror.*

Guastalla How could we take it, Ma'am?

She appeals to Stephen Czernyak, who responds like a man half hypnotised.

The Queen Count Czernyak?

Czernyak It wouldn't be a very pretty trick.

The Queen Do you want us to win, Mr Bruckner?

Bruckner There are things I want less.

Guastalla Shall I fetch his Majesty, Ma'am?

The Queen No.

Czernyak General Horvath is waiting for me, Ma'am.

The Queen He can wait.

*We could detect then a slight tremor in **Czernyak**'s voice; in hers, none.*

Bruckner Here's what I'm after . . . it's simple enough. That starved pedant Madrassy has tangled me up in his politics too. I want him sent back to his school books. So do you.

Czernyak And further.

Bruckner Very well. I've been for fighting and making you fight. Let's know who's to be master. This wretched country needs to know . . . for it needs one. I mean to be its master if I can be . . . and there are men that will back me. Yes . . . tell my colleagues in the Ladies' Waiting-Room that, Colonel Guastalla . . . if you think it's news to them. If I can't be . . . I'd as soon have you rattling your sabre. Or you, Madam! You seem to believe in yourself. That's the first thing. People with nothing better to believe in will believe in y o u.

Her Majesty stiffens against such familiarity.

The Queen Possibly! What can you do for us . . . what can you do? Don't interfere, please. Don't speak! I need no advice.

*For to **Guastalla**'s – and even **Czernyak**'s – horror, though to **Mr Bruckner**'s grim amusement, she is unfastening from her neck the pearls she always wears; and it is obvious what she means to do with them.*

Bruckner Do you want to bribe me?

The Queen Yes. If this isn't enough . . . tell me how.

*And **Bruckner** finds the necklace in his hands. He smiles very grimly indeed.*

Bruckner What's it worth?

The Queen I'm afraid I don't know. Quite a lot. I could sign something as well.

But he hands it back, with what is very nearly a bow.

Bruckner I respect you, Madam, for the attempt. I am not above bribes. But you haven't my price in your pocket for the moment . . . and I shouldn't like to cheat you. Besides . . . once a man has taken his bribe he's no longer worth it, remember! No . . . I must fight you for a bit . . . and beat you if I can. Thank me for that, at least.

Czernyak *has taken his decision.*

Czernyak Tell your colleagues in the Waiting-Room, Mr Bruckner, that I'm taking your advice. But if I beat you and have my way . . . I'll skin you alive.

Bruckner You'll be quite right to.

Czernyak I don't ask your Majesty's approval.

The Queen You have it.

Guastalla For God's sake don't say that, Ma'am.

The Queen You have it.

Czernyak, *with her clarion note to hearten him, has gone. She says swiftly to* **Guastalla**.

I'll tell the King.

Guastalla Very well, Ma'am.

Bruckner *notes this.*

Bruckner There's nothing more then, I fancy, that I can do for your Majesty.

The Queen You'll do what best pays you . . . I understand that. If you find a little later it might pay you better to be beaten . . . I'll see that you're paid.

She says it with such contempt that he cannot resist a masked retort.

Bruckner Your Majesty is too kind. A post at Court, perhaps . . . in uniform.

Captain Dod, *at this moment, comes from the carriage, his arm beautifully bandaged. The* **Queen,** *having turned her back upon the unspeakable* **Bruckner,** *greets him graciously.*

The Queen That's right, Captain Dod. Come and have it dressed again, please . . . tomorrow morning.

And she enters the carriage. **Bruckner** *finds that* **Guastalla** *is staring at him in no friendly way. So he says with a certain briskness . . .*

Bruckner We'd better be getting back to our lines before trouble starts. Or will you make us prisoners? Etiquette apart, I don't recommend it. Horvath in command is worth ten thousand men to the other side, any day.

He departs, jauntily for him. **Dod** *is a little puzzled.*

Dod What's up now?

Guastalla God knows!

Dod Light me a cigarette . . . there's a good chap. (*For his bandaged arm makes this a hard job.*) I wonder if they looted the printer's. We could get in first with this mutiny story. If I give it a twist our way it might even do us a bit of good. Better copy than an armistice, anyhow! That's old Hadik's, isn't it? (*His eye has caught the sword still lying where the* **King** *flung it.*)

Guastalla Yes . . . I had to borrow one.

Dod Don't leave it lying about, then. Besides . . . it looks so silly.

Guastalla *stiffens with correctitude.*

Guastalla I can't touch it.

Dod Can't you? I can.

And he picks it up without more ado.

Act Four

*A railway carriage is cramped quarters for a three weeks' stay;
but, by dint of removing some of the fixed furniture, this
twenty-year-old saloon has been turned into a tolerable sitting-
room for the **King** and **Queen**. A table with inkstand and
papers on it, set against one of the line of windows that look
out, drearily enough, to the farther side of the station, shows
that he conducts his business there. Another little table in the
corner may be **Guastalla's**; another by the odds and ends on
it, is the **Queen's**. It is afternoon, and a cold grey autumnal
afternoon at that. The place is empty. But **Colonel Hadik**
opens one of the narrow doors to usher in **Sir Charles
Cruwys**, saying as he does so . . .*

Hadik Colonel Guastalla, sir, is not yet back from the
funeral.

Sir Charles The funeral?

Hadik But I was to tell his Majesty at once of your arrival.
The British Minister?

Sir Charles Yes.

Colonel Hadik *passes across to the other narrow door and
passes through it to find the **King**. We notice that he is
carrying a large official-looking letter. He has become, by sheer
devotion to his simple duties, the perfect butler.*

Sir Charles Cruwys *is no more than fifty, one supposes, but
he has already acquired the silvery hair and silky benevolence
of the distinguished diplomat. He is due for promotion as soon
as these Carpathian troubles are settled – though when will
that be? He would not, in fact, have been left here these four
years but for the need of a good man at such a post. He is, you*

discover after a little, a very 'good man' indeed. Do not be deceived by that air of taking everything more seriously than his business, with which the diplomatist learns to avoid the risk of indiscreet talk about it. (Sometimes, of course, appearances are not deceptive.)

Sir Charles, *awaiting his Majesty, gives a glance round; then, apparently, he finds the place remarkably cold, for he starts to put on the motoring coat, carried over his arm. While he is doing so* **Colonel Guastalla** *arrives, hurriedly, as if he knew he was late.* **Sir Charles,** *caught with one arm in the coat and one out, asks politely . . .*

Sir Charles May I?

Guastalla Please! It is chilly. The heating won't work without the engine . . . and the oil-stoves I asked for smell. You've not been kept waiting, I hope. (**Guastalla,** *oddly enough, is carrying a bunch of flowers; red and yellow chrysanthemums. He puts this down on the table in the corner.*)

Sir Charles I've been having a brisk half-hour with the Commandant . . . your head gaoler here. He has been treating you civilly . . . has he?

Guastalla He thinks so, I'm sure.

Sir Charles Not quite the sort of fellow they should let represent them.

Guastalla But suppose he does?

Sir Charles *appreciates this riposte, and the disdain that inspires it. But his talk to the Commandant has worried him a little.*

Sir Charles That opens up unpleasant vistas.

Guastalla We're cut off from news, of course. I gave my parole before they passed me through the wire not to ask for any. We've to thank you, Sir Charles, for my little outing, I think.

Sir Charles I shan't be sorry to be back in Karlsburg before dark. My government escort, even, does not inspire confidence.

The **Queen**'s *entry interrupts him. She is paler than she was, visibly strained by this ordeal; graver and quieter too, her old unquestioning confidence abashed. She has a smile for* **Sir Charles**, *though, as she gives him her hand.*

The Queen Sir Charles Cruwys. We met long ago . . . at Stuttgart.

Sir Charles Good of your Majesty to remember.

The Queen The King wishes me to be present. Do you play tennis still?

Sir Charles Oh yes, Ma'am.

The Queen Can you still jump the net standing?

Sir Charles *postures comic despair.*

Sir Charles No, Ma'am. Ah . . . no!

Guastalla *has retrieved his flowers from the table.*

Guastalla A woman ran out of a shop and asked me to bring your Majesty these.

The Queen Oh! Did you thank her for me? I hope you thanked her.

The break in her voice tells us much. We should not have heard it but that she was taken by surprise. The **King** *comes in. He is as cool and cheerful as ever; rather brusquer perhaps. He shakes hands with* **Sir Charles** *in a businesslike way. In his other hand is that official-looking letter delivered to him by* **Colonel Hadik**.

The King How do you do, Sir Charles? You've had a cold drive. Please sit down. What can I do for you?

For all this easy civility, there is a certain ring of challenge in the **King**'s *voice.* **Sir Charles** *and he face each other, as they sit, duellist-wise. The* **Queen** *has turned away and seated* *herself apart; her pale face is outlined against the pallor of the windows; she holds that simple gift of the flowers as if it were a friend's hand. As to the challenge,* **Sir Charles** *neither accepts nor declines it. He measures his words.*

Sir Charles Upon your Majesty's abdicating I am authorised by my government to offer you a suitable asylum.

The King That's very civil of them. And this that you've brought me . . . is the form I fill up? (*He gives an almost jaunty twirl to the official-looking letter.*)

Sir Charles I believe so, Sir. I did not bring it. It came with me.

The King A nice distinction.

Sir Charles's *reply has its edge too.*

Sir Charles One clings to the correct thing . . . as long as may be.

The King I expected it sooner.

Sir Charles This has been a troublesomely uncertain week.

The King So I gather from what reaches me of our cook's conversation with her favourite sentry. Who may I ask . . . if anyone . . . is now governing the country?

Sir Charles You may well ask, Sir! Dr Madrassy is still in office. He'll come tomorrow, I presume, to ask that back from you . . . if he's still in office.

The **Queen** *turns her head.*

The Queen I think, Sir Charles, that, whatever else happens, you'll find Dr Madrassy in office . . . till we put him out once and for all.

This last phrase draws a quick glance from the **King**; *while* **Sir Charles**, *still courteous, grows stern.*

Sir Charles Will your Majesties please face the facts of the situation? You're prisoners here . . . and helpless. Madrassy and his mongrel government are at such odds that they're as helpless . . . all but! In the country the bottom's dropping out of things. The mark's going to glory . . . the towns can't buy food . . . the peasants are digging up their guns again. And here's winter suddenly . . . to make all worse!

The King And where is Count Czernyak, if you please?

Sir Charles *vents a little hiss of exasperation.*

Sir Charles I told them it was childish not to tell you! Czernyak and his mutineers are fifteen miles from Karlsburg.

The King Thank you. So the cook and her sentry were right. There's been fighting?

Sir Charles Gunfire . . . and a casualty or two, I suppose. Enough to give the newspapers headlines.

The soldier in the **King** *says to* **Guastalla** *with a certain satisfaction . . .*

The King That's fifteen miles a day, Guastalla.

Guastalla Rather more, Sir.

Sir Charles Horvath had orders to keep out of range. But he can't get back any further.

The King How many mutineers?

Sir Charles A couple of thousand still.

The King And what happens next?

Sir Charles That's the question. They won't surrender.

The Queen Surrender!

High indignation is in the word. The **King** *explains.*

The King Her Majesty approves of their conduct. I, of course, cannot.

The Queen Why should they surrender?

Sir Charles They can be surrounded and shot to pieces at any moment, Ma'am. My wonder is the order's not been given. Before I get back it may be. But Madrassy won't court-martial more than a dozen of them . . . Czernyak apart, of course . . . I've his word for that . . . if they'll surrender.

The King . . . and I abdicate.

The Queen Do you really think, Sir Charles, that we're to be tricked like this?

It is an unpleasant moment, which the **King** *has to redeem by asking good-humouredly* . . .

The King Are you tricking us?

Her Majesty is implacable.

The Queen Or being tricked himself!

Sir Charles The diplomat finds that still less complimentary, Ma'am.

The Queen Madrassy daren't fight . . . he never has dared. And here's his last chance to cheat us . . . and then tell men that will fight for us that there's nothing left to fight for. Isn't that the trick? Hurry back, Sir Charles . . . or you may find Count Czernyak in Karlsburg before you . . . and his Majesty proclaimed.

Sir Charles Good God, Ma'am . . . you can't think that's possible! Two thousand men . . . all but starving . . . and not much more than their bare fists left them to fight with! D'you want them massacred? Do you, Sir?

A moment's silence before the **King** *answers.*

The King They know they can't win. They must know that. But they'd sooner be killed to a man than give in.

Foolish of them . . . and I must abdicate to save their
skins. Will they thank me? What if they've the right of it?
Is the battle that's worth losing . . . and the cause . . . the
one battle we must fight . . . and the cause that can't be
lost? Thank Madrassy for holding his hand – It has been
hard to, I'm sure. But I almost wish I had my sword again
. . . and that he'd put me among them . . . so that I could
be foolish too.

Another moment of silence before **Sir Charles** *returns to
practical politics.*

Sir Charles By tomorrow, Sir, I'm promised two boats'
crews from the Firefly. She was within reach, thank
goodness! They'll go on guard here . . . and if I don't like
the look of things I shall pack you across the frontier
whether you abdicate or not.

*'The impudence!' is probably what springs to his Majesty's lips
at this; but he translates it into . . .*

The King You can't do that! No government worth its salt
will let you.

Sir Charles I can, Sir . . . and I shall.

The King I shall formally protest.

Sir Charles That will make no difference.

The King Really, Sir Charles . . . what business is this of
yours?

Sir Charles Sir . . . Carpathia may shoot her ministers
and generals or her bankers and editors if she finds them a
nuisance . . . by the dozen . . . and welcome! It's a
method of government like any other . . . and there's a lot
to be said for it. But we can't have your throat cut. There
may not be much belief left in kings nowadays . . . but
there's still a lot of sentiment about them . . . pleasant,
wholesome sentiment. We don't want that churned up
into passion . . . and other passions churned up to clash
with it. We can't afford to have this affair of yours turn

tragedy. Europe's nerves aren't braced to it for the
moment. You'll be ready to leave, please, tomorrow.

The King gives a bitter little shrug.

The King Lock the doors. Start the train. What can I do?

Sir Charles We kept our fingers out of the pie as long as
we could. I don't say we'd not have welcomed your
success. But what less could you expect us to welcome?

The King However I'd come by it? Whatever I'd done
with it?

Sir Charles This mess won't clear up yet awhile . . . and
you're well out of it, Sir, believe me.

The King seems to speak from far away.

The King There are two ways of looking at this world,
aren't there? As a chaos that you fish in for your profit
. . . you can always pull something up. Then there's the
world of your idea . . . and some of us would sooner go on
to the end, hoping that may come true. Have you ever
been possessed by an idea, Sir Charles?

Sir Charles *can afford now to return to the amenities of
conversation, and most readily he does.*

Sir Charles In my youth I believed I was a poet.

The King And were you?

Sir Charles My friends thought the evidence insufficient.

The King They may have been wrong.

Sir Charles I still feel sometimes that they were.

The King And the further the reality slips from you . . .
the better you know the idea was true. I came back set not
to fight . . . and with nothing I wanted to win. But I did
come to think for a little that there was something for me
to do here. I shall never do it. Who wants it done? Yet
I've never felt so much a king as I do now. As a poet . . .
you'll understand that. I'll walk to the gate with you . . .

I'm glad of the exercise. If I'd still faith enough in my idea
. . . would the barbed wire be down when we reached it?

But **Sir Charles** *cannot let these pretty metaphysics fog the
business that's in hand.*

Sir Charles What's your answer to Madrassy, Sir?

The King Poor Madrassy! Finessing for my skin all the
week with Bruckner and his catastrophic friends! And
now that your Firefly's over the horizon . . . here's his
reward. (*Once more he twirls that official envelope.*) He's to
flourish it signed and sealed in their faces tomorrow. A
respectable Republic in being! Stocks and shares mounting
again! And their only excuse for letting hell loose spirited
away! Yes . . . I think you'll have dished the new
revolutionaries very nicely, between you.

Sir Charles Your Majesty has it pat.

He says this with genuine admiration; the **King** *would be a
master at the game, that's clear. They have all risen.* **Sir
Charles** *is moving towards the door, when suddenly, with a
side glance at the* **Queen** . . .

The King Shall I sign now, Rosamund . . . or wait till
tomorrow?

She does not look at him.

The Queen Why ask me?

To this, very noticeably, he does not reply.

The King Have we made the best bargain we can? Once I
started bargaining I'd be a very Jew. Can't I have my
mutineers amnestied . . . Czernyak and all?

Sir Charles He'd let off the lot if he dared, Sir. But
Bruckner's nominee took over Horvath's command this
morning.

The **King** *watches the* **Queen** *still. She makes no move.*

The King It's a close game.

Suddenly she turns, to ask lightly . . .

The Queen Sir Charles . . . will you take a note for me to Karlsburg? And could Dominica come out to see her mother, Henry?

The King (*interpreting*) Countess Czernyak.

Sir Charles I'm sure she can.

The Queen I'll fetch it.

She goes out, with unexpected swiftness. They begin the casual talk of men kept waiting.

The King How's Captain Dod, by the way?

Sir Charles In hospital . . . and I mean to keep him there. They'll save his arm . . . but it's badly poisoned.

The King I'm sorry . . . I'm glad! (*His mind does not seem to be on the subject.*) And what happened at the funeral, Guastalla?

Guastalla I walked behind the bier. Your Majesty's wreath was a very pretty one.

The King In the country here, did you know, a child's body's carried by children. There's no coffin . . . they cover it with flowers.

Sir Charles I didn't know, Sir.

The King This happened the day of the mutiny . . . our one casualty, I'd hoped! Her father kept the toll-gate. She used to sit on his shoulder to take the pennies. When she heard the firing she ran out to see the soldiers . . .

He stops. He pretends to no sentimental grief. But still . . . !
Sir Charles *is tactful.*

Sir Charles No one holds your Majesty responsible for that sorry affair.

The King That is sound constitutional doctrine, I know. Karlsburg's cursing me pretty roundly, I suppose, though. Martial law?

Sir Charles No . . . everyone's enjoying the crisis, I think. Spending money! Why not . . . when it may be worthless tomorrow? The opera's crowded. I dropped in last night . . . to show I'd nothing on my mind.

The King What were they giving?

Sir Charles *Tosca*.

The King Terrible stuff. Cats on the tiles! What's this new woman like?

Sir Charles She can do everything but sing. Mozart would put her in her place. No . . . Madrassy has been very sensible. Even the Stock Exchange panic has gone on long enough now for as many people to be doing well out of it as badly. And the knowing ones must have done very well indeed.

The King Will my backers in Paris go bankrupt?

Sir Charles Not, Sir, if for this last week they've been backing you to lose . . . as I should suppose they have.

The King I hope they have.

The **Queen** *returns with the letter.*

The Queen Here it is. Thank you.

Sir Charles I'll seal it.

The Queen No need. It's to ask her to bring me some stockings.

Sir Charles Tomorrow, Ma'am.

He turns towards the door again, the **King** *with him.*

The King Suppose you do find Czernyak in Karlsburg? Garibaldi worked just such a miracle . . . and gave a nation faith in itself for fifty years.

Sir Charles Then Madrassy would need no answer, Sir.

The King But Carpathia would be asking for another sort of king. We'd like news of the children . . .

They all go out together. Left alone, her Majesty and **Guastalla** *turn to each other, like conspirators, glad of each* *other's support but none too pleased that they need it, nor with each other.*

The Queen Why did he make me listen? I couldn't bear it another minute. How much does he know?

Guastalla You've not told me yet how much you've told him, Ma'am.

The Queen If he guesses why doesn't he say so! He has hardly spoken to me these three days.

Guastalla I've a message from Czernyak. It was in the flowers. I've burnt it.

The Queen Weren't they sent to me? (*She puts them aside a moment later, as if they had won a little gentleness from her on false pretences.*)

Guastalla He's in touch with Bruckner.

The Queen Did he get the money?

Guastalla I suppose so.

The Queen I'm beginning not to care.

Guastalla Will you please warn me, Ma'am, when you mean to tell his Majesty?

The Queen Why?

Guastalla I'll ask for my dismissal. I won't wait for it.

The Queen Why should he dismiss you?

Guastalla I'm deceiving him, Ma'am.

The Queen looks him up and down.

The Queen If I can deceive him . . . surely you can.

Guastalla There's a difference.

Her Majesty grows colder still.

The Queen You should not be doing what you think it wrong to do, Colonel Guastalla.

Guastalla I am glad to be of service . . . to your Majesty.

*As she looks at him standing there, his eyes averted, most shocking thoughts surge in her mind, recollections of the **King's** mild chaff about his adoring her. Surely he cannot imagine that . . . !*

The Queen You will please not think of it in that way.

Guastalla Very well, Ma'am. Was that letter about stockings?

As a fellow-conspirator he has every right to know. But he is frozen with a . . .

The Queen You heard me say so. You should not ask such a question.

And, to their mutual relief, the conspirators part. She leaves him standing there.

*   *   *

The carriage is empty. The window-blinds are drawn, and the grey light of morning filters through them. **Ella**, *the maid, bustles in and begins snapping them up in great haste.* **Countess Czernyak** *follows her, hastily too.*

Countess Czernyak Who is it, Ella?

Ella I don't know, my lady.

By the other door in comes **Colonel Hadik**.

Countess Czernyak Who is it, Basil?

Hadik Bruckner.

Countess Czernyak At this hour! They're not out of bed.

By the doorway from which **Countess Czernyak** *came comes* **Colonel Guastalla**.

Hadik Mr Bruckner to see his Majesty.

Guastalla I know. I've told him.

Countess Czernyak He must wait.

Guastalla He's to come in.

At which moment **Mr Bruckner**, *who has not waited, even for this, does come in. He stands there, glum and bodeful. After a moment* **Countess Czernyak** *says . . .*

Countess Czernyak Run along now, Ella. You can tidy later.

Ella *runs along.* **Countess Czernyak** *follows her.*

Bruckner Was that Countess Czernyak?

Guastalla Yes.

Bruckner I thought so.

The **King** *enters, shaved and spruce, but still in his dressing-gown. He greets his visitor with very cool politeness.*

The King Good morning, Mr Bruckner. Your business is pressing?

Bruckner Can I speak to your Majesty alone?

The King Certainly. Will you have some coffee?

Bruckner No, thank you.

The King Please do. Then I can finish mine with a better grace.

Bruckner Very well.

The King Let Ella bring it in, please, Colonel Hadik. Get your own, Guastalla. It's a headache for me if I start work first.

Colonel Hadik *has left the room.* **Guastalla** *follows him. But* **Mr Bruckner** *is not to be disconcerted by these civilities. He is of very set purpose indeed. So the* **King**, *still studying him, changes tactics with a more familiar . . .*

The King Out with it!

Mr Bruckner *comes out with it; purpose in every word.*

Bruckner If you'll do as I tell you I'll have you in Karlsburg within the week.

The **King** *duly digests every word; then queries with the politest irony . . .*

The King In my coffin?

Bruckner As king. On your white horse . . . with your crown on . . . in a week or two!

The King Really! This is a familiar promise. Count Czernyak made it me last. I'll own I didn't think I'd next hear it from you.

Bruckner Czernyak's dead.

Then something has happened at last. The **King** *shows neither surprise nor grief, but brings all his wits to bear.*

The King Killed?

Bruckner Yes.

The King When?

Bruckner About two o'clock this morning. He'd been with me till past one. I had him brought back to my quarters. Here's all I found in the pockets. (*He takes from his own pocket a carefully wrapped up little packet.*)

The King Who killed him?

Before **Bruckner** *can answer* **Colonel Hadik** *comes in with the tray of coffee, which he puts down upon a convenient table.*

Hadik If your Majesty will forgive me . . . Ella is not yet properly dressed.

He departs; the perfect butler! **Bruckner**, *put out by the interruption, says rather sourly . . .*

Bruckner Does he l i k e carrying trays?

The King I daresay.

He says it with the ghost of a smile; but his eyes are sternly questioning still, and it is to them **Mr Bruckner** *half replies with . . .*

Bruckner He came in to make terms.

The King Not with my knowledge.

Bruckner Granted.

The King And rashly . . . it seems!

Bruckner D'you think I had him killed?

The King Did you come to terms?

Bruckner I thought his offer too good to be true.

The King As yours, Mr Bruckner, seems to me.

Bruckner You've come pretty near beating us, though. D'you know how near?

The King I think I know.

This may have a meaning for him, which escapes **Mr Bruckner**.

Bruckner I've been wondering all this week if the very legend of you locked up here mightn't beat us! Why didn't Madrassy make terms with you? He has missed his chance. Czernyak has missed his . . . once and for all. I see mine now. That's frank.

The King Admirably!

The **King** *hands him his coffee; he is surprised to find how glad he is of it.*

Bruckner You'll have to trust me a bit. But if I fail I'm done for.

The King That's a fair pledge. But what use can I be to you?

Bruckner The two of us can stop things here stampeding to perdition. If we don't . . . and pretty quickly . . . I don't know now what else can.

The King We make . . . politically . . . an odd pair, Mr Bruckner.

Bruckner Does that matter?

To which the **King** *makes frank and respectful response.*

The King No. But I thought things were going so well with you.

Bruckner Yes . . . I've the troops in hand . . . I can wipe out these men Czernyak has left stranded. I've purged my own party and I can turn out Madrassy if I want to. Yes . . . everything's going well with me, thank you! But where am I going? When I'm where I want to be . . . what next? That's the one question most men won't ask in time, isn't it? What has brought me here? I'll tell you. Count Czernyak wasn't over civil . . . he meant me no good . . . I don't blame him. He didn't like talking terms . . . but he knew I meant fighting . . . so his game was up . . . though he'd have had a last fling at me, I suppose, with any men that would have followed him. I sent two young hopefuls of mine to see him through the lines. They picked a quarrel with him and shot him. I was planning today's work with the staff when the news came back. It took me ten minutes to find out I daren't punish them for it. Daren't! I've not pushed my way and other men out of it without knowing what that means! I lay down an hour to think things over . . . then I started here to you. I won't be hustled to the devil if I can help it. Can we shake free and make a fresh start and do the sensible thing between us? That's the question. I must be back by midday to carry on.

All this gulping his coffee. Now he puts the cup down, and waits response. What the **King** *is thinking of it all who can say? Not* **Mr Bruckner***, for the moment.*

The King Have you a practical plan?

Bruckner I think so. I'll bring you to Karlsburg. There's clamour enough to put you on trial and make a martyr of you. I shall let things go hang for a week till everyone's pretty frightened . . . for that'd mean stiff reprisals. Then I'll march in the troops for a day's shooting. Then I'll risk it . . . I'll proclaim you. And you'll proclaim peace and the union of parties and the rest. Your own manifesto! That Englishman dropped twenty on my head one day.

The King And what next?

Bruckner We'll work a plebiscite to take the wind from Madrassy's sails. Then we must govern and stand no nonsense.

The King That will be for you to do.

Bruckner Yes. By what right? Because I can. If I can't . . . I'll take the consequences.

The King I should find myself sharing those with you, at least. Who is to support us?

Bruckner The men that are sick of this never-ending muddle called politics.

The King Quite a large following!

Bruckner . . . that'll do a hand's turn or so to put an end to it.

The King Ah . . . not quite so large!

Bruckner . . . if we make it worth their while. Not with money. Stuff men with money when they're no more use. I want young men . . . kept on the stretch. Bully them a bit . . . and let them do a bit of bullying.

The King Your two young murderers may still be useful.

Bruckner I'll bring them to book for you . . . once things are safe.

The King Would that be quite fair? Yes . . . it all sounds most practical.

Mr Bruckner *is not over-susceptible to irony; but he becomes conscious of the fact that he has, at least, not stirred his Majesty to any enthusiasm. His brows twist into a frown and he begins to undo the little packet of the things found in* **Czernyak**'s *pockets.*

Bruckner I'll hand you these, I think.

As he bends over, loosening the string, the **King** *studies him curiously.*

The King Did we ever meet in the old days, Mr Bruckner?

Bruckner Remember the top of my head, do you? I was boot-black at the Vigado Club when you were Crown Prince and used to come there. I've blacked your boots many a time.

For the first time the **King** *feels a little drawn towards him.*

The King So you were! You were famous as a boot-black. And always reading!

Bruckner It was dull between-times.

The King I used to bring you books. You kept a little stack of them under a duster in the corner. Didn't you go up to some university later? We all subscribed.

Bruckner Yes . . . and a bit later, when the war came, to prison. And when peace came . . . into exile.

The King Were we fellow-exiles?

Bruckner I came back when you left.

The King What did you go to prison for?

Bruckner Optimism. Belief in the millennium . . . in the brotherhood of man and the rest of it. I'm quite cured.

He has the contents of the parcel spread out now: a paper or so, two bundles of banknotes, and a little something twisted up in tissue paper.

Czernyak tried to bribe me with silly promises. But here's his list . . . and a pretty full one . . . of my underlings. These (*the banknotes*), I daresay, were for paying a couple of them to cut my throat. And these, I think, are her Majesty's.

The tissue paper, untwisted, shows the **Queen**'s *pearls. Were it a mislaid umbrella brought back, his Majesty could not say more casually . . .*

The King I believe so.

Bruckner The letter she wrote sending them . . . isn't a very discreet letter.

He hands it to the **King**, *who glances it over.*

The King Not very.

Bruckner No one else has read it . . . as far as I know.

The **King** *hands it back.*

The King Thank you. I doubt if I can pay your price for it.

Bruckner Take it! Take the lot! I'm not driving a bargain. I want no hold on you. I'll take these if you like and write a receipt for them. Then you'll have bought m e and paid for me. (*He swings the pearls in his hand.*)

The King That would give you a very tight hold on me.

These finessing scruples are more than **Mr Bruckner** *can bear.*

Bruckner What is it you want, then? Here's all you've been asking for . . . if you'll trust me to give it you. You wouldn't think the better of me if I'd come to you talking loyalty and patriotism.

The King The worse!

Bruckner I'm not gentleman enough? It can't be that . . . in these days.

The King No. You are a man of some talent, Mr Bruckner . . . and I, at least, am a king. We can both afford not to be snobs.

Bruckner If you'd brought back your old gang . . . if you took on Madrassy's nondescripts . . . how long would that last? There's more to be done now, I tell you, than look wise and say smooth things while the old machine clanks round. There's one way to govern a country . . . just one. Find where its real power is . . . and give that play. It's in me for the moment . . . and the men of my mind. When I've done all I can . . . when I lose grip . . . the next good man may scrap me. I give him leave.

The King But what is your need of m e?

What can **Mr Bruckner** *do but answer such a candid question?*

Bruckner I shouldn't count myself clever if it weren't for the fools around . . . but I do try to see things as they are and not as I'd fancy them. Once I get to work . . . I shan't be very popular.

The King Oh . . . why not?

Bruckner With the middle-class mob that never wakes up to anything till the virtue's going out of it? But keep the shops open and the trains running on time . . . and they'll think all's well with the world! Not with your friends. Not with my horny-handed kith and kin, I promise you! For we've to get this country to work again . . . and to fight again, maybe. Men are children, mostly, and . . . give them a chance . . . wicked children . . . and as lazy as they're let be. Put tools and guns in their hands . . . you must! But take care the ideas in their heads aren't dangerous toys to play with.

The King The sight of me with a crown on occasionally would keep them amused, you think.

Bruckner It all counts. You're impressing me now, you know . . . even in your dressing-gown.

At this his Majesty laughs outright.

The King I'm so glad.

Bruckner But there's more to you than that. You like people . . . I can't! . . . and they like you. That counts. They believe in you. And that counts . . . doesn't it?

The **King** *weighs this in his mind for a moment. Then* . . .

The King Mr Bruckner . . . when you sent your two young friends off with Count Czernyak did you think . . . or didn't you . . . they might murder him? Will you answer me that?

Mr Bruckner *wonders if he shall, then decides that he will.*

Bruckner Yes . . . I did.

The King Thank you.

He is sitting at his table. He rings a little bell on it. Then he takes from a despatch-case that long official envelope we have already seen, and from it the document.

Bruckner Is that what's troubling you? He's as well out of the way. He'd done his best for you. What more was he doing but mischief . . . flinging his men to their death?

The King And he m i g h t have beaten you.

Bruckner Yes . . . and then where should I have been? I'm sorry. But half measures were no use with him. It was the best thing to do . . . and the best way to do it.

Colonel Guastalla *comes in. The* **King** *is now signing the document.*

The King Will you witness this please, Guastalla? It's my abdication.

Mr Bruckner – *though he was beginning to expect this – is at loss for a juster comment than* . . .

Bruckner That's useful!

But, indeed, what comment could be juster? The **King** *yields his place to* **Guastalla**, *who sits and signs. He turns to* **Mr Bruckner** *again.*

The King I shall watch your career with interest, Mr Bruckner. This body-politic's corrupt enough, perhaps, to need your medicine. When you're cured of your modesty . . . I think you may be very popular indeed. But you'll do well enough without me for a puppet. And I shall find poultry-farming pleasanter . . . and far more dignified. How much belief in me was to be left when we'd shaken hands over Czernyak's dead body? Enough for your purpose! I could serve that well enough, no doubt . . . as the dumb sign of a faith made tame and ridiculous . . . its loyalties turned to the breeding of snobs. No, I'll betray my cause in my own way.

Guastalla is at his side with the document of abdication. He takes it and hands it to **Mr Bruckner**.

Will you give this to Madrassy? He's still your chief, isn't he? But you'll be fighting him in the open soon.

Bruckner I hope so.

The King You may beat him. With the best intentions he betrays his beliefs. But the belief that has been betrayed may then beat you. I'll give it a chance to. Czernyak has been killed, Guastalla.

Guastalla Yes, Sir.

Bruckner I trust the news won't upset her Majesty very much.

The **King** *is surprised – though really he should not be – at this little touch of common humanity.*

The King Thank you.

Mr Bruckner *weighs the abdication in his hand.*

Bruckner You've missed y o u r chance.

The King Do you think so? I could hardly tell you, Mr Bruckner, how fantastically unreal all you've been saying has seemed to me. If ill-luck ever sends you abroad again

. . . look me up. I'd much like to know if it doesn't come to seem so to you. Goodbye.

Bruckner I wish your Majesty a pleasant journey.

As **Mr Bruckner** *nears the door which* **Guastalla** *is holding open for him, the* **King**, *turning to the table where the débris from* **Czernyak**'*s pockets is still lying, asks . . .*

The King You're sure you've no use for these . . . spoils of war?

Bruckner None.

And so, with some dignity, he departs, **Guastalla** *following him. The* **King** *goes to the other door and calls . . .*

The King Rosamund!

When the **Queen** *comes in he is standing again by the table.*

These are yours, I think. I should burn the letter. Stephen Czernyak has been killed.

The Queen Fighting?

The King No. Did you send him the money as well?

The Queen All I had.

The King He went in with it to bargain and they shot him in cold blood. You're not to blame for that.

The Queen I'll take the blame. I'm very sorry.

The King Shall I tell his mother . . . or will you?

The Queen I must.

The **Queen** *has the necklace in her hand and the letter. The* **King**, *half-automatically, has opened one of the packets of notes.*

The King But what was he to do with t h e s e?

The Queen Bribe people.

He gives an exasperated sigh.

The King How many more times am I to tell you that this old note with my head on it is worthless?

The Queen Not if we'd won! And if the people he bribed cheated us and we didn't . . . I wanted them to be cheated too. Don't always think me a fool, Henry.

*At this moment – fortunately perhaps – **Guastalla** reappears; and the **Queen** before she turns to go (she is glad to go) says . . .*

Colonel Guastalla has been in no way to blame.

*And she leaves them. The **King** is a little brusque with **Guastalla**, who is evidently preparing, metaphorically, to surrender h i s sword.*

The King Now, Guastalla . . . don't apologise. I knew you were up to something. You can't keep a secret to save your life. And don't try and resign. That does no good. We must clear up these papers. They may pack us off at any moment now.

So they set to work.

* * *

*It is dusk, and the arc lamps of the station, already lighted, flare through the windows. Near one of them stands the **Queen**, tense and still. She is gazing out, but she has just turned away from **Dominica Czernyak**, who, by the door, and in some distress, drops a departing curtsey.*

Dominica Then may I please take my leave of your Majesty?

*The **Queen** turns back, remorse quenching anger.*

The Queen No . . . don't go like that, child. I didn't mean to hurt you. But if your mind's made up . . . why ask me to approve . . . when you must know I don't? Don't stand there tongue-tied as if you were afraid of me. I've had you about me since you were a baby. There's nothing to make me very terrifying now!

Dominica I've never been afraid of your Majesty. But of course I don't talk to you as I would to any one else.

She does not mean her candour to cut so deep. But it does; though a while ago her Majesty might have thought this was just as it should be.

The Queen I see. Well . . . your mother thinks it her duty to go with us . . . and you don't think it your duty to be with her.

Dominica She doesn't think it, Ma'am.

The Queen She thinks you'd better stay, perhaps, and keep a few friends here. Then here's a retreat for her. And if I approve . . . then our friends can't blame you. Yes . . . a very good plan! Why do you humiliate me by making me say bitter things to you?

Under the sudden storm of anger and pride and pain with which this ends, poor **Dominica***, who is, after all, very young, bursts into tears.*

Dominica I didn't mean to . . . I didn't! I'm so sorry for your Majesty . . . but I thought it would make you angry if I said so. And Mamma's going with you because she loves you . . . more than anyone in the world except Stephen and me. And Stephen's dead!

The **Queen***, remorseful again, even, perhaps, shamed a little, sinks into a chair.*

The Queen Come and sit by me a minute. Forgive me. Stephen's death has been a great shock . . . to the King . . . and to me. I've been trying all day to break it to your mother. I never thought I could be such a coward. I'll tell her now . . . before you go. Or will you tell her?

Dominica But she knows, Ma'am. She has known since this morning.

The Queen Are you sure?

Dominica She said when she kissed me: You've heard Stephen's dead. I said: Yes. There wasn't time for more. She had to announce me to you.

The Queen She has been with me all day. I ought to have known she knew!

Dominica I think she'd rather not talk about it . . . if you don't mind, Ma'am.

The Queen He died for his country . . . and for us . . . just as truly as if he'd died fighting. You can always remember that. See that Masses are said for him. Your mother's so busy packing she mayn't think of it. I'll send you the money. (*Then with simple affection for the girl she adds . . .*) But come with us . . . won't you? There's still time.

Dominica *shakes her head.*

Dominica No, Ma'am . . . I can't.

The Queen You're behaving very foolishly. You don't know what may happen here. We're leaving the country to its fate . . . and it deserves no better . . . to Socialism . . . and Communism . . . or even worse. You may find yourself a waitress in a tea-shop . . . or anything. What good can you do by staying?

Dominica The worse things were, I think, the more I should have to stay.

The Queen Dominica . . . you're not in love with anyone undesirable, are you?

Dominica No, Ma'am, not with anyone at all. But . . .

The Queen Well? Tell me the truth.

Dominica *tells it.*

Dominica It's my country, you see.

The **Queen** *has no more to say.* **Colonel Hadik** *appears. He carries some bundles of newspapers.*

The Queen What are those, Colonel?

Hadik The newspapers his Majesty asked for. Sir Charles Cruwys has just come. He brought them in his car. He will wait upon your Majesty whenever it is convenient. The engine is now being attached. But there may be a little delay . . . for something, it seems, is broken. And his Majesty asks you to allow Jakab to take leave of you also.

The Queen Who? I remember. Yes.

Hadik The farmer. And could your Majesty perhaps find a goodbye present for him?

The Queen I'll try.

Count Hadik *goes out again. He is a little excited and upset by the bustle of departure, a little shaky.*

The Queen What's to become of him?

Dominica He'll go back, Ma'am, to his garden and his gun . . . and do his sums. He was quite happy.

The **Queen** *sighs rather enviously.*

The Queen Once you're old, nothing matters much. You've (*She pats the girl's hand.*) all sorts of things to hope for. I'm not afraid for you, my dear. You're good. Yes . . . be gallant . . . be gay! And never let anyone pity you. Pray for us sometimes, won't you? We shall be so far away. Give me a kiss. Go to your mother now. Stay with her till we start.

She looks up to see **Jakab** *standing in the doorway. He is an old farmer; of the earth earthy, and it is hard caked earth at that. He is in his working clothes, for it is a weekday; but they have been brushed to rights very strenuously by somebody.* **Dominica** *has obediently risen, dropped her curtsey and gone. What the* **Queen** *is to do with the mute old man, who stands* *rigidly staring at her from the doorway, she cannot think. She is nearing the end of her resources of tact. At last she says helplessly . . .*

The Queen Goodbye.

Then the image finds a slow tongue.

Jakab This is your Majesty?

The Queen Yes.

Jakab Happy to have a look at your Majesty . . . as my wife . . . and his Majesty . . . said I ought . . . it being the last chance there'll be. And his Majesty's been a lot about the farm . . . very friendly.

*This gives the **Queen** her cue.*

The Queen Thank you for the butter and the eggs . . . such good eggs . . . and the milk you've sent us.

Jakab (*encouragingly*) They've been paid for . . . I'll say that.

*The **King** comes in. He is brisk and lively. The one great change in him is that he no longer wears his uniform. He had instead to send into Zimony for a reach-me-down, and, frankly, the cut and the pattern of Zimony clothes leave a little to be desired. But he carries them with ease and dignity. He could be dignified and easy in a bathing-dress, it seems.*

The King Just seen Sir Charles! Bermuda's where they're sending us. And our naval escort's parading on the platform. He wants me to inspect it. Very civil of him!

The Queen Henry! You can't!

The King Why not?

The Queen Dressed like that! (*The horrors of war pale before the scene she imagines.*)

The King Oh, nonsense! Goodbye, Jakab. Six months here with you . . . and I'd know something of farming. He tells me I've an eye for a calf. Poultry I'm not to be flattered about . . . but who'd have thought I'd an eye for a calf.

*The **King**'s good spirits and the familiar topic bring the old farmer to life a little, and he winks portentously at the **Queen**.*

Jakab I said it to please him. But you've not a bad eye for a calf.

The King And he's going to keep Snowjacket.

*Countess Czernyak **has come in and is waiting in silence.** The **Queen** turns to her with an affection that she tries to keep from seeming remorseful.*

The Queen Yes . . . dear Ja-ja?

Countess Czernyak We're starting at once, Ma'am. Your hat-box hasn't come from the town. Shall I ask if we may send for it?

The Queen No . . . we'll manage.

Countess Czernyak Very well, Ma'am.

*Her face calm and unchanging, she goes. The **Queen** says swiftly to the **King** . . .*

The Queen Henry . . . she knows.

He is amazed; rather shocked.

The King Who told her?

The Queen I can't think. Say nothing to her tonight.

The King Very well.

*Jakab **has been waiting to pursue the only subject that interests him; but he never cares how long he waits.***

Jakab Not that he'll earn his keep!

*The **King** is jovial but firm.*

The King Now . . . not one penny do you bluff out of me by that tale!

Jakab He's no use for ploughing. He'll go in the small muck-waggon. But how often do I have it out?

The King You'll ride him to market every Friday.

Jakab I won't. My son's got a motor car.

The Queen Snowjacket should be shot, Henry.

But this **Jakab** *takes very badly.*

Jakab Oh . . . I'll shoot him . . . and thank you! He'd fetch a bit as horseflesh.

Colonel Guastalla *comes swiftly in with* . . .

Guastalla The escort's paraded, Sir.

The King Jakab, don't be surly. Very well . . . I'll come.

Jakab Surly!

The **Queen** *makes a last, almost tearful appeal.*

The Queen Henry . . . won't you . . . please . . . ?

The King What, my dear?

The Queen Put on your uniform?

Jakab Me surly!

The King Certainly not. I've abdicated. It would be most improper.

Jakab And well I might be surly with all these carryings-on! My barns made barracks of! Sentries and pickets . . . !

The King You've coined money out of us.

Jakab But you're going now.

The King You farmers talk as if you were the only people on earth that mattered.

Jakab So we are. Governments! I've seen 'em come and I've seen 'em go. Red . . . white . . . all colours! There's nothing I ask of 'em but to let me alone. Politics! My son's for politics . . . my wife'd be if she got about. He sneaks

into Zimony to see your Majesties. Your Majesty gives
him a pretty smile . . . well, he thought so! . . . so he's for
politics. God help the land when I'm gone! Will politics
grow corn . . . or raise beef? Jacks-in-office come round
badgering me! Will I plant this . . . will I sow that? Why
won't I pay taxes? I won't pay no taxes. I'll feed you or
starve you . . . take your choice . . . according as you
worrit me or let me alone. But no politics! My work's cut
out watching the weather. That's chancy enough for me.

He now finds that the **King** *has missed the greater part of this
discourse, having gone to inspect the parade. He wags a head
at the door.*

Is he coming back?

Guastalla Not till we start, probably.

Jakab Oh!

Even **Guastalla's** *tact seems exhausted; the* **Queen's**
endurance is ebbing, and there **Jakab** *still stands. At last she
says, helplessly . . .*

The Queen Guastalla . . . I've nothing to give him.

Jakab Yes . . . I did understand there was something
might be given me.

The Queen I'm sorry.

Jakab I'd thought of an order.

Her Majesty's mind weakens.

The Queen But what more can we order?

Jakab To wear. Lots used to have 'em. And his Majesty
being so friendly . . . my wife says: You ask for an order.

She can bear no more.

The Queen Please go away.

Jakab *turns on her grimly, yet with no intended unkindness.*

Jakab It's not me that's going away.

Guastalla *comes to the rescue.*

Guastalla His Majesty has abdicated, Mr Jakab . . . and cannot confer decorations. They would not be valid.

Jakab When did he?

Guastalla This morning.

Jakab Oh! I ought to have asked sooner . . . when my wife told me. Well . . . I wish your Majesty a good journey.

He makes a rough bow and is going. But the **Queen** *rallies. Life shall not outmock her. She goes to her little table, finds there a small morocco case, opens it and presents it to him, saying . . .*

The Queen Mr Jakab! Yesterday you would have been a Knight of St Andrew.

Jakab *is delighted.*

Jakab Now that's most ladylike of your Majesty . . . and I'm much obliged . . . and so'll my wife be. Of course if it's not valid it don't do you any good. But you mean it kindly. Much obliged to your Majesty, I'm sure.

Guastalla *manœuvres him out; for the* **Queen** *is near a breakdown, might break down now did not* **Countess Czernyak** *return. A little courage is due to her.*

The Queen Yes . . . dear Ja-ja?

Before an answer can be given **Jakab** *and* **Guastalla** *are back again. This is unendurable.*

Guastalla Forgive me, Ma'am . . . the inspection . . . I forgot! May we go the other way?

Jakab Cold weather for the time of year! And your Majesty feels it . . . boxed up like this. To be sure you must!

They are gone again – thank God! – by the other door.

Countess Czernyak The hat-box has come, Ma'am. I've not money enough to pay for it, I'm afraid.

The Queen I've none. Ask Guastalla.

Countess Czernyak *hurries after him. And now the* **Queen** *does utterly and irretrievably break down, collapses, shaken with weeping, into the nearest chair, where, unluckily,* **Sir Charles Cruwys** *finds her. She looks up to discover him standing there.*

Sir Charles I most humbly beg your pardon, Ma'am.

The Queen It's the first time . . . it is indeed! I've stood up to the worst. But little things happen you're not ready for . . . silly things. Did they laugh?

Sir Charles *is puzzled.*

Sir Charles Who, Ma'am?

The Queen The escort. He shouldn't have inspected them in that suit, should he? It doesn't fit him . . . it was ready-made. They didn't laugh?

Sir Charles No, indeed!

The Queen Sailors are so kind.

Sir Charles He's talking to my French and Italian colleagues. I've left them to have their say . . . there's been a little feeling! I ought to have given them more of a show. I brought you these, Ma'am. (*He hands her a few letters.*)

The Queen From the children? Oh . . . thank you!

Sir Charles They're to join you at Toulon . . . with both governesses and the head nurse. It's the shortest train journey.

The Queen Where is Bermuda?

Sir Charles It's an island . . . a small island . . . near America. An excellent climate. No mosquitoes.

The Queen I've never been across the sea . . . not even to England. We don't travel like other people, you know . . .

and I was married so young. It's a very small island, I
expect. Do sit down, Sir Charles . . . please. One of my
bad dreams when I was a child was that I was left on a
piece of land no bigger than a dinner plate . . . for the
lesson books never said it need be any bigger . . .
surrounded entirely by sea. And I'd wake up screaming.
(*She has dried her tears; but, they being dry, pain and anger
flush through her again.*) Oh this wicked country! Thank
God it's not mine . . . not really mine! Better have none!
But why do they let us go . . . why haven't they killed us?
I want to stop hating them . . . it poisons you to have to
sit still and hate people. (*And again pain and anger have
exhausted her.*) We've been putting petrol on the ponds
here because of the mosquitoes. They don't all give you
malaria . . . you tell them by their legs. I can't die fighting
. . . but they could have found some way to kill me. Tell
me more about Bermuda.

Sir Charles *is about to, when the* **King** *enters, alert and
cheerful.*

The King Honoured, my dear Sir Charles, by such an
escort. A very smart body of men! A little pale, some of
them. These modern ships do coop them up. What's that
young officer's name again?

Sir Charles Anstruther.

The King Say it once more.

Sir Charles Anstruther.

The King Thank you . . . I shall remember it now. He
knows Bermuda, Rosamund. Charming place! Houses
built of coral. Not much rain. American tourists. British
Atlantic Fleet. No mosquitoes to speak of.

Sir Charles I must bid your Majesties goodbye.

The **King** *shakes hands warmly.*

The King You've been most kind!

The Queen Most kind!

The King Next year . . . if we've behaved ourselves . . . you might let us run over to America for a week or so.

Sir Charles It's possible, Sir.

The King Incognito.

Sir Charles That would not be so easy.

The King I've to think of the future. We've seven children to marry. And I expect I'm a pauper.

The Queen Henry . . . don't joke about such things.

The King I'm serious. Europe must face democracy . . . and America's problem is to leaven the social lump.

Sir Charles Our policy, Sir, has long been to bring in the New World to redress the bank balances of the Old. The War brought the process to some confusion.

The King And we may yet see the South American states weary of revolution and dictatorship and demand constitutional kings. Goodbye.

Sir Charles But there's to be no confiscating your private funds.

The King The farm at Zurich will take some winding up. I put a pile of money into it. What about Bermuda for poultry now?

Can the **Queen** *bear it one moment more?*

The Queen Why don't we start? Why don't we go?

Sir Charles They're waiting, I fear, for me to get out. Something comes from Bermuda. Potatoes! I'll ask about poultry. We shall be in touch with you till you leave Toulon. Your Majesty.

He bows to the **Queen**, *who gives him her hand to kiss.*

The King Goodbye, again.

He gives **Sir Charles's** *hand another cordial shake.*

Sir Charles Goodbye, Sir.

*He departs. The **King** and **Queen** are alone. All's over.*
Nothing more to do. After a blank incomprehensible moment
they sit down and turn to the letters and newspapers that have
been brought for them.

The King Pleasant fellow!

The Queen Yes. What does he care?

The King We're off!

For the train has given a jerk, which nearly upsets them.

The Queen No.

For it jerks no more.

The King Something went wrong with the connecting
rod. Funny if they couldn't start the train!

The Queen At least they might give us a good engine.
The state this country's in!

The King If it were the best engine in the world I
couldn't drive it.

The Queen Henry . . . don't be sententious. Hildegarde
sends you her love . . . she has pulled out three teeth . . .
and you owe her fifteen francs.

The King She shall have it.

How quickly letters and newspapers can make life
commonplace again! But yet another spasm of wrath shakes
*the **Queen**.*

The Queen Carted away like cattle!

The King You should have come the round with me just
now. Everyone friendly and cheerful!

The Queen Thankful to be rid of us!

The King I suppose they are.

The Queen And you're glad to go.

The King I suppose I am. Bermuda may be interesting. There'll be lots of things to do . . .

The door bursts open and in comes **Colonel Hadik**, *in great distress.*

The King Why don't we start?

Hadik You're starting, Sir. I must bid your Majesties goodbye.

The King You're coming to the frontier.

Hadik That's countermanded. God keep your Majesties!

King *and* **Queen** *are on their feet in a minute.*

The King My dear Colonel! I'd so much more to say to you. You've been goodness itself . . . ever since you wanted to shoot me! God bless you.

The **Queen** *catches both his hands.*

The Queen Dear Colonel Hadik . . . dear, dear Colonel Hadik! You knew we'd fail . . . you never minded. Oh, such a strength to me!

The King And we won't forget our chess.

Hadik Out of my grave, Ma'am . . . to be your servant! Back to it! But your Majesty's most humble servant . . . to the end . . . to the end!

And even in the haste of his departure, the old man manages, totteringly, to make that triple bow Court etiquette prescribes. But the effect of it on the **Queen**, *when he has vanished . . . !*

The Queen No . . . he did that to mock me! He did! God forgive me . . . I'm wicked. But I think my heart's broken.

The **King** *puts a comforting arm round her.*

The King My dear . . . my dear! You're always so plucky. We've our lives to live.

She pulls herself together. They are alone; and now surely all is over, for the train gives a more purposeful jerk. And the **King** *says . . .*

There! We're off now!

The Queen Read your papers.

He settles himself comfortably and opens the first one to hand.

The King It has been a tiring day.

The Queen You never thought we'd win. I think I've believed we should . . . till this very minute.

The King But, my dear . . . I came back to stop civil war. I've stopped it . . . and there won't be another. All the men are to be sent home. No reprisals . . . no court-martialling! I've done what I came to do. I have won.

The Queen Don't be paradoxical, Henry.

The **King** *puts his hand out to one of the radiators, and says with some satisfaction . . .*

The King The heat's coming on.

The Queen The whole world's laughing at us!

The King It'll all be forgotten in a month or so.

The Queen That's comforting!

He has found something of import in his newspaper.

The King Do you remember my seeing some journalist the day we left?

The Queen But I'd do it again. I'm not sorry for anything but the failure . . . not for Czernyak being killed . . . nor anything. Misfortune doesn't soften us. I did tell myself: If we're beaten I'll at least be a better woman. But I'm not that either. I haven't changed a bit.

He is deeper still in the newspaper.

The King Did I tell him I wasn't going back to Carpathia?
Well . . . I wasn't. So perhaps I did.

The Queen I could have done my duty here. You're either
a queen or you're not. I'm no use as anything else.

The King I must write and apologise.

The Queen If we're to live like common people I shall nag
at you, Henry . . . I know it . . . and be horrid to the
children! Apologise? What for? (*For her ear has belatedly
caught the objectionable word.*)

The King I misled him.

The Queen Apologise to a journalist!

He reads, with a half-enjoyable dismay . . .

The King But spite of the smooth démenti his Majesty's
eye flashed, I thought, towards the map of Carpathia
behind the rococo writing-table and he fingered the hilt of
his sword.

The Queen How vulgar!

The King It isn't rococo . . . and I wasn't wearing one.

The Queen The table's rococo.

The King Louis Seize furniture is not rococo. Clever of
him to guess at the map though! I never had it down
before strangers.

Suddenly they are shaken in their chairs: almost out of them.

The Queen Are we stopping?

The King No . . . this is where the line was cut. Bumpy,
isn't it? (*He reads on.*) At which moment her Majesty
swept into the room. A stately blonde, a woman in whom
mothercraft goes hand in hand with high political
intelligence . . .

The Queen Show me!

*She takes the paper and is soon deep in it herself. The train
moves on through the night towards the frontier.*

Farewell to the Theatre

1916

Farewell to the Theatre was produced at the Royal Lyceum Theatre, Edinburgh, on 20 August 1992, as a rehearsed reading with the following cast:

Dorothy	Susan Engel
Edward	Tenniel Evans
Scene Narrator	Christopher Good

Directed by William Gaskill

*This talk took place in **Edward**'s office. He is a London
solicitor and his office reflects his standing. It is, that is to say,
a musty dusty room in a house two hundred years old or so,
now mercilessly chopped into offices. The woodwork is so old
and cracked that new paint looks old on it and fresh paper on
the walls looks dingy in a day. You may clean the windows
(and it is sometimes done) but nothing will make them shine.
The floor has been polished and stained and painted and
scraped and painted again till it hardly looks like wood at all.
And the furniture is old, not old enough to be interesting, old
enough to be very respectable. There are some pictures on the
wall. One is a good print of Lord Mansfield, one represents a
naval battle, the third a nondescript piece of mountain scenery.
How the battle and the nondescript came there nobody knows.
One pictures some distracted client arriving with them under
his arm. They were left to lean against the wall ten years or so;
then a clerk hung them up. The newest thing in the room and
quite the strangest seeming there is a photograph on the
mantelpiece of **Edward**'s daughter, and that has been here
nine years or so ever since she died. A pretty child.*

*Well, the papers renew themselves and the room is full of
them, bundles and bundles and bundles. They spread about
poor **Edward** like the leaves of a forest; they lie packed close
like last year's leaves and in time are buried deep like leaves of
the year before last. His **clerk** knows what they all are and
where everything is. He flicks a feather duster over them
occasionally and has been observed to put some – very
reluctantly – away. Very reluctantly. For, after all, these are
the fabric of a first-class practice and it is his instinct to have
them in evidence. **Edward** has never thought about it. Thus
was the room when his uncle walked out of it and he walked*

*in and thus he will leave it in a few years for some junior
partner.*

*Note the signs then by which a lawyer marks himself above
reproach. Beware the businesslike well-polished office, clicking
with machinery. There works a man who does not practise law
so much as make a practice of it. Beware!*

Edward *is at his desk. Wherever else is he, unless he rises
wearily to stretch his long limbs before the fire? Thin,
humorous and rather more than middle-aged, a sensitive,
distinguished face. One likes* **Edward**.

His **clerk** *shows in* **Dorothy Taverner**. *Everybody knows*
Miss Dorothy Taverner. *The* **clerk** *beams at her with
forgetful joy – shamelessly a t her while he tries to say to*
Edward, *'Miss Taverner, sir'. Then he departs.*

Edward How punctual!

Dorothy Twelve ten by the clock out there. Your note
said eleven thirty.

Edward And I said 'How punctual!'

*They shake hands like the oldest friends. He bends a little over
her pretty hand.*

Dorothy You have no right to send for me at all when I'm
rehearsing . . . and you know it.

Edward It was urgent. Sit down.

Dorothy My dear Edward, nothing is more urgent than
that my rehearsals should go right . . . and if I leave the
company to the mercy of my understudy and this author-
boy . . . though he's a nice author-boy . . . they don't.

Edward I'm sure they don't.

Dorothy His beating heart tells him that we must all be
bad actors because we don't live and move just like the
creatures as he began thinking them into being. He almost

weeps. Then I tell him God called him into collaboration
fifty-three flying years too late as far as I'm concerned.

Edward Oh . . . oh!

Dorothy Fifty-four will have flown on November the next
eighteenth. And that cheers us all up and we start again.
Well, dear friend, you are fifty-seven and y o u . . . look it.

Having made point pause for effect. **Edward** *carefully places
legal documents on one side.*

Edward My dear Dorothy . . .

Dorothy That tone means that a little business talk has
now begun. Where's the rickety paper-knife that I play
with? Thank you.

Edward Vernon Dix and . . . Boothby, is that the name of
your treasurer? . . . paid me a formal visit yesterday
afternoon.

Dorothy Behind my back! What about?

Edward They complain you won't look at your balance
sheets . . .

Dorothy (*with cheerful charm*) But they're liars. I look at
them every week.

Edward . . . That you won't study them.

Dorothy I'm studying a new part.

Edward They brought me a pretty full statement. I spent
some hours over it.

Dorothy More money wanted?

Edward They also brought me the estimate for this new
play.

Dorothy It'll be exceeded.

Edward Can more money be found?

Dorothy We can search.

Edward You remember the last search.

Dorothy The rent's paid till Christmas.

Edward Trust your landlord!

Dorothy This play may do well.

Edward It may not.

Dorothy *gives a sigh. With an impatient gesture or two she takes off her hat and puts it obliviously on* **Edward**'s *inkstand. She runs her fingers through her front hair, takes out a hairpin, and viciously replaces it. Signs, these are, that she is worried.*

Dorothy Yes, I remember the last search. Nearly kissed by old James Levison for Dear Art's sake. At my age! I wonder did he guess what an even choice it was between five thousand pounds and boxing his flat white ears.

Edward There was Shelburne's five thousand and Mrs Minto's . . .

Dorothy Well, I did kiss Lord Shelburne . . . he's a dear. Blue-eyed and over seventy or under twenty . . . then I always want to kiss them. Why?

Edward My eyes . . . alas . . . were never blue and never will be now.

Dorothy Because I suppose then they don't care whether I do or not. All that money gone? I'm sorry. Mrs Minto can't afford it.

Edward No, it's not all gone. And another five thousand will make you safe through this season. Another ten thousand unless you've very bad luck should carry you to Christmas . . . otherwise, if this new play isn't an instant success, you must close.

Dorothy *sits upright in her chair.*

Dorothy I have been in management for sixteen years. I have paid some dividends. 'Dividends' is correct, I think.

Edward I keep a sort of abstract which reminds me of the fearful and wonderful way you have been financed.

Dorothy Dear Edward, I should have cheated everybody but for you.

Edward I have also managed mostly to stop you from cheating yourself. Dorothy, it is odd that the people who put money in only to make some did often manage to make it out of you, while the people who stumped up for art's sake and yours never got anything at all.

Dorothy I don't see anything odd in that. They got what they wanted. People always do. Some of them got the art . . . and one of them nearly got me.

Edward Why didn't you marry him, Dorothy? A good fellow . . . a good match.

Dorothy Oh, my dear! Marry him? Marry! Confound him . . . why did he ask me? Now I can't ever ask h i m for a penny again. Yes . . . on that bright Sunday morning the manageress was tempted, I won't deny.

Edward But the record of the past five years does not warrant your promising more dividends . . . and that's the truth.

Dorothy Well . . . shall we hide the balance sheets away and shall I gird myself with boastfulness once more . . . once weary more? What is our record for Dear Art's sake? Shakespeare . . . w i t h o u t scenery . . . Molière, Holberg, Ibsen, Strindberg, Maeterlinck, Shaw, Hauptmann, d'Annunzio, Benavente, Giacosa, Parraval, Ostrovsky, Lavallière, Chekhov, Galsworthy, Masefield, Henniker and Borghese, Brieux, Yeats, van Arpent and Claudel. Some of it sounds quite old-fashioned already . . . and some has begun to pay. When a Knight of the Garter dies, you know, they proclaim his title over his tomb. You'll have to come to my burning, Edward, and through a trumpet of rolled-up balance sheets proclaim my titles to fame. 'She, here deceased, did her duty by them, Shakespeare, Ibsen' . . . How I hate boasting! And boasting to millionaires to get money out of them. I'm as vain as a peacock still . . . but boasting I hate.

Edward Then consider. You can see through the production of this . . . what's it called?

Dorothy *The Salamander*. Good title!

Edward If it fails . . . shut up . . . finally.

Dorothy Yes . . . I've been thinking of doing that, Edward. *The Salamander* won't succeed in the fine full business sense . . . though now I've whispered that for the first time it most perversely may.

Edward Then what on earth are you putting it up for?

Dorothy Because it's good enough . . . and then the next can be better. It won't succeed because I've only a small part in it. Say Egoist . . . say Actress.

Edward Wiser to keep out altogether.

Dorothy And then it wouldn't succeed because the dear Public would think I didn't believe in it enough. Queer silly children the dear Public are, aren't they? For ten years now my acting is held to have grown steadily worse, so quite rightly they won't rush to plays with me in them. But then they won't have my plays with me out of them either. So what's a poor body to do?

Edward I don't hold that your acting has grown steadily worse.

Dorothy Well . . . not steadily perhaps. But I never was steady, was I? And you don't like the parts I choose?

Edward Not when you hide yourself behind them.

Dorothy I never do.

Edward Your old self! But I want you to finish with it all anyway.

Dorothy Why?

Edward Because I fear I see heartbreak ahead.

Dorothy That you need never look to see . . . for the best of reasons.

Edward You still do care . . . far too much.

Dorothy Do I hanker for the old thrill . . . like wine bubbling in one's heart . . . and then the stir in the audience when . . . on I came. Dear friend, you now prefer my acting . . . off the stage. My well-known enthusiasm. It seems to me it rings more tinny every day. I'm glad it takes you in. Still, even that's only an echo . . . growing fainter since I died.

Edward My dear Dorothy.

Dorothy Oh . . . but you knew I was dead. You own now to mourning me. You know the day and hour I died. Hypocrite . . . I remember how you congratulated me on the tragic occasion . . . kissing my hand . . . you're the only man that does it naturally. Doesn't that abstract remind you when we produced *The Flight of the Duchess*?

Edward Many of us thought you very good.

Dorothy Because I was far, far better than many a bad actress would have been. It is the queerest sensation, Edward, to be dead . . . though after a while you get quite used to it. Are you still alive, by the way?

Edward There is the same feeble flicker that there has ever been.

Dorothy Burn on, dear Edward, burn on . . . that I may warm my poor hands sometimes at the flame you are.

Edward It can serve no better purpose.

Dorothy No . . . so I'm sure I think.

There falls a little silence. Then **Edward** *speaks, the more bitterly that it is without anger.*

Edward Damn them! I'd damn their souls, if they had any. They've helped themselves to you at so much a time for . . . how many years? Dorothy . . . what have they ever given you in return?

Dorothy Oh, if that were all my grievance I'd be a happy ghost this day. If I'd a thousand souls and they wanted them . . . the dear Public . . . as they n e e d them . . . God knows they do . . . they should have every one, for me. What does the law say, Edward? Is a soul private property?

Edward There are decisions against it.

Dorothy Then I prefer your law to your religion. It's more public-spirited.

Edward My ancestral brand of religion, my dear, taught me to disapprove very strongly of the theatre.

Dorothy And after watching my career you've found out why. How long have you been in this office, Edward?

Edward Thirty years, nearly.

Dorothy The weight of them! Do you remember having tea at Richmond . . . at The Roebuck at Richmond . . . when they'd offered you this billet and we talked wisely of the future?

Edward I do.

Dorothy And I made you take it, didn't I?

Edward You did.

Dorothy And I wouldn't marry you.

Edward *looks at her. One side of his mouth twitches a little. You might charitably call it a smile. But his eyes are smiling.*

Dorothy Don't say you didn't ask me to marry you.

Edward On that occasion?

Dorothy Yes . . . on that occasion, too. That's what one calls the Past, isn't it? How right I was . . . and what successes we've both been.

Edward My son Charles tells me that I have done very well. Do you know, I was moved to ask him the other night as we sat in the box whether he wasn't in love with you?

Dorothy Do you think it's hereditary?

Edward He said he had been as a boy.

Dorothy How old is he?

Edward Twenty-three.

Dorothy Bless him! If young things love you, be quite sure that you're alive. I do regret sometimes.

Edward What did happen . . . so suddenly?

Dorothy What happens to the summer? You go walking one day and you feel that it has gone.

Edward You've been that to the Theatre.

Dorothy A summer day . . . a long, long summer day. Thank you. I prefer the sonnet which calls me a breath of spring. But truly he died . . . oh, that lion's head of his! . . . before I was full blown.

Edward I know it by heart.

Dorothy It's a good sonnet.

Edward It makes history of you.

Dorothy And it never made me vain a bit because indeed I knew it was true. Yes, I like to be standard literature.

Edward Easy enough for a poet to be public-spirited over you.

Dorothy But from the time I was born, Edward, I believe I knew my destiny. And I've never quarrelled with it . . . never. I can't imagine how people get along if they don't know by sheer instinct what they're meant to be and do. What muddles they must make of life!

Edward They do . . . and then come to me for advice. It's how you told me to earn my living.

Dorothy You only tell them what the law says and what two and two make. That's all you ever tell me. But what I was alive for I have always known. So of course I knew when I died.

Edward Dorothy, my dear, it hurts me to hear you say it.

Dorothy Why? We must all die and be born again . . . how many times in our lives? I went home that night and sent poor old Sarah to bed. And I didn't curse and break things . . . I'd always let myself do that a little on occasion . . . it seemed so much more human . . . when I was alone . . . oh, only when I was quite alone. But that night it had all been different . . . and I sat still in the dark, . . . and wondered . . . wondered what was to happen now. It's a frightening thing at best to lose your old and well-trained trusted self . . . and not know what the new one's going to be. I was angry. I had rehearsed the wretched play so well too. Why do people think I've no brains, Edward?

Edward I suppose because you're so pretty.

Dorothy Or perhaps because I don't use them for the things they were never meant to be used for. I've sometimes thought, since I can't act any longer, I might show the dear Public my rehearsing. That'd teach them! But there . . . I've come down to wanting to teach them. Time to retire. For, you see, after that night I wasn't born again. Something . . . didn't happen. And a weary business it has been finding out what. With the dear Public helping me to discover . . . hard on them, they've thought it. And you so patient with my passion to keep on failing . . . hard on you. For you've not understood. I've disappointed you these later years. Own up.

Edward If it's admitted that all my heart is your most humble servant I'll own up again to disapproving of the Theatre . . . to disapproving most thoroughly of acting and of actors too . . . and to doubly disapproving when any new nonsense about them is added to life's difficulties.

Dorothy Yes . . . if the life you call life's so important! Well . . . I have four hundred a year . . . s a f e . . . to retire on, haven't I, Edward?

Edward As safe as money can be.

Dorothy I do think that money ought to learn to be safe. It has no other virtues. And I've got my Abbey.

Edward Milford Abbey is safe for you from everything but earthquake.

Dorothy How utterly right that I should end my days in a shanty built out of the stones of that great Abbey and buttressed up in its shell.

Edward Is it?

Dorothy Oh. Edward, if you had but the artist's sense of the eternal fitness of things, you'd find it such a help . . .

Edward . . . To imagining Miss Dorothy leading the Milford monks a dance.

Dorothy Well . . . their religion was not of this world, nor is mine. But yours is, dear Edward. Therefore the follies of art and saintliness must seem to you two sorts of folly and not one. St Francis would have understood me. I should have been his dear sister Happiness. But you and the railway trains running on time would have puzzled him no end.

Edward What foolishness makes you say you're dead, my dear?

Dorothy While . . . if I'd lived the cautious life, I shouldn't be. If I'd sold my fancies for a little learning, virginity for a gold ring, likings for good manners, hate for silence . . . if I ever could have learnt the world's way . . . to measure out gifts for money and thanks . . . well, I'd have been married to you perhaps, Edward. And then you never could have enjoyed my Imogen as you used to enjoy it. You used to say it was a perfect tonic.

Edward So it was!

Dorothy Yes, dear, you never had a gift for subtle expression, had you?

Edward From the beginning I suppose you expected more of life than ever I could find in it.

Dorothy Whatever I expected, my friend, I bargained for nothing at all.

Edward I'd like you to know this, Dorothy, that . . . for all my rectangular soul, as you used to call it . . . when I asked you to marry me . . .

Dorothy On which of those great occasions?

Edward On the various occasions I did ask you before I did . . . otherwise . . . marry.

Dorothy I think there were five . . . or six. I recall them with pride.

Edward But not with enough of it to ensure accuracy.

Dorothy And was it never just for the sake of repeating yourself?

Edward No. When I was most ridiculously in love I used to think three times before I faced a life with you in that . . .

Dorothy Well?

Edward That flowery wilderness which was your life. I knew there were no safe roads for me there. And yet I asked you . . . knowing that very well.

Dorothy I'm glad . . . for your sake . . . that you risked it.

Edward Glad, for your own, y o u didn't?

Dorothy Did you really only marry her because I told you to?

Edward I fear so.

Dorothy That was a wrong reason for doing the right thing. But I could not have one of the ablest men of his set in everything else said at his club to be sentimentalising his life away about an actress . . . I really couldn't. They told me she was desperately in love with you. And I never would have spoken to you again if you hadn't. Edward, it was never hard on her, was it?

Edward No, Dorothy, I hope and think it never was. I made her happy in every ordinary sense . . . at least I felt she felt so.

Dorothy And you did love her, didn't you, Edward?

Edward I shouldn't put this into words perhaps. I thought through those twenty-five years I gave her all the love that her love asked for. But the world of . . . folly, one calls it . . . into which your laugh had once lifted me . . .

Dorothy Or was it wisdom?

Edward That, my dear Dorothy, was the problem you would never consent to try and solve.

Dorothy She never could have liked m e, Edward.

Edward She thought you a great artist. She had judgment and taste, you know.

Dorothy Yes . . . she thought me an attack of scarlet fever, let us say . . . and that it was a very beautiful scarlet.

Edward Dorothy, somehow that hurts.

Dorothy I'm sorry.

Edward Some years before she died, her nature seemed to take a fresh start, as it were. It shot out in the oddest ways . . . over a home for horses and cooking reforms . . . and a most romantic scheme for sending strayed servant girls to Australia to get married. If there had been any genius in my love for her . . . would she have had to wait till forty-five and then find only those crabbed half-futile shoots of inner life begin to show? While her children were amused . . . and I was tolerant! For quite incurably middle-aged she was by then . . .

Dorothy Had she dreaded that?

Edward Not a bit. Not even in fun . . . as we made such a fuss of doing.

Dorothy Admirable Ethel! Clear-eyed and so firm footed on this spinning earth. And Life her duty . . . to be punctually and cheerfully done. But over-trained a little, don't you think . . . just for her happiness' sake.

Edward She didn't count h e r happiness.

Dorothy She should have.

Edward She shouldn't have died when she did.

Dorothy The doctors were fools.

Edward Well, it was a while after . . . remembering my love for you . . . I suddenly saw how perhaps, after all, I had wronged her.

Dorothy It was just three years after that you asked me to marry you again.

Edward You forgave me. Let's forget it. It was good to feel I was still a bit of a fool.

Dorothy Folly for certain, it was then?

Edward And not so old at heart as you thought.

Dorothy I like your declarations, Edward. They're different. But never from the beginning have you been like the others.

Edward And I was never jealous of any of the three.

Dorothy Four.

Edward Four?

Dorothy One that you never knew about. I told you though I should never marry . . . and I never have. Perhaps I'm as frightened at the meaning I might find in it . . . as you ought to have been.

Edward They made you just as miserable at times, Dorothy, as if you had married them.

Dorothy Poor dears.

Edward And two out of the three were really perfect fools.

Dorothy Three out of the four, my friend, were perfect fools . . . helpless fools.

Edward Then which wasn't?

Dorothy The one you never guessed about. Don't try to, even now. He never really cared for me, you see . . . and I knew he didn't . . . and so I was ashamed to tell you.

Edward Now when was that?

Dorothy You're trying to guess.

Edward No, honestly . . .

Dorothy Do you remember a time when I was very cross with life and wouldn't act for a whole year . . . in the days when I still could? I went down to Grayshott and started a garden . . . a failure of a garden. And you came down to see me . . . and we talked into the dark. And I said I ought to have married father's scrubby-headed assistant and had ten children . . .

Edward I vaguely remember.

Dorothy Well, it wasn't then . . . but shortly after.

Edward You wanted that experience . . .

Dorothy No, no! How dare you? Am I that sort of a creature . . . collecting sensations? Sometimes, Edward, I

find you the biggest fool of the lot . . . a fool at heart,
which is worse than a fool at head . . . and wickeder.

Edward I'm sorry!

Dorothy Never mind, it's not your fault now if fresh air
disagrees with you. And you can't open the window here,
for only dust comes in.

Edward Is the room stuffy?

Dorothy Yes . . . but so's London . . . and so's life.

Edward I do remember there was a time when I thought
you were hardening a little.

Dorothy Well, it wasn't from that bruising. No man or
woman in this world shall make me hard.

Edward Dorothy, will you marry me?

Dorothy (*her voice pealing out*) Oh, my dear!

Edward That's what you said to Blackthorpe when he
offered you his millions on a bright Sunday morning.
Don't say it to me.

Dorothy I never called him My Dear . . . I was much too
proper . . . and so is he! But you are the Dear of one
corner of my heart . . . it is the same old corner always
kept for you. No, no . . . that sort of love doesn't live in
it. So for the . . . seventh? . . . let's make it the seventh
time . . . oh, yes, I wear them on my memory's breast like
medals . . . no, I won't.

Edward Very well. If you don't want to raise five thousand
pounds you'd better close the theatre after this next play's
produced.

Dorothy Heavens above . . . that's what we started to
discuss. What have we been talking of since?

Edward Dear Dorothy . . . I never do know what we talk
of. I only know that by the time I've got it round to
business it's time for you to go.

Dorothy Yes, I said I'd be back at the theatre by half-past twelve.

Edward It's long after.

Dorothy I'm so glad. They'll finish the act without me and lunch. I never want food. Isn't it odd?

Edward Do you decide to close the theatre after this next play?

Dorothy I decide not to ask man, woman or devil for another penny.

Edward Then you close.

Dorothy But if it's a success?

Edward Then, when it's finished, you may have a few pounds more than four hundred a year.

Dorothy I don't want 'em.

Edward But you'll close?

Dorothy I will. This time I really will and never, never open again. I want my Abbey. I want to sit in the sun and spoil my complexion and acquire virtue. Do you know I can have fourteen volumes at a time from the London Library?

Edward Yes . . . don't spoil your complexion.

Dorothy Well . . . when it is really m y complexion and no longer the dear Public's I may get to like it better. To acquire knowledge for its own sake! Do you never have that hunger on you? To sit and read long books about Byzantium. Not frothy foolish blank verse plays . . . but nice thick meaty books. To wonder where the Goths went when they vanished out of Italy. Knowledge and Beauty! It's only when you love them for their own sake that they yield their full virtue to you. And you can't deceive them . . . they always know.

Edward I'm told that the secret of money making's something like that.

Dorothy Oh, a deadlier one. Money's alive and strong. And when money loves y o u . . . look out.

Edward It has never wooed me with real passion. Six and eightpences add up slowly.

Dorothy *throws herself back in her chair and her eyes up to the ceiling.*

Dorothy You've never seen me asking for money and boasting about my art, have you?

Edward That has been spared me.

Dorothy I'm sorry you've missed it for ever. It is just as if the millionaire and I . . .

Edward Though they weren't always millionaires.

Dorothy They were at heart. I always felt we were striking some weird bargain. For all I'd see at his desk was a rather apologetic little man . . . though the Giant Money was outlined round him like an aura. And he'd seem to be begging me as humbly as he dared to help save his little soul . . . though all the while the Giant that enveloped him was business-like and jovial and stern. I shouldn't like to be the marrow of a shadowy giant, Edward . . . with no heart's blood in me at all.

Edward That's why our modern offices are built so high, perhaps.

Dorothy Yes, he reaches to the ceiling.

Edward And are very airless, as you say.

Dorothy Ah . . . it's he that breathes up all the air. You have made rather an arid world of it, haven't you, Edward . . . you and Henry and John and Samuel and William and Thomas?

Edward Will Mary Jane do much better?

Dorothy Not when you've made a bloodless woman of her. And you used to bite your pipe and talk nonsense to me about acting . . . about its necessarily debilitating effect, my dear Dorothy, upon the moral character! Edward, would I cast for a king or a judge or a duchess actors that couldn't believe more in reigning or judging or duchessing than you wretched amateurs do?

Edward We 'put it over', as you vulgar professionals say.

Dorothy Do you think so? Because the public can't tell the difference, as the voice of my business manager drones. I've fancied sometimes that poor actors, playing parts . . . but with real faith in their unreal . . . yet live those lives of yours more truly. Why . . . swiftly and keenly I've lived a hundred lives.

Edward No . . . the trouble with my patients . . .

Dorothy Of course they are! That's why I've to be brought here by force. I never feel ill.

Edward Never a pain in the pocket!

Dorothy I never f e e l it.

Edward The trouble when most people do is that it's all they can feel or believe in. And I have to patch them up.

Dorothy Put a patch on the pocket . . . tonic the poor reputation.

Edward What can I say to them? If they found out that the world as they've made it doesn't exist . . . or perhaps their next world as they've invented it either . . .

Dorothy Oh but I think that exists . . . just about as much. And that you'll all be there . . . bustling among the clouds . . . making the best of things . . . beating your harps into coin . . . bargaining for eternity . . . and saying that of course what you go on in hope of is another and a better world.

Edward Shall we meet?

Dorothy I think not. I flung my soul over the footlights before ever I was sure that I had one . . . well, I was never uncomfortably sure. As you warned me I should . . . biting your pipe. No, thanks, I don't want another. I have been given happier dreams. Do you remember that letter of your father's that I would read?

Edward No . . .

Dorothy Oh yes! Think twice, my dear boy, think twice before you throw yourself away on this woman.

Edward Old innocent! Y o u were the cautious one.

Dorothy But you never knew, Edward, how tempted I was.

Edward Dorothy, don't! The years haven't taught me to take that calmly.

Dorothy Every woman is what I was more or less . . .

Edward Less.

Dorothy So they seem. And you won't pay the price of more.

Edward What was it? I was ready . . . and ready to pay.

Dorothy The price to you of my freedom when you love me! Why . . . dear Edward . . . your jaw sets even now. And so . . . for your happiness . . . that your minds may be easy as you bustle through the world's work . . . so we must seem to choose the cat-like comfort of the fireside, the shelter of your cheque-book and our well-mannered world. And, perhaps I should have chosen that if I could have had my choice.

Edward Dorothy!

Dorothy Had not some ruthless windy power from beyond me . . . blown me free.

Edward Dorothy . . . I've loved you . . . and I do . . . with a love I've never understood. But sometimes I've been glad you didn't marry me . . . prouder of you as you were. Because my love would seem a very little thing.

Dorothy It is.

Edward I never boasted . . . never of that.

Dorothy But the more precious . . . a jewel. And if we're to choose and possess things . . . nothing finer. My dear . . . what woman wouldn't love you? You've not been flattered enough. Never mind . . . you lost no dignity on your knees. I had no choice though but to be possessed . . . of seven angels. Oh, my dear friend . . . could you ever have cast them out?

Edward I've watched them wear you through . . . the seven angels of your art that kept you from me.

Dorothy Yes . . . I'm a weary woman.

For a moment there is silence.

Edward But sometimes I've wondered . . . what we two together might have done. Dorothy, why didn't you try?

Dorothy Not with these silly self-conscious selves. Poor prisoners . . . born to an evil time. But visions do come . . . of better things than we are . . . of a theatre not tinselled . . . and an office not dusty with law . . . all rustling with quarrelsome papers. How wrong to tie up good lively quarrels with your inky tape! Oh, shut your eyes . . . it's easier to see then. Are they shut?

Edward Close. And the grip of your hand is wonderful for the eyesight.

Dorothy Aren't you an artist, too, Edward . . . our fault if we forget it. For Law is a living thing. It must be, mustn't it?

Edward Yes . . . I had forgotten.

Dorothy My dreams and the stories of them are worthless unless I've a living world to dream of? What are words and rules and names? Armour with nothing inside it. So our dreams are empty, too.

Edward Dorothy, my dear, it may sound as silly as ever when I say it . . . but why, why didn't you marry me?

Dorothy Yes . . . I should have made a difference to this habitation, shouldn't I?

Edward Would you have cared to come here then?

Dorothy Always . . . the spirit of me. And I do think you were a better match than the looking-glass.

Edward I promise you should always have found yourself beautiful . . . in my eyes.

Dorothy But I'm widowed of my looking-glasses, Edward. Have you noticed that for fifteen years there's not been one in my house . . . except three folding ones in the bathrooms?

Edward I remember my wife remarking it.

Dorothy Some women did . . . and some men were puzzled without knowing why.

Edward She wondered how you studied your parts.

Dorothy I could have told her how I learnt not to . . . and it's rather interesting.

Edward Tell me.

Dorothy This is perhaps the little bit of Truth I've found . . . my little scrap of gold. From its brightness shines back all the vision I have . . . and I add it proudly to the world's heap. Though it sounds the silliest thing . . . as silly as your loving me at fifty-seven, more babyishly than you did at seventeen.

Edward Please heaven my clerks don't see me till . . .

Dorothy Till you're quite self-conscious again. Well . . . before the child in me died . . . such an actress, as you all thought, as never was . . .

Edward 'O breath of Spring! Our wintry doubts have fled.'

Dorothy But, remember, all children could be like that.

Edward I deny it.

Dorothy And that's why they're not. Well, growing older, as we say . . . and self-conscious, Edward . . . I found that the number of my looking-glasses grew. Till one day I counted them . . . and big and small there were forty-nine. That day I'd bought the forty-ninth . . . an old Venetian mirror . . . so popular I was in those days and felt so rich. Yes . . . then I used to work out my parts in front of every mirror in turn. One would make me prettier and one more dignified. One could give me pathos and one gave me power. Now there was a woman used to come and sew for me. You know! I charitably gave her jobs . . . took an interest in her 'case' . . . encouraged her to talk her troubles out for comfort's sake. I wasn't interested . . . I didn't care one bit . . . it didn't comfort her. She talked to me because she thought I liked it . . . because she thought I thought she liked it. But, oddly, it was just sewing she liked and she sewed well and sewing did her good . . . sewing for me. You remember my Lily Prince in *The Backwater*?

Edward Yes.

Dorothy My first real failure.

Edward I liked it.

Dorothy My first dead failure . . . dear Public. Do you know why? I hadn't found her in the mirrors, I'd found her in that woman as she sewed.

Edward I didn't think it a failure.

Dorothy Well . . . the dear Public wouldn't pay to see it . . . and we've found no other word. But I knew if that was failure now I meant to fail . . . and I never looked in a mirror again. Except, of course, to do my hair and paint

my poor face and comically comfort myself sometimes . . .
to say . . . 'Dorothy, as mugs go it's not such an ugly
mug.' I took the looking-glasses down . . . I turned their
faces to the wall. For I had won free from that shadowed
emptiness of self. But nobody understood. Do you?

Edward If I can't . . . I'll never say that I love you again.

Dorothy What can we understand when we're all so
prisoned in mirrors that whatever we see it's but ourselves
. . . ourselves as heroes or slaves . . . suffering,
triumphant . . . always ourselves. Truth lives where only
other people are. That's the secret. Turn the mirror to the
wall and there is no you . . . but the world of other people
is a wonderful world.

Edward We've called them your failures perhaps . . .
when we wouldn't follow you there.

Dorothy And I that have, proudly, never bargained was so
tempted to bargain for success . . . by giving you what
your appetites wanted . . . that mirrored mannequin
slightly oversize that bolsters up your self-conceit.

Edward But you had meant our youth to us, Dorothy . . .

Dorothy I'd given you that . . . the flower of me. Had I
grudged it?

Edward I think we're frightened of that other world.

Dorothy Well you may be!

Edward If we couldn't find ourselves there with our
virtues and our vanity . . . the best and worst of what we
know.

Dorothy So you all failed me, you see . . . for I'd given
you my life and what other had I? And I failed . . . died
. . . not to be born again. Oh, my poor theatre! Keep it
for a while then to patronise and play with. But one day it
shall break you all in pieces. And now my last curtsey's
made . . . (*The paper knife she has been playing with snaps.*)

Edward Dorothy . . . what an omen! Not your last visit here, too!

Dorothy A fine omen. I do not surrender my sword! But I shouldn't march off quite so proudly, Edward, if it weren't for a new voice from that somewhere in me where things are born saying . . . shall I tell you what it says?

Edward Please.

Dorothy The scene is laid in Dorothy's soul. Characters . . . A voice . . . Dorothy. Dorothy discovered as the curtain rises in temper and tears. The voice: 'Thirty-five years finding out your mistake! But that's a very short time.' Dorothy: 'Boohoo! . . . but now I'm going to die.' The voice: 'Who told you so?' Dorothy: 'Oh . . . aren't I? . . . or rather Am I not?' The voice: 'Dorothy, my dear . . . what led you that November day to your ruined Abbey? What voice was it called to you so loud to make it yours? Yours! What are you beside the wisdom of its years? You must go sit, Dorothy, sit very patiently, in the sunshine under the old wall . . . where marigolds grow . . . and there's one foxglove . . . (hsh! I planted it!) Did it trouble those builders . . . who built it not for themselves . . . not for you . . . but to the glory of God they built it . . . did it trouble them that they were going to die?' Dorothy: 'If they'd known that the likes of me would one day buy it with good hard cash they'd have had heart failure on the spot. Besides they did die and their blessed Abbey's a ruin.' Two thousand five hundred pounds it cost me to do it up!

Edward Well?

Dorothy If I say anything like that, of course, the voice is silent. But if I sit there after sunset when the world's all still . . . I often sit to watch the swallows, and if you keep quiet they'll swoop quite close . . . then I can hear the voice say: 'They built the best they could . . . they built their hearts into the walls . . . they mixed the mortar with their own hearts' blood. They spoke the truth that was in

them and then they were glad to die.' 'But was it true?' I
ask. 'And see how the wall is crumbling.' And then the
voice says, 'What is Truth but the best that we can build?
. . . and out of its crumbling other truth is built. Are you
tired, Dorothy?' I answer: Yes, that I am very tired. I sit
there till the stars shine and there are friendly spirits
around me. Not the dead . . . never . . . but the unborn
. . . waiting their heritage . . . my gift to them . . . mine,
too. That's the true length of life . . . the finished picture
of his being that the artist signs and sells . . . gives . . .
loses! It was his very soul and it is gone. But then he is
glad to go . . . to be dust again . . . nothingness . . . air
. . . for he knows most truly . . .

Edward What?

Dorothy Why, I told you. That he was always nothingness
called by some great name . . . that the world of other
people is the only world there is. Edward . . . what's the
time?

Edward Past one.

Dorothy Well, I'm hungry. Take me out and give me
lunch.

Edward Bless you . . . I will.

*With three fine gestures she puts on her hat again. Time was
when one would sit through forty minutes of a dull play just to
see* **Dorothy** *take off her hat and put it on again. Much less
expressively he finds his and they go out together. The clerks
all stare ecstatically as she passes.*